The Empiricists

Critical Essays on the Classics
Series Editor: Steven M. Cahn

The volumes in this new series offer insightful and accessible essays that shed light on the classics of philosophy. Each of the distinguished editors has selected outstanding work in recent scholarship to provide today's readers with a deepened understanding of the most timely issues raised in these important texts.

Descartes's *Meditations*: Critical Essays
    edited by Vere Chappell
Kant's *Groundwork on the Metaphysics of Morals*: Critical Essays
    edited by Paul Guyer
Mill's *On Liberty*: Critical Essays
    edited by Gerald Dworkin
Mill's *Utilitarianism*: Critical Essays
    edited by David Lyons
Plato's *Republic*: Critical Essays
    edited by Richard Kraut
Kant's *Critique of Pure Reason*: Critical Essays
    edited by Patricia Kitcher
The Empiricists: Critical Essays on Locke, Berkeley, and Hume
    edited by Margaret Atherton

Forthcoming in the series:

The Rationalists: Critical Essays
    edited by Derk Pereboom
The Social Contract Theorists: Critical Essays on Hobbes, Locke, and Rousseau
    edited by Christopher Morris
Aristotle's *Ethics*: Critical Essays
    edited by Nancy Sherman

The Empiricists

Critical Essays on Locke, Berkeley, and Hume

Edited by
Margaret Atherton

ROWMAN & LITTLEFIELD PUBLISHERS, INC.
Lanham • Boulder • New York • Oxford

ROWMAN & LITTLEFIELD PUBLISHERS, INC.

Published in the United States of America
by Rowman & Littlefield Publishers, Inc.
4720 Boston Way, Lanham, Maryland 20706

12 Hid's Copse Road
Cumnor Hill, Oxford OX2 9JJ, England

British Library Cataloguing in Publication Information Available

Library of Congress Cataloging-in-Publication Data

The empiricists: critical essays on Locke, Berkeley, and Hume /
edited by Margaret Atherton.
    p.   cm. — (Critical essays on the classics)
    Includes index.
    ISBN 0-8476-8912-3 (cloth : alk. paper). — ISBN 0-8476-8913-1
(pbk. : alk. paper)
    1. Empiricism—History.   2. Philosophy, British—History.
3. Locke, John, 1632–1704.   4. Berkeley, George, 1685–1753.
5. Hume, David, 1711–1776.   6. e-uk.   I. Atherton, Margaret.
II. Series.
B1302.E6E46   1998
146'.44—dc21   98-39077
                                                              CIP

Printed in the United States of America

∞ ™ The paper used in this publication meets the minimum requirements of
American National Standard for Information Sciences—Permanence of Paper
for Printed Library Materials, ANSI Z39.48-1984.

Contents

Introduction

The three philosophers with which this volume is concerned have several things in common. They lived and wrote during the "long eighteenth" century, the period known as the Enlightenment. They all came from the British Isles—John Locke from England, George Berkeley from Ireland, and David Hume from Scotland—and they wrote their best-known books in their native language, English. And they are leading or even founding members of the school of thought known as Empiricism. While this term is the label under which all three are most usually grouped, it has recently come under criticism as introducing unwarranted distinctions between these and other thinkers of this period. It is certainly misleading to think of these three as members of a "school" in which later members attempted to carry out the purposes and projects of earlier members. Instead Locke, Berkeley, and Hume must be understood as carrying out individually conceived projects with motivations that differ significantly one from another. Nevertheless, they all share a general view in common that can fairly be called "Empiricist." Consider Locke's claim expressed early in Book II of the *Essay Concerning Human Understanding*, in which he enlarges on the statement that our minds are blank paper, furnished by experience:

> Our observation, employed either about *external sensible objects, or about the internal operations of our minds perceived and reflected on by ourselves, is that which supplies our understanding with all the materials of thinking.* These two are the fountains of knowledge, from whence all the *ideas* we have, or can naturally have, do spring. (*ECHU* 2.1.2)

Compare this with Berkeley's opening sentence of *The Principles of Human Knowledge*:

vii

It is evident to anyone who takes a survey of the objects of human knowledge, that they are either ideas imprinted on the senses, or else such as
are perceived by attending to the passions or operations of the mind,
or lastly ideas formed by the help of memory and imagination, either
compounding, dividing, or barely representing those originally perceived
in the aforesaid ways. (*PHK* 1)

And finally Hume, in the first section of Book I of the *Treatise of
Human Nature*, tells us that the contents of the human mind are either ideas or impressions and that

> Ideas produce the image of themselves in new ideas: but as the first ideas
> are supposed to be derived from impressions, it still remains true that
> all our simple ideas proceed either mediately or immediately from their
> correspondent impressions. (*THK* 1.1.1)

And like Berkeley and Locke, Hume identifies two sources of impressions, sensation and reflection. Thus Locke, Berkeley, and Hume share
a common genetic account of the contents of the understanding:
There are no mental contents that cannot be derived from sensation
or reflection. This common approach can reasonably be called Empiricism.

In addition to this common methodology, there are other aspects of
their thought that all three share. Not surprisingly, they all tend to
be empiricist in a broader sense as well; they all tend to assume that
knowledge is advanced through experience. Although their motivations differ, they are all engaged in roughly the same project, that of
laying down the framework for a science of human nature. Their approach to the science of human nature shares loosely the same empiricist method: an introspective examination of the ideas that form the
content of the understanding. It also might be said that they are all, in
one way or another, interested in exploring the limitations of human
mental faculties. After these general areas of commonality, however, it
must be said that John Locke, George Berkeley, and David Hume have
written very different books.

Locke

Locke's *Essay Concerning Human Understanding*, the work in which
he developed his version of Empiricism, was published in 1690, when

Locke was fifty-eight years old. He tells us in his "Epistle to the Reader" that he began work on what was ultimately to become the *Essay* after a meeting with "five or six friends" who, finding themselves at a standstill "on a subject very remote from this," agreed that before further progress could be made "it was necessary to examine our own abilities and see what objects our understanding were or were not fitted to deal with." This project, many years later, found fruition in the *Essay*. The purpose of this work was, through an investigation of the nature of the human cognitive faculties, to achieve some understanding of how far our own faculties can reach, so as to identify the limitations of our knowledge. In an often quoted passage from this Epistle, Locke describes himself as an "underlabourer" to the great natural scientists of his day (he mentions Boyle, Sydenham, Huygens, and Newton), clearing away rubbish before their progress. It is reasonable to assume, then, that Locke saw the sort of psychological investigation on which he was embarked as a necessary preliminary to the study of the natural world. Before making pronouncements about the character of the natural world, Locke thought it necessary to understand more clearly the character of the knowledge we are equipped to develop—to see, in his sort of words, how far our ideas can take us. Locke's relationship to these physical scientists is somewhat complex. He was not intending to engage in physical enquiries himself, nor did he intend either to clarify or to justify the pronouncements of the physical scientists. Rather, it was his goal to indicate those areas where the physical scientists had overstepped their mark, either by inappropriately demanding certainty or by employing concepts for which our faculties do not make adequate provision.

Locke carries out his analysis of the scope and limitations of human mental faculties almost entirely in terms of ideas. While it is only Book II that is explicitly labeled "On Ideas," the other three books concern the impossibility of innate ideas (Book I), words which stand for ideas (Book III), and knowledge, which consists in the agreement or disagreement of ideas (Book IV). Clearly, Locke's notion of ideas provides the basic framework of the *Essay*. Unfortunately, understanding exactly what Locke means by an idea has proved both difficult and controversial. This unclarity can be, and often is, blamed on vagueness in Locke's language in talking about ideas, but some of the blame must be attributed to the sheer difficulty of the issues involved. Locke defined 'idea' as "the object of understanding when a man thinks" and expressed the hope that, since no one can think without being conscious of the ideas thought, that everyone would, through their own experience, be able to recognize what an idea is. That this has nevertheless proved difficult has to do with the dual nature of ideas. Ideas are subjective states of mind and they also inform of or represent objective states of the external world. The problem is to see how these things we are supposed to be able to find within ourselves, mind-dependent states of the knower, are able to acquaint us with mind-independent states of the physical world. How much of what we are conscious of in thinking is to be understood as states of ourselves, reflecting our own subjective nature, and what is left to be the objective world we know? To stress that we know with ideas seems to leave knowers trapped and unable to get at the world of things, while to stress that we know things, not ideas, seems to leave the activity of the mind unaccounted for. Much of the commentary on Locke's use of the term 'idea' has been an attempt either to convict Locke of one of these two untenable positions or to work out an appropriate middle path.

If Locke's belief that we know by means of ideas has proved puzzling, so has his further claim that we know no further than our ideas can take us. It is Locke's view that our knowledge is limited to the ideas provided us by the five senses we happen to have, and to the various ways in which our experience has shown us these ideas coexist or combine. Identifying exactly how much these limitations allow us to know about the natural world has proved controversial. This controversy has included in its sweep many important and heavily discussed concepts and distinctions in Locke, including 'substance', 'real and nominal essence', 'primary and secondary qualities', and 'personal identity'.

Locke says that when a number of ideas are found in our experience to go regularly together, we treat them as one thing and suppose them to inhere in a substance. We do this because we take the coexisting ideas to be dependent upon a "particular internal constitution, or unknown Essence of that Substance" (2.23.3). Substance seems to be, for Locke, that something in the world from which our ideas "flow." We have the ideas we do because of something in the outside world Locke wants to call substance. But he also says we don't know what substance is. We don't know what it is about the outside world that accounts for the ideas we have. Locke is very clear that this ignorance we have about substance holds not only for material substance, but also for minds or immaterial substances.

Exactly why we are so ignorant is a matter of some dispute. One very plausible clue is Locke's claim that we don't know the essence of substance. After all, if we did know—as Descartes, for example, thought we did—that the essence of material substance was extension, and that of immaterial substance was thought, then we presumably would have the sort of knowledge about bodies or minds that Locke denies we have. Locke distinguishes between the 'real essence' and the 'nominal essence'. The real essence he describes as the "real Constitution, on which any Collection of simple *Ideas* co-existing, must depend" (3.3.15). The nominal essence is the abstract idea under which things are gathered into kinds. In Locke's view, we don't know the real essence of any thing. We don't know what it is that, being true of that thing, determines its properties, and so we don't know what properties it must have. We will know what ideas go into the name we use to pick out things of that kind but this is not the same as knowing that all the things picked out by the name share the same inner constitution. So according to Locke, we don't know the essence of bodies; we don't know what determines bodies to have the properties they do. We have an abstract idea of bodies, including, for example, that bodies are extended and movable, but we don't know how the parts of bodies cohere to form extension and we don't know in virtue of what they are movable. Similarly, although we are aware of our minds as thinking and willing, we don't know what about minds determines them to think and will.

Locke's famous distinction between primary and secondary qualities can be understood to form a part of this general account of the limitations on our knowledge. Locke's account notoriously identifies a set of qualities, usually extension, solidity, motion and rest, figure, and number, as primary qualities, while a range of sensible qualities such as red, soft, sweet, and loud are identified as secondary qualities. As long as Locke is taken to be describing on the one hand a set of qualities characterizing mind-independent physical substance, and on the other a set of mind-dependent qualities having no counterpart in nature, then he seems to be making some quite far-reaching claims. How Locke is in any position to know which qualities are the primary qualities of body becomes an urgent question. It is important to notice, however, that Locke's account depends upon a distinction between ideas in us and qualities in bodies. His distinction is intended to be between ideas of primary and ideas of secondary qualities, and his ideas of primary qualities in fact constitute the nominal essence of bodies, the ideas of bodies that in our experience go constantly together. The purpose of the distinction is not to teach us something about the qualities of bodies, but to show how a painter or dyer has better ideas of colors than a philosopher worried about their unknown causes. This issue too is actually about limitations in our knowledge. Similarly, Locke's account of personal identity is designed to tease out what we can know about ourselves as persisting entities, given our ignorance of the nature of our immaterial substance. Thus one dominant theme running through many of Locke's discussions is that the way in which we are built to have ideas does not permit us to construct a natural science of essences for those ideas.

It is also important to notice that these limitations on knowledge of the natural world do not extend to moral knowledge. Since moral knowledge is not knowledge of substances but, in Locke's terminology, of "mixed modes," abstract ideas which we make without trying to capture some externally existing thing, our ignorance of real essences does not stand in the way of our having demonstrative moral knowledge. Since, according to legend, the original topic of discussion among Locke and his friends that spurred the existence of the *Essay* is said to have been a piece of moral knowledge, this result may be the conclusion toward which the *Essay* was heading.

Berkeley

George Berkeley published the work in which he laid out his views most substantially, *Treatise Concerning the Principles of Human Knowledge*, in 1710, when he was still a young man of twenty-six. Disappointed in the rather negative reception of this work, which he thought reflected a lack of understanding of the ideas he had been trying to put forth, he rewrote his theory in a more accessible dialogue form, *Three Dialogues Between Hylas and Philonous*, which he published in 1713. Despite the second attempt, Berkeley's views have often had trouble finding a sympathetic hearing. Berkeley's claims have often been taken to be too counterintuitive to be remotely plausible. This reaction is to some extent ironic, since Berkeley took it as his purpose to vindicate common sense against the challenges of skepticism and atheism. Although he shared with Locke the broad outlines of an account of our cognitive faculties and how they operate, he did not accept Locke's conclusions about the limited nature of the knowledge we can acquire. To the contrary, it was Berkeley's view that "the far greater part if not all, of these difficulties which have hitherto amused philosophers, and blocked up the way to knowledge, are entirely owing to ourselves. That we have first raised a dust, and then complain, we cannot see" (*PHK, Intro*, 3). Berkeley's purpose in writing the *Principles* is to show that conclusions about the limitations on knowledge are themselves based on faulty assumptions.

While Berkeley shared Locke's view that we are limited in our knowledge of the natural world to what we can gain through our senses, he also denied Locke's claim that the natural world somehow outruns our sensory knowledge. Berkeley's denial rests on a rather striking existence claim: The natural world does not outrun our sensible ideas because to be is to be perceived; the only things that exist are minds and ideas. Thus Berkeley has saved the world from skepticism, but at what looks like a considerable cost: He has turned everything into ideas. Berkeley himself denies this allegation. Responding to it in *Three Dialogues*, he writes: You mistake me. I am not for changing things into ideas, but rather ideas into things" (*3DIII*, 244). Before Berkeley's self-defense can be accepted, however, it is necessary to understand the argument by which he turns ideas into things.

Berkeley's argument has two components, an idealist component and an immaterialist component, each of which requires some discussion. The idealist component says our ideas cannot exist outside the mind. Understanding this claim depends to an important degree on what Berkeley means by idea in this context. From the examples he provides, it seems relatively clear what he has in mind are sense qualities or sensations. But in this case, the idealist claim amounts to the relatively uncontroversial claim that sensations cannot exist independently of minds with a sensory apparatus. Sensings or sensations cannot exist in the absence of perceivers, so sensations do not exist without the mind. This claim is in fact so uncontroversial that Berkeley shares it with numerous other thinkers.

What is controversial in Berkeley's theory, then, rests on his immaterialism. Berkeley claims not just that ideas exist in minds but that there is nothing that ideas stand for except that which exists in minds. As he puts it in his notorious Master Argument in the *Principles*: "If you can but conceive it possible for one extended movable substance, or in general, for any one idea or anything like an idea, to exist otherwise that in a mind perceiving it, I shall readily give up the cause" (*PHK* 22). This argument clearly involves a negative component: Our ideas cannot be held to stand for an extended, movable mind-independent substance, for such a notion is inconceivable. Any attempt to frame a concept of such a substance will be necessarily in terms of sense-derived ideas, which are themselves, as sensory, mind-dependent. There is no way in which we can start from our sensings and peel off from them some way in which the world is independent of any mind. The idea of a world as it would be if all minds were annihilated is itself inconceivable. While we are often driven to postulate the existence of such a mind-independent world, because we think our ideas must have a cause, it is Berkeley's view that any account of the cause of our ideas in terms of material substance is incoherent. Any account that, for example, describes material substance as extended and movable is of necessity derived from our ideas, and as such describes something passive. There is no way in which we can understand how such an inert being could initiate power and there is no way in which such an unthinking being could be a cause of thought. So the negative side of Berkeley's immaterialism consists in a demonstration of the incoherence of any account that attempts to ground our understanding of the nature of reality in material substance.

Berkeley's immaterialism has a positive element as well. In place of the picture of the world as a mechanical device of extended moving parts, he wants to substitute a picture of the world as a language. The world we live in is a real world because it makes sense. The ideas I have occur in meaningful patterns or regularities. Our ideas of trees or tulips do not represent some mind-independent essence, but rather represent other ideas. When I perceive a tree or a tulip, I immediately perceive or sense some ideas I make sense of in terms of other ideas, those ideas which have regularly recurred in the presence of the ideas I am now having. Understanding the nature of the physical world is a matter of understanding how our ideas go together. Berkeley conceives the task of the physical scientist not as uncovering unknown essences but as discovering those regularities which allow us to predict the course of nature. The second or positive half of Berkeley's immaterialism is a theory about the representational function of ideas.

Although Berkeley thinks we have been led into skepticism through an unwarranted belief in material substance, he does not think the same can be said for minds or immaterial substances. Instead, he holds that through my own introspective capacities I have an immediate acquaintance with myself as a mental agent, capable of having ideas and of willing and understanding. Mental agency, unlike the problematic notion of corporeal agency, is something with which I am perfectly familiar and which makes perfect sense. Berkeley argues that when I try to give an account of the cause of those of my ideas of which I am not the cause, it must be in terms of mental agency. Such an account is readily forthcoming. My ideas and the ideas of all finite beings are caused by the Supreme Intelligence, God, who speaks to us via the "Language of Nature." Berkeley conceived his system to be the antidote not only to skepticism but also to atheism.

Hume

Like Berkeley before him, Hume laid out his basic position in a work published when he was still quite young. *A Treatise of Human Nature* appeared in 1739/40 when Hume was twenty-five years old. Hume too was disappointed at the reception of his first work, and tried to make his ideas more acceptable in two further volumes, *An Enquiry Concerning Human Understanding*, published in 1748, and *An Enquiry Concerning the Principles of Morals* in 1775. Although Hume himself in later life went so far as to recommend to his readers that they confine themselves to the two Enquiries, subsequent generations of readers have tended to ignore this advice and concentrate their attention on the rather fuller expression of Hume's ideas found in the *Treatise*.

Hume's project in the *Treatise* is to develop a "science of man," to give an account of the qualities and powers of the human mind as they are revealed through observation and experiment. It seems Hume shared Locke's view that by investigating human mental capacities he was serving as an underlabourer to the sciences. It is clear, however, that Hume did not adopt this project in any spirit of humility. To the contrary, it is Hume's contention all the sciences—that is, all bodies of knowledge, including mathematics, natural philosophy, and natural religion—rest on the science of man as their foundation. Hume is developing an observationally based account of human cognitive capacities because he thinks an understanding of progress in the sciences requires that we know something about the nature of human ideas and mental operations. What Hume is after is a naturalistic account of human knowledge, in which the beliefs we end up with are the result of those cognitive capacities with which we are endowed. While this is also the project with which Berkeley was engaged, Hume took a very different attitude toward skepticism than Berkeley. While Berkeley took it as an important part of his project to lay skeptical doubts to rest, Hume highlights a number of skeptical conclusions to his investigations. It has been a complicated and controversial matter among readers of Hume to balance his claims to be able to lay the sciences on a firm foundation against his expressions of skepticism.

Hume begins by making some terminological refinements in the view he shared with Locke and Berkeley: that we are limited in our ideas to what we can acquire by means of the senses. Hume proposes we reserve the term 'perception' as an umbrella term for all of our mental contents, and then, within this framework, he distinguishes between two kinds of perceptions, impressions and ideas. Hume's account of this distinction is disappointingly brief and appeals to the introspective experience of the reader. "Every one of himself" he says, "will readily perceive the distinction between feeling and thinking" (*T* 1.1.1). And indeed, everyone probably will admit being able to distinguish between feeling pain (having an impression) and thinking about pain (having an idea of pain). Hume tells us he wants to characterize this distinction in terms of force and vivacity: impressions are more forceful and lively than ideas. He further wants to distinguish between simple and complex impressions and simple and complex ideas in order to call to our attention what is for him an important principle, that we have no simple ideas that are not derived from and do not copy simple impressions. Hume supports this principle by urging the reader to engage in introspective experiments, to find a simple idea that does not resemble its corresponding impression. Again, it is relatively easy to perform the kind of thought experiment he points us to; people are not likely to be able to form an idea of the taste of some fruit they have never tasted, and the idea of the taste of the fruit they have tasted seems to derive from the impression gained by actually biting into the fruit. What we know when we know what a pineapple tastes like is like what we experience in tasting a pineapple. Although Hume's confidence that what he is talking about is introspectively obvious is not entirely misplaced, it has not been easy to put these various claims together in a way that is similarly obvious. Even though introspection reveals that something less lively is occurring when we think than when we feel and even though introspection also reveals that what we can think about depends upon and reflects what we have felt, it is by no means clear, for example, that when thinking about pain we uncover a kind of foggy duplicate of what we feel. Indeed, it becomes hard to understand how to discriminate thinking of a very great pain from feeling a faint twinge. It has proved easy to provide unacceptable ways of understanding Hume's copy theory of ideas and much harder to provide interpretations that save what is introspectively satisfying as an account of our cognitive capacities.

While the principle of no ideas without their corresponding impressions provides a starting point for Hume's investigations of our cognitive capacities and constitutes a complete account of the origin of simple ideas, a more interesting question concerns the origins of our complex ideas. Complex ideas must ultimately be traced to simple impressions, but we also need to know something of the processes by means of which the mind forms complex ideas from simple ones. Hume calls this constructive faculty the imagination and he holds it is possible to discover that it operates by means of only a few associative principles: resemblance, continuity, and causation. It is possible to uncover in Hume a thoroughly naturalistic project. Hume is exploring the origins of some of our complex ideas, such as causation, the continued and distinct existence of bodies and personal identity, to name some of the most frequently discussed. His answer is going to show starting from which impressions, and by means of which principles, the complex idea is framed. This naturalistic project, however, is not carried out in an entirely straightforward manner. Hume is at pains to show that the question, From which impressions is the idea of, say, causation, derived? has an unexpected answer. Although our idea of causation seems to be of a necessary connection between contiguous events, we have actually no impressions of the necessary connection of cause and effect, but only the impression of resembling sequences of contiguous events. Or, similarly, although our idea of bodies is of something existing continuously and independently, our impressions are only fleeting and mind-dependent. There is no impression of continuous, independent existence. Again, Hume says that when he looks within himself, all he can find is a succession of ideas and no permanently existing self. There is no impression or set of impressions corresponding to our idea of personal identity. Hume gives an account of the origin of these problematic ideas in terms of the enlivening effects of our associative principles themselves. We can find the missing impressions as part of the contribution of the constructive mind. Hume does provide an answer to the question, From which impressions are these ideas derived? He also stresses, however, that there can be no basis found in reason for our belief in causation or in the continued existence of bodies or even the continued existence of ourselves. Subsequent generations of readers have disputed whether Hume's account of the origins of these ideas is the account of a skeptic showing how we are tricked into supposing there are causation and external bodies or the account of a naturalistic psychologist, showing the mental mechanisms by means of which these ideas are generated.

In giving this account of the important ideas of Locke, Berkeley, and Hume, I have stressed how frequently an interpretation of their thought remains controversial. That there is no widespread agreement about the nature of the theories of these major thinkers might seem surprising, but I think should not be. The issues with which they are engaged are difficult ones and do not lend themselves to an easy or straightforward expression. The ideas being laid out are the result of long and arduous thought and, in return, take more than a little thought to understand. It is also important to keep in mind that the authors of these ideas lived at a time several centuries removed from us and operated on the basis of assumptions we do not share, using language that is no longer in common usage. The various articles included in this anthology provide help in understanding difficult issues, but more importantly, they provide models for how to go about reading a historical text so as to profit from it. The authors of the articles included engage the thinkers of the past with respect and show sensitivity to the historical period in which these thinkers lived. The reader of these pieces will not find all controversies laid to rest, but will have had the opportunity to learn a great deal about how to read the history of philosophy.

Acknowledgments

Ian Tipton, " 'Ideas' and 'Objects': Locke on Perceiving 'Things' " from *Minds, Ideas and Objects*, edited by Phillip D. Cummins and Guenter Zoeller, Ridgeview Publishing Co., 1992. Permission to reprint granted by the North American Kant Society.

Michael R. Ayers, "The Foundations of Knowledge and the Logic of Substance in Locke's General Philosophy" from *Locke's Philosophy: Content and Context*, edited by G. A. J. Rogers, Oxford University Press, 1994. Permission to reprint granted by the author.

G. A. J. Rogers, "Locke, Law and the Law of Nature" from *John Locke: Symposium Wolfenbuettel 1979*, edited by Reinhard Brandt, Walter de Gruyter, 1981. Permission to reprint granted by the author.

Edwin McCann, "Locke on Identity: Matter, Life and Consciousness," *Archiv fuer Geschichte der Philosophie* 69 (1987). Permission to reprint granted by the author.

Phillip D. Cummins, "Berkeley's Ideas of Sense," *Nous* 2 (1975). Permission to reprint granted by Basil Blackwell, Inc.

Margaret D. Wilson, "Did Berkeley Completely Misunderstand the Basis of the Primary-Secondary Quality Distinction in Locke?" from *Berkeley: Critical and Interpretive Essays*, edited by C. M. Turbayne, University of Minnesota Press, 1982. Copyright 1982 by the University of Minnesota. Permission to reprint granted by the University of Minnesota Press and by the author.

George Pappas, "Berkeleian Idealism and Impossible Performances" from *Berkeley's Metaphysics: Structural, Interpretive and Critical Essays*, edited by Robert G. Muehlmann (University Park: Pennsylvania State University Press, 1995, pp. 127–145). Copyright 1995 by the Pennsylvania State University. Permission to reprint granted by the Pennsylvania State University Press.

Charles J. McCracken, "Berkeley's Notion of Spirit" from *History of European Ideas*, vol. 7, no. 6, 1986. Permission to reprint granted by Elsevier Science.

Don Garrett, "The Representation of Causation and Hume's Two Definitions of 'Cause' " from *Nous* 27 (1993). Permission to reprint granted by Basil Blackwell, Inc.

Kenneth Winkler, "Hume's Inductive Scepticism" has not been previously published.

Robert Fogelin, "The Soul and the Self" appeared as chapter 8 of *Hume's Scepticism in the Treatise of Human Nature*, Routledge and Kegan Paul, 1993. Permission to reprint granted by the author.

Barry Stroud, "Hume's Scepticism: Natural Instincts and Philosophical Reflection" from *Philosophical Topics* 19, no. 1 (Spring, 1991). Permission to reprint granted by the author.

1

"Ideas" and "Objects": Locke on Perceiving "Things"

Ian Tipton

The problem of understanding Locke's idea of "idea" is clearly not confined to the area of sense-perception. But there is supposed to be an issue there, with commentators apparently divided over whether we should interpret him in what is often called the "traditional" or "orthodox" way, according to which Locke accepts "the representative theory of perception," or, rather, see his ideas as "perceptions," or "appearances" perhaps, or at least not as what M. A. Stewart has described as "those dummy objects of that dummy Locke beloved of the critics."[1] Among those who have been associated with the "traditional" view are Thomas Reid in the eighteenth century, and Reginald Jackson, R. I. Aaron, H. A. Prichard and D. J. O'Connor in our own; while amongst its critics we might list William Swabey, Douglas Lewis, Douglas Greenlee, A. D. Woozley and John Yolton.[2] Both lists could be extended, and in a way which might cast doubt on the notion that *either* view was ever strictly "orthodox," but the impression one gets, certainly, is that while fifty years ago, or about the time that Aaron published his *John Locke*, few would have dissented from his view that, for Locke, we are acquainted with ideas and not external things, most Locke scholars today would have doubts. However, the issue remains a live one and one we find it difficult to agree on. I want to consider why.

One problem of course is that if one combs the text of the *Essay*, the letters to Stillingfleet, and so on, looking for clues as to precisely what Locke takes ideas to be, one is bound to be struck by his clear reluctance to pronounce on the issue. His complaint to Norris that "If you once mention ideas you must be presently called to an account *what kind of things you make these same ideas to be*"³ inevitably resurfaces as a rebuke to any enquiring commentator, including oneself. And the well-known passage in the *Essay* in which he explains his use of the term turns out to be surprisingly unhelpful. Thus his explanation that he uses it "to express whatever is meant by *Phantasm, Notion, Species,* or whatever it is, which the Mind can be employ'd about in thinking,"⁴ *may* suggest to us, as it did to Reid for example, that Locke's view is "built upon" the view of the Peripatetics and only intelligible in terms of it,⁵ or it *can* be read as introducing the term in a more or less theory-neutral way to replace the theory-loaded terms of the schools. The passage can, in short, hardly be said to *settle* anything, though, like many other passages in the *Essay,* it may seem to if we approach it with some preconceived idea of what Locke's ideas must be.

That, however, is not the only problem. Another, which I want to dwell on here, is that the picture we have of two "camps," adopting more or less clearly defined yet competing interpretations of Locke, is itself problematic, and this for two reasons. Less interestingly, there is the fact that those thought of as being representative of the opposing camps often waver, conceding that the textual evidence is inconclusive, and that Locke may not consistently adhere to the view they attribute to him. More interestingly, there is the fact that the battle-lines between the two supposed camps are often not clearly drawn. As just one example, I note that Gibson, who has certainly been listed alongside Aaron and others as accepting the "traditional" view, and who does indeed say that Locke accepts "a theory of representative perception,"⁶ *also* says that Locke's ideas are "essentially signs, which point beyond themselves to a realm of real being,"⁷ a view which hardly makes them "dummy objects"; while, on the other side, Woozley, who sees himself as opposing the "orthodox" view that Locke's ideas are "entities," does nonetheless concede that "he held *some kind* of representationalism."⁸ It would be rash to conclude that there are no genuine disagreements, but I at least hope that if we correct certain definite mistakes that have been made in outlining Locke's position we shall get clearer on what the real issues are. I shall start by looking at Aaron's position, for there are complications even there.

Certainly Aaron starts off confidently enough, claiming that, for Locke, "The mind does not see the real physical object. It sees an object which somehow exists in the mind, and yet it is not the mind itself, nor a modification of the mind";[9] a claim echoed by D. J. O'Connor for example, though now referring to "observation," when he says that, for Locke, "we can never look behind the curtain of ideas to observe the physical objects which cause our ideas."[10] If we combine this claim with the thought, which is again echoed by O'Connor, that this gives rise to serious problems—"it becomes possible to deny the ultimate object supposed to be copied by the idea"—and that Locke recognized this, we might seem to have a definitive statement of what *counts* as the "traditional" view, with Aaron a clear proponent of it. The trouble with that, however, is that, first, as Woozley notes, the view *as stated* is one that Locke clearly didn't hold, and, secondly, that Aaron himself does not see Locke as consistently adhering to it. Both points are important.

First, then, Woozley is surely right to point out that Locke does not normally talk of "seeing" ideas of things such as tables, though he does talk of "having" them; to which we can add that, when pressed on his view of ideas, he happily talks of seeing, not ideas, but the external things themselves. As he says impatiently to Norris, "what difference a man finds in himself, when he sees a marygold, and sees not a marygold, has no difficulty, and needs not be inquired after: he has the idea now, which he had not before."[11] The issue, as Locke presents it there, is whether, as Norris thinks, the mind sees "the divine idea in the understanding of God," or, "as the ignorant think," and quite simply, "the marygold in the garden"; and, far from disassociating himself from "the ignorant" here, Locke pointedly includes himself among "we vulgar" who, he says, "have the ingenuity to confess their ignorance" as to what the alteration in the mind consists in, beyond saying that it is the mind's "having a perception, which it had not the moment before." Here, then, what the mind "sees" *is* the external thing, and, as so often in the *Essay*, the idea is simply "a perception." When it comes to "observing," we need only recall Locke's pronouncement that "the Extension, Figure, Number, and Motion of Bodies of an observable bigness, may be perceived at a distance *by* the sight" (*E*:2.8.12), together with the fact that, from the outset, it is "Our Observation employ'd . . . about *external, sensible Objects*" that is said to be one of our two sources of ideas (*E*:2.1.2). For Locke, if we "see" the marigold, we "observe" it too.

In fact, the only moral we can safely draw at this point is that Aaron is certainly incautious here, for obviously one could hold what Woozley calls a "picture-original theory of sense-perception" and still *say* that we "see" the originals, while, conversely, and perhaps less obviously, a philosopher who holds that ideas are "perceptions" may deny that we "see" the external things. Thomas Brown comes at least close to that, for we find that, though he vigorously opposes the view that Locke's ideas are "images" or "things," insisting, against Reid, that they are simply "perceptions," or "states of the mind," and that he is applauded by Yolton for so doing, he also describes talk of "seeing the sun," for example, as no more than "popular and very convenient phraseology."[12] For, Brown, it is "that which acts immediately upon the organs" that is "the real object of sense"; "All of which we are truly conscious, in sensation, is the mental affection, the last link of the series, in the supposed process"; and belief in external things derives from "suggestion." Which "camp" that puts Brown in is unclear, but that is because the battle-lines are so poorly drawn. Yolton certain welcomes him as an ally.

Returning to Aaron, though, we now have to face the second of the complications I referred to earlier, which is that, while the passage already quoted suggests that he belongs in the"traditional" camp if anyone does, he not only softens that interpretation by conceding that Locke was not an enthusiastic advocate of representationalism, and indeed that "The truth or falsity of empiricism . . . has nothing to do with the truth or falsity of representationalism," but eventually asserts that in Book Four, Chapter Eleven, the very chapter in which Locke faces up to the question of our knowledge of *the existing of Things without us,*" he departs from his earlier representationalism by rejecting the view that "we know through ideas only," and taking the line that, "Whenever we sense we are *directly* assured that things exist independently of us" (my emphasis). This is, Aaron thinks, quite inconsistent with what Locke says elsewhere, so, as he sees it, Locke leaves us with "two theories of knowledge standing side by side." *One* of these involves the representative theory of perception, but the other holds that "knowledge, on occasion at least, is a direct apprehension of the real."

Now of course one conclusion we could draw from this is simply the obvious one that if there are two "camps," taking clearly opposed views on how Locke should be interpreted, Aaron in fact straddles them by suggesting that it all depends on which part of the *Essay* one is looking at. But if we left it there we'd be missing the point that Aaron is surely rash to suggest that Book Four, Chapter Eleven involves a rejection of the view that "we know through ideas only," in that, even there, it is "the actual receiving of *Ideas* from without, that gives us notice of the *Existence of other Things"* (*E*:4.11.2), and it is "when our Senses do actually convey into our Understandings any *Idea"* that we are sure that something exists "without us" (*E*:4.11.9). Given that it is thus the "receiving" of ideas that is supposed to give us the assurance Locke certainly thinks we have, this is still, it seems, knowledge by way of ideas. And that leaves two possible interpretations open. The first is that Locke is still committed to what Aaron would think of as the earlier representationalism, but now naively underestimating the seriousness of the problems it poses, which would at least have him consistent; while the second, which would also have him consistent, is that Locke's earlier representationalism has been misinterpreted. Perhaps Locke never meant to suggest that we are not acquainted with things.

For the moment, however, that can only be a suggestion, for my aim is still to get clearer on what divides the two "camps" on this issue, a problem that has perhaps become that of pin-pointing some feature or features of a position that might with *some* plausibility be attributed to Locke, and which would justify the talk of "screens" or "barriers" we have become accustomed to. And given that we can't locate such a feature in a claim that, for Locke, we don't "see" the real things, the most likely candidates would seem to be:

(a) that his very definition of "knowledge" in *E*:4.1.2 *should* rule out knowledge of *"the existing of Things without us"*;

(b) that he does apparently believe that our seeing a man for example will require that (b-1) we have an idea in our minds, but that, in addition, (b-2) the idea must be causally dependent on the existence of the man;

(c) that there is therefore, as R. S. Woolhouse has put it, "a merely contingent connexion between our ideas and the presence of a man";[13]

(d) that such an account must make the existence of external things problematic;

(e) that Locke himself recognizes that he holds a view of perception that creates difficulties;

(f) that his talk of ideas as the "immediate" objects of perception shows clearly that he is not a direct realist;

(g) that he says quite explicitly that we perceive ideas, and, on occasion, that we perceive *only* ideas;

(h) that these ideas must be "things," "objects" or "entities," and perhaps,

(i) that they are *pictures*.

That is quite a mixed bag, and I am not suggesting that anyone who we would be inclined to include in the "traditional" camp must accept all of (a) to (i), though all these claims are common in the literature. Nor am I saying that anyone who accepts *any* of (a) to (i) must have at least a foot there. Woozley, for example, accepts that (b) is attributable to Locke, and it would be difficult to deny that it is, while, (g) is a straight-forward statement of fact, though we may differ as to how it is to be interpreted. One problem, certainly, is that of deciding which of the above we should accept; but another is that of deciding how many we would have to accept before we agreed that the "orthodox" interpreta-tion was at least not wildly out. I can illustrate what I have in mind by looking at J. L. Mackie's interpretation of Locke.

Mackie is one recent commentator who certainly says that Locke held a representative theory of perception,[14] and it is clear that he ac-cepts a number of the items on the above list, including (b) to (e), while he probably rejects (h), but apparently not (i). One has to be a little careful here, for in general Mackie is less concerned with exegesis than with what he takes to be the underlying philosophical issues, but he at least seems to be accepting (i) when he quotes from *E*:4.11.1— "the having the *idea* of anything in our mind no more proves the exis-tence of that thing, than the picture of a man evidences his being in the world"—to show how "Locke himself compares 'the having the idea' with a picture," adding, in a way that links (i) to (e), that here he "openly admits holding a view for which the problem arises whether there is something external answering to our ideas." Given that the context is apparent scepticism about Woozley's view that Locke did *not* hold a "picture-original theory of sense-perception," this might seem to be sufficient to place Mackie in the "traditional" camp. In fact, I want to suggest that the situation here parallels the one we found when we considered Aaron. In the first place, there is some questionable exege-sis at the outset, and, secondly, Mackie's Locke turns out to adopt a position rather different from that which Mackie's earlier comments might lead us to expect. I shall cover both points.

So far as the question of exegesis is concerned, the point is not sim-ply that comparing the having of an idea with a picture is not the same as saying that Locke's ideas are "literal pictures," which is what Wooz-ley is concerned to deny, but that, in the statement quoted, Locke is talking about ideas as they occur in thought (in the narrow sense), and in particular "any *Idea* a Man hath in his Memory," and that, whether or not he took talk of "pictures" seriously in that context, the basic point he is making is the uncontroversial one that having the idea (conception) of a mermaid, say, most certainly does not evidence the existence of a mermaid, any more than a picture of a mermaid would. That quite innocent claim betrays no sceptical anxieties about sense perception,[15] and indeed no sceptical anxieties are present when he turns from thought (in the narrow sense) to sense perception, dropping any analogy with pictures, and announcing that it is "the actual receiving of *Ideas* from without, that gives us notice of the *Existence* of other Things." Here of course Locke confidently refers to "the certainty of our Senses" and "the Testimony of my Eyes," and pours scorn on any challenge from the sceptic. There is thus no evidence in Book Four, Chapter Eleven for (e), or, I should say, for (i) either, at least if we are talking about sense-perception. From that point of view, Mackie gets us off to a bad start.

What follows, however, suggests that Mackie himself may not take (i) very seriously. For we find that after an excursus on "a crude picture-theory," which Mackie does *not* attribute to Locke, we are offered a view which he holds is "fairly close to what Locke was trying to state," according to which ideas are simply "intentional objects." These are, Mackie explains, "not a special kind of entity," but "contents of states of perceptual awareness," or "appearances," where "to speak of appearances is just to speak generally of such matters as how-it-looks or how-it-feels." This means, apparently, not that we *don't* perceive things (it seems that Mackie does not interpret (g) as entailing *that*), but rather that we can only perceive them *through* becoming aware of how they look and feel to us. It is the sort of point I take Woozley to have in mind when he says that, "If a God's eye view of the world is possible at all, it is possible only to God," so it is perhaps hardly surprising that Mackie envisages a critic claiming of this position that, "Far from being a crude representationalism, it is not a picture-original analysis of perception at all." His reply is that "it seems to me that this is still a representative theory in the sense that has provoked some of the stock objections" in that "it leaves room for sceptical doubts, more or less extreme." So, in effect, what Mackie offers us is an interpretation of Locke's position which rests, it seems, on (b), (c), and perhaps (f), together with an insistence on (d), which is just the claim that the theory does give rise to problems. And my objection now is really just the one Mackie anticipates, though I would put it by saying that, though he started off as if he were disagreeing with Woozley, it has become very difficult to distinguish his position from that of others who see themselves as *opposed* to the "traditional" view. As already noted, Woozley allows that Locke "held *some kind* of representational-ism," and I should say that the position Mackie outlines is pretty much the one Woozley has in mind; while it comes as no surprise to find Yolton greeting Mackie's contribution with only slightly qualified en-thusiasm.[16] If there is anything distinctive about Mackie's contribution, that seems to me to lie primarily in the stress he puts on (d), which is not really part of the theory attributed to Locke, but points, rather, to an alleged consequence of holding it. That supposed consequence, however, is one that requires special comment.

The crucial point here, I think, is that while both Mackie and Wooz-ley see Locke as not being a "direct" realist, on the basis that he obvi-ously does take sense-perception to be mediated by ideas, even if these ideas are not "entities," it seems clear that both see the view they attri-bute to him, not as some philosophical extravagance, but as involving little more than a recognition of the obvious *fact* that our knowledge of objects can only be based on how they appear to us. Given, however, that an alternative view of perception—a view which would regard it as "a mode of awareness that is so direct as to be self-guaranteeing and unproblematic"—is, in Mackie's opinion, quite untenable, even if it makes sense, his claim that Locke's view of perception leaves us with problems loses much of its sting. As Mackie himself sees it, *anyone* who accepts, as he thinks we all must, that there is "a logical gap be-tween . . . how we see things and how they are" will be open to a challenge from the sceptic, with the consequence, it would seem, that there is nothing *specially* problematic about *Locke's* view which, as Mackie is now presenting it, merely emphasizes the inescapable facts. It therefore becomes understandable if Woozley for example does not stress these problems, or indeed if Locke is not acutely aware of them as problems which it is incumbent on *him* to solve.[17] In so far as he has an answer, it seems to be not incompatible with the one Mackie himself goes on to propose, but at root his conviction is that we can only rely on the testimony of our senses. That won't of course satisfy the deter-mined sceptic who presses what Descartes himself recognized as "hy-perbolical" doubts centered on the Dream Argument, but it is far from clear that any view or theory could.[18] Mackie's recognition of that fact seems to be quite insufficient to put him in the "traditional" camp, unless, that is, Woozley and Yolton belong there too. It follows, I think, that if there are to be genuine battle-lines, more must be incorporated, so we should perhaps look at (a). Aaron is certainly just one commentator who holds that Locke's definition of "knowledge" rules out knowledge of the existence of things.

There are two preliminary points that should perhaps be made about this suggestion. The first is that even if Locke's definition of "knowledge" in *E*:4.1.2 in fact ruled out knowledge of external things, that on its own would not show that he was a representationalist as traditionally conceived, for Locke's definition leads him to deny that we have knowledge in other areas where we would normally say we had it, where the denial has nothing to do with representationalism but everything to do with his special requirements for "knowledge." An obvious case is his insistence that if I am not now perceiving any men, I do not at present "know" there are other men in the world, even though, as he says, "the great likelihood of it puts me past doubt" (*E*:4.11.9). *That* assertion clearly has nothing to do with representative realism, but depends on a decision to use the word "knowledge" in such a way that, with one possible exception, only intuitive and demonstrative knowledge will count. It is, in short, just what we should expect, given the original definition, and though it might give us grounds for criticizing the definition, as Leibniz soon did,[19] it has and is supposed to have no sceptical implications whatsoever. It follows that Locke might have said that we never "know" that any external object exists, even when we are perceiving it, while still referring to "assurance." Indeed, the second point is that he comes close to saying just that. Thus we have the definition of "knowledge" in *E*:4.1.2, and then an account of intuition and demonstration which culminates in the claim that "These *two*, (*viz.*) Intuition and Demonstration, *are* the degrees of our Knowledge; *whatever* comes short of one of these, with what assurance soever embraced, is but Faith, or Opinion, but *not* Knowledge" (*E*:4.2.14, emphases added). Again, that is, I think, what we might expect, given the definition, but then he relents, noting that this is so "at least in all general Truths." There is, he says, something else that "passes under the name of Knowledge," and that is sensitive knowledge. Just as in Book Four, Chapter Eleven, where we are said to have "an assurance that *deserves the name of Knowledge*" in this area, Locke seems almost to be making this "knowledge" by special dispensation. It is arguable, I suggest, that the need to do this has nothing to do with ideas as "pictures," or indeed with "knowledge" in the ordinary sense, any more than does his refusal to make that dispensation in the case of what I would ordinarily take to be my knowledge that Julius Caesar lived. To that extent, Locke's definition of "knowledge" may be irrelevant to the matter in hand.[20]

Those are, however, only preliminary points, for it is clear that many in the "traditional" camp would argue that, even if we take them on board, the real issue remains. What they find disturbing is a thought they find lying *behind* Locke's definition of "knowledge," which they think *should* rule out knowledge of things on *any* definition of the term. Thus Locke does open Book Four with a clear statement, not just that "*the Mind*, in all its Thoughts and Reasonings, hath no other immediate Object but its own *Ideas*," but that it is these alone which it "does or can contemplate," and it is this that raises all the familiar difficulties. Obviously, it will be said, it is this view that leads to Locke's offering the definition he does, but we don't need to read that far, for knowledge of things has already been effectively ruled out. It is *that* notion which I take to lie behind the acceptance of (a) on my original list, and I think that here we do have something that divides Woozley, Yolton, and indeed Mackie too, from those in the "traditional" camp. It follows, however, that (a) in effect collapses into (g) on my list, for the appeal is to the fact that Locke can indeed be found admitting that we "perceive" (or "contemplate") nothing but ideas. In turn, that means that the issue is going to concern the interpretation of such passages, for as it stands (g) is uncontroversial. Whatever he *means* by it, Locke can be found saying that we perceive only ideas. This is something we must return to, but only after a brief look at (h). For if the interpretation of (g) does divide the "camps," so, it might seem, does the question as to whether Locke's ideas are "things." One difficulty there, however, is that it isn't as clear as it might be what (h) amounts to, or what it *is* to be an "entity" or a "thing."

There are for example many references under the headings "entity" and "ideas as entities" in the index to Yolton's *Perceptual Acquaintance,* but the only point at which the question of what that term means is raised comes in a note on p. 41 which includes the words "The term 'entity' or 'thing' designates 'substance,'" suggesting at least that what is at stake is whether ideas are *substances.* Even here, however, there is a reference to Malebranche, who is said to be a champion of the view that ideas are "entities," so it seems significant that Yolton himself observes later that, even in the case of Malebranche, "there was no clear category in his metaphysics for characterizing these beings" and "they were substance-like, if not substances,"[21] and that he also describes them as "thing-like,"[22] Given, then, that in Yolton's view it is unclear that even Malebranche's ideas are actual substances, rather than "substance-like," it would seem most unlikely that this is the real issue we face when we turn to Locke. However, the term "substance-like" is clearly deplorably vague, and it seems to me that this vagueness permeates the literature. So here I can only suggest that when we find references to the words "proxy objects," or "dummy objects," we need to put more stress on the word "proxy," or "dummy" than on "objects." In the case of Woozley, for example, the denial that Locke's ideas are "entities" seems to be more or less equivalent to the denial that they are "literal pictures," but, more generally, I take the thought to be that Locke *may* believe that, though most of us naively assume that sense-perception acquaints us with external things (and typically substances), this is a mistake because we are in fact acquainted only with ideas. What will make them "things" (or, better, "thing-like") will be nothing more or less than their standing in the relation to perception that we normally suppose the real things do. If that is right, (h) will, perhaps rather surprisingly, again collapse into (g).[23]

I take it, however, that even if I am right about that, very little is settled, for, to repeat, nobody could deny that Locke *does* say that we perceive only ideas, so everything is going to hang on the interpretation of (g), and whether, as those in the "traditional" camp have assumed, he is committing himself to the claim that we do not perceive the "outward" things. Given that my main aim in this paper has been to clarify the basic issues rather than to settle them, I could perhaps be excused from pronouncing on that here. There are, however, a number of points to be made.

One is that, if a great deal hangs on the interpretation of (g), those in the "traditional" camp might still claim that their interpretation receives all the support it needs from evidence supporting other items on my original list, and that I haven't done justice to them all. And on that I can only say that it seems clear to me that Locke *is* committed to (b), (c), and (f) too, at least on some reading of "direct" realism, but that these are insufficient to give those in the "traditional" camp what they want; that (a) and (h) do not seem to me to raise issues that can be settled before we have agreed on an interpretation of (g); that the claim made in (d) that Locke's view of perception is (specially) problematic can again not be settled before we determine what his view of perception is; and that of course I have not *shown* that either (e) or (i) is false. All I have in fact said about those is that they seem not to be

supported by anything in Book Four, Chapter Eleven; but of course
some have argued that they do receive ample support elsewhere, and
in particular that (e) is supported by what Locke says in *E*:4.4.3. Discussing that section brings us round to what is clearly well-worn
ground, but I shall say something about that.[24]

Some comment on that particular section does seem to be required
for it is the section that has been most frequently cited by those we
think of as being in the "traditional" camp as containing the clearest
possible statement of (g)—"the Mind . . . perceives nothing but its own
Ideas," *and* what they judge to be clear evidence for (e), when Locke
raises the question as to how we can know that the ideas "agree with
Things themselves." This section is indeed cited by Mackie as evidence
for (e), and by Aaron too, who suggests that it is Locke's failure to deal
convincingly with the difficulty when he raises it there that leads him
to set aside his representationalism in 4.11 and give an answer that is
inconsistent with it. The section has of course been discussed too by
others who take a quite different view, so, to repeat, I shall be covering
well-worn ground. We need to be clear on at least two things.

One is that even if Locke's claim that "the Mind . . . perceives nothing
but its own *Ideas*" is indeed to be taken at face-value, and as entailing
that we do not perceive external objects, or things which are not ideas,
it must at least be recognized that often, as in *E*:2.8.12 for example, he
clearly contradicts that by stating that we perceive the things themselves.[25] Indeed, the situation is somewhat similar with his claim in
E:4.1.1 that we "contemplate" only ideas, for that too has to be set
against the claim in *E*:4.21.4 that ideas are necessary as signs precisely
because "the Things, the Mind contemplates, are none of them, be-
sides it self, present to the Understanding." Whatever else Locke may
be saying in that section, it is at least clear that his actual words clearly
commit him to the view that we *do* "contemplate" the things the ideas
are *of*, which leaves us free just accuse him of straightforward inconsistency, or, alternatively, to make a greater effort to understand what his
real view is. Clearly it won't do to simply assert without qualification
that Locke holds that we don't "perceive" or "contemplate" the things,
given that he asserts the contrary.

That, however, is only one point. It is just as important to be clear
that in Book Four, Chapter Four, Locke's eye is not focused, primarily
at least, on the issue of whether we can be sure that external objects
exist (an issue he doesn't raise until Book Four, Chapter Eleven), but
on general truths and, more particularly, the relationship between our

conceptions of things and their natures.[26] Now clearly that *is* an issue for Locke throughout the *Essay*, and it is one that deserves a fuller treatment, but just to illustrate, it will concern the thought that our conception of gold as having, for example, the familiar colour we see individual lumps of gold as having (with no suggestion that we don't see lumps of gold) does not reveal the ultimate or corpuscular nature of the substance itself. Here, then, the *existence* of lumps of gold, let alone of the particular piece of gold I might have in front of me, seems not to be at issue, and those who have concentrated on the few sentences in Section Three that might *seem* to suggest that it is might, I think, have been more puzzled than perhaps they have by what follows. For we find that, after a section in which it is taken as evident that our simple ideas (e.g. our idea of yellow) correspond to powers *in things,* Locke dwells on mathematical and moral truths, before turning at last to our ideas of substances, arguing, in effect, that general propositions concerning gold, for example, will latch on to reality just so long as our abstract ideas include only ideas we have found co-existing in nature. What is striking here is that when Locke does turn to our knowledge of substances, the existence of which should be at issue on one reading of *E*:4.4.3, we find that he is concerned only with *sorts* of things and our *abstract* ideas and that at no point does he question that certain ideas (yellowness and malleability would be examples) have been "discovered to co-exist in Nature" or "found" there (*E*:4.4 12). It is also significant that what Locke says we have found co-existing "in Nature" are *ideas*, for this gives us the clue that the claim that "the Mind . . . perceives nothing but its own *Ideas*" (*E*:4.4.3) is not necessarily incompatible with the view that the mind perceives what is found in nature, or the phenomenal qualities of things, which I take it is what Locke believes. Perhaps this needs a fuller defence, but it can at least be said that, on a quite plausible reading, what Locke takes it we do *not* perceive is, in fact, not lumps of gold, or other external things, but rather the "real Constitution . . . of Substances, whereon our simple *Ideas* depend" (*E*:4.4.12). On this reading, we find little support for the "traditional" interpretation of (g).

In his recent book on Locke and Boyle, Peter Alexander cites Yolton and me as among those who have opposed what I am calling the "traditional" interpretation of Locke; argues that "ideas are simply the appearance of . . . objects to us"; and endorses the notion I had supported that an acceptance of the scientific account of how perception takes place presupposes that we perceive the external things,

rather than suggesting that we do not.[27] And, though I feel a little uneasy about that reference to me, for in my book on Berkeley I in fact
avoided committing myself on whether or not Locke got this wrong, I
do think we should by now be clear that Locke does say that the objects
themselves are "perceived at a distance *by* the sight," as well as that
ideas are then produced in us (*E*:2.8.12); that it is these *two* facts that
he suggests should lead us to accept the scientific account of the perceptual process; and that here, and throughout the *Essay,* the existence of the external objects is taken for granted, on the basis that we
observe them. So to the extent that the "traditional" interpretation
denies these things, that interpretation fails. That is, I think, widely
accepted by now, so as a final point I will just stress that Locke's view
does *not* entail that we are as certain of the existence of objects as we
are that we have ideas, and that he does accept (c) on my original list.[28]
That point is worth making, not so much because it is clear that many
would deny it, but because it is easy to fall into the trap of supposing, or
at least suggesting, that, with the "traditional" interpretation defeated,
scepticism is ruled out of court. It is indeed merely to avoid any misunderstanding that I note that Locke's pragmatic dismissal of scepticism
based on the Dream Argument in particular does *not* amount to a refutation of it, and that doubts at that level survive the translation from
"entity" to "perception," "mental content," and "appearance" too, so
that if *that* were what was at issue, those in the "traditional" camp
would win. It is, I submit, not what they usually say.

Notes

1. M. A. Stewart, "Locke's Mental Atomism and the Classification of Ideas:
I," *The Locke Newsletter* 10 (1979), p. 54.
2. It should not of course be supposed that the philosophers in each of
the groups are in total agreement over what Locke means by "idea," or that
each individual takes him to mean just one thing by it. Claims that Locke uses
the term in various senses are common, and there is broad agreement that it is
not easy to characterize his view adequately. The account of the two competing
interpretations in this paragraph grossly oversimplifies the issues involved, but
lists such as the above *are* common, and one of my aims is to bring out just
how misleading they can be.
3. *JL Answer to Mr. Norris's Reflections* has been printed by Richard Ac-
worth as "Locke's First Reply to John Norris," in *The Locke Newsletter* 2 (1971).
4. *Essay:* 1.1.8. Unless otherwise stated, references to Locke are to the P.

H. Nidditch edition of *An Essay Concerning Human Understanding* (Oxford: Clarendon Press, 1975) by book, chapter and section following *"E"* for *Essay*.

5. Thomas Reid, *Essays on the Intellectual Powers of Man*, in *The Works of Thomas Reid, D.D.* ed. Sir William Hamilton, 2 volumes (6th edn., Edinburgh: Maclachlan and Stewart, 1863), 1, p. 226. In a note at this point, Hamilton protests that "If by this it be meant that the terms of *species* and *phantasm*, as occasionally employed by Gassendi and Locke, are used by them in the common meaning attached to them in the Schools, Reid is wrong."

6. James Gibson *Locke's Theory of Knowledge and Its Historical Relations* (Cambridge: University Press, 1917), p. 222.

7. Gibson *Locke's Theory of Knowledge*, p. 172.

8. References to A. D. Woozley in this paper are to the section "The New Way of Ideas" in the introduction to his abridged edition of the *Essay* (London: Fontana, 1964), pp. 24–35.

9. References to R. I. Aaron are to his defence of the view that Locke was a representationalist in his *John Locke*, third edition (Oxford: Clarendon Press, 1971), pp. 101ff, and to qualifications made in the same book, pp. 114–5 and 237ff.

10. D. J. O'Connor, *John Locke* (New York: Dover Publications, 1967), p. 65.

11. The quotations at this point are from Section Two of Locke's *Remarks upon Some of Mr. Norris's Books . . .* in *The Works of John Locke* (London: Thomas Tegg, 1823), volume 10.

12. Brown discusses these issues at length in his *Lectures on the Philosophy of the Human Mind*, twelfth edition (Edinburgh: William Tait, 1840). Lectures 18–31 are particularly relevant. The reference to "convenient phraseology" is on p. 120. Yolton devotes a paragraph to Brown in his *Perceptual Acquaintance from Descartes to Reid* (Oxford: Basil Blackwell, 1984), p. 99.

13. R. S. Woolhouse *Locke's Philosophy of Science and Knowledge* (Oxford: Basil Blackwell, 1971), p. 35. In the passage from which this is taken, Woolhouse is outlining what we think of as the "traditional" view rather than arguing for it, but it may be worth noting that he immediately glosses (c), above, by comparing the connection to that "between shadows on a screen and a man behind it." This *might* suggest that if we see Locke as holding (c) we will *thereby* be accepting that the "traditional" reading is right. Now it may be that this is not the suggestion here, for Woolhouse also refers to the view that "we do not directly perceive objects in the external world" and that our ideas "represent" them; but it is only fair to say that suggestions that everything does hang on (c) can be found in the literature. My difficulty there is that it seems to me not only that Locke is committed to (c), but that writers such as Woozley and Yolton need not deny it. I shall return to the point.

14. References to Mackie in this paper are to his *Problems from Locke* (Oxford: Clarendon Press, 1976), chapter 2, "Representative Theories of Perception."

15. Cf. Locke's complaint to Stillingfleet that, in seeing Locke's claim that "the idea in the mind proves not the existence of that thing whereof it is an idea" as inviting scepticism, Stillingfleet has missed the distinction between "the idea that has by a former sensation been lodged in the mind" and "actu-

ally receiving any idea." The former does not prove that the thing exists; the latter, Locke repeats, gives knowledge (*Works* 4, p. 360).

16. Yolton *Perceptual Acquaintance*, p. 101. If Yolton's approval of Mackie's contribution is, as I said, "slightly qualified," it is only because, where Mackie talks of "appearances," Yolton says he would "prefer" an account in terms of "perceptual acquaintance," or "act and content." No doubt it is important to get this right, but it is worth noting that in the course of his discussion Mackie does talk of Locke's ideas as making up "experiential content," and that in his *John Locke* (Oxford: Basil Blackwell, 1985), pp. 148–51, Yolton puts the emphasis on "appearances."

17. Towards the end of the chapter Mackie in fact concludes that "We can see that at least in principle Locke was right not to be disturbed by what he admitted to be initial difficulties for this sort of view." This, together with an earlier recognition that Locke always thought that the supposed problems could be solved, clearly means that Mackie's acceptance of both (d) and (e) on my original list is qualified, though, in relation to (e) he does talk of Locke's awareness of "difficulties." The evidence for this awareness is found, supposedly, in *E*:4.11.1, which I have already commented on, and in *E*:4.4.3, which I shall return to.

18. The thought here connects with the point, often made in the literature, that even a view of perception that we might naturally call "direct" realism is not immune from challenges from the sceptic. Even if we hold that when we see things we perceive them "directly" (whatever exactly that turns out to mean), the sceptic can still perplex us with the thought that we may only be dreaming that we are having this "direct" perception, or even that we have ever had it. If there is some way of *refuting* this sort of suggestion, it is clear that Locke does not know it. In pouring scorn on the sceptic's position, he is in fact really only echoing Descartes's own view that such doubts are in a sense absurd; though, unlike Descartes, he does not believe that they can serve any useful methodological role in philosophy, or that we should try to elevate the degree of assurance we do have in this area to the status of demonstrative knowledge. I must leave unexamined the claim, also sometimes found in the literature, that far from the "direct" realist being immune from sceptical attacks, the representationalist is no worse off.

19. The reference is to Leibniz's *New Essays on Human Understanding*, Peter Remnant and Jonathan Bennett, translators and editors (Cambridge: University Press, 1981), pp. 444–5. When Leibniz argues that the terms "knowledge" and "certainty" could be extended to cover cases where "to doubt in a practical way" would be "insane," or even "very blameworthy," and that, on this basis, we are certain, for example, that there are men in the world, and that Julius Caesar lived, it is clear that the dispute is about how the word "knowledge" should be used, not over whether or not there are genuine grounds for doubt.

20. This point stands even though, in replying to Stillingfleet (*Works* 4, p. 360), Locke himself suggests that his initial definition of "knowledge" allows for sensitive knowledge. I join those commentators who have doubts, but if we accepted what Locke says at this point, it would become even less clear than I think it is that (a) supports the "traditional"interpretation of his view.

21. Yolton, *Perceptual Acquaintance*, p. 136.
22. Yolton, *Perceptual Acquaintance*, p. 102.
23. In elaborating on this I would say that if we put very little stress on the word "things" when asking "Does Locke hold that there are such things as ideas?" the natural answer is that *of course* he does; while if we read "thing" as "substance," the answer is almost certainly that he does not. Beyond that, the conclusion we are likely to come to is that he was vague about, and probably not interested in, their precise ontological status, so that really the only live issue does concern the interpretation of (g). That said, someone could claim that there may be more to the notion that an idea may be "substance-like" than I have suggested. When Thomas Brown for example denies that Locke's ideas are "things," rather than states of mind, part of what he is suggesting seems to be that they are not, as they were for Berkeley and Malebranche as he interprets them, "separate" things. They might merit that description if, as he has Berkeley supposing (Brown, *Lectures*, p. 153), they were said to be "capable of existing in other minds, but in them alone," or to have "permanent existence . . . when they have ceased to exist in the individual mind." The difficulty here is that, while this might indeed make ideas more substance-like, or even, as Brown puts it, turn them into "foreign independent substances," it does not seem that those in the "traditional" camp have interpreted Locke's ideas in *that* way. Aaron for example does say that Locke's ideas are "objects," but I doubt that he ever thought they were "separate things" in that sense, or in Malebranche's sense where, as Yolton notes, ideas were "totally distinct essences . . . resident in God" (*Perceptual Acquaintance*, p. 106). If distancing Locke from the notion that ideas are "things" came down to distancing him from that, the task would be very easy indeed.
24. It will be clear that I am being selective here and not, for example, covering what Locke says about ideas as "resemblances" when discussing primary and secondary qualities in Book Two, Chapter Eight. That is again well-worn ground and I will do no more than refer to an observation M. A. Stewart makes on it in the paper cited earlier, pp. 60–61, where he claims that Locke's talk of "a copy or resemblance relation between ideas and originals" in the case of our ideas of primary, but not secondary qualities, actually militates *against* the view that ideas are "images."
25. In *E*:2.8.12 the claim concerns primary qualities, for it is "the Extension, Figure, Number, and Motion of Bodies of an observable bigness" that are said to be "perceived at a distance *by* the sight," but elsewhere we find him holding that "we immediately by our Senses perceive in *Fire* its Heat and Colour" (*E*:2.23.7). Locke's later assertion that we perceive only ideas looks rather less worrying when we recall that these may include the perceived heat and colour of fire. In *E*:2.23.7 the immediate/mediate contrast is of course between different sorts of *powers*, but it should be noted that what he goes on to stress in the following section is that we "distinguish Substances one from another" on the basis of these, rather than on the basis of their "real Constitutions." In this context anyway, the notion is that what we fail to perceive is, not bodies, but their "minute parts."
26. This point is developed by Kathy Squadrito in her "The *Essay* 4.4.3,"

The Locke Newsletter 9 (1978). She presents an interpretation of the chapter which sees Locke's concern as being with "the extent to which our concepts adequately represent the world," with "representing" here being "not . . . a matter of imitating or copying objects," but of classifying them (p. 60 and n. 3).

27. Peter Alexander, *Ideas, Qualities and Corpuscles: Locke and Boyle on the External World* (Cambridge: University Press, 1985), pp. 187–8. Alexander refers to passages in my *Berkeley: The Philosophy of Immaterialism* (London: Methuen, 1974).

28. The point is of course epistemic. If I am indeed seeing a man there must, for Locke, be a *causal* connection between the idea and the man perceived. However, neither the fact that I have an idea of a man, nor the fact that I seem to be seeing a man, *entails* that there is a man there. I take it that Locke's recognition that sensitive knowledge falls short of either intuition or demonstration basically amounts to an acceptance of (c), at least as it is understood here.

2

The Foundations of Knowledge and the Logic of Substance: The Structure of Locke's General Philosophy

Michael R. Ayers

1. The Foundations of Knowledge

Gassendi, Hobbes, and Locke all categorically asserted the independent authority of the senses as knowledge-producing faculties. As Hobbes put it, *"Knowledge of Fact . . .* is nothing else but Sense and Memory, and is *Absolute Knowledge."*[1] Locke announced the senses' immediate authority on questions of existence just as bluntly: They are "the proper and sole Judges of this thing."[2] On the other side, Platonistic or Augustinian philosophers such as Mersenne, Descartes, and Arnauld firmly subordinated the senses to the intellect. This division constitutes one of the great watersheds of early modern epistemology, and is well illustrated by Locke's response, as we may suppose it to be, to an argument in the Port Royal *Logic*. The *Logic* had argued, in effect, that the doctrine of transubstantiation does not contradict the senses, since even ordinarily the senses must be interpreted by reason. In the case of the Eucharist we simply have special reasons for taking the body of Christ to be behind a wafer-like appearance.[3] Locke brought the independent authority of the senses in the Protestant cause. Because the Romanist is indoctrinated from childhood with the principle that Church and Pope are infallible, "How is he prepared easily to swallow, not only against all probability, but even the clear evidence of his Senses, the Doctrine of Transubstantiation? This Principle has such an influence on his Mind, that he will take that to be Flesh, which he sees to be Bread."[4]

It is well known that Gassendi's mature epistemology was built on Epicurean and Stoic sources. Locke's similar debt to ancient empiricism was less explicit and may or may not have been less direct, but it is no less certain. His treatment of "sensitive knowledge of existence" is an example. He identified the "evidence" of such knowledge with our immediate knowledge in sensation "that something doth exist without us, which causes [an] *Idea* in us": accordingly, "I have by the Paper affecting my Eyes, that *Idea* produced in my Mind, which whatever Object causes, I call *White*; by which I know, that that Quality or Accident (*i.e.* whose appearance before my Eyes, always causes that *Idea*) doth really exist."[5] This direct causal realism has much the same general structure, and is expressed by means of the same example, as the theory attributed to the Stoic Chrysippus in a work present in Locke's library: "An impression is an affection occurring in the soul, which reveals itself and its cause. Thus, when through sight we observe something white, the affection is what is engendered in the soul through vision; and it is this affection which enables us to say that there is a white object which activates us."[6]

Even more convincing evidence of an ancient source is provided by Locke's argument that metaphysical mistrust of the senses is mistrust of a basic cognitive faculty, and is therefore self-destructive: "For we cannot act any thing, but by our Faculties: nor talk of Knowledge it self, but by the help of those Faculties, which are fitted to apprehend even what Knowledge is."[7] The suggestion that the senses are the source of the sceptic's own capacity to conceive of knowledge itself echoes the Epicurean onslaught on the sceptic in *De Rerum Natura*: "If he has never seen anything true in the world, from where does he get his knowledge of what knowing and not knowing are?" For Lucretius, the concept of (or acquaintance with) truth "has its origin in the senses." Since reason is the product of the senses, "if the senses are not true, all reason becomes false as well."[8]

A more pervasive debt, however, was to the doctrine of signs, notes, or marks through which we can have knowledge of things not evident in themselves. A distinction was widely drawn in ancient philosophy between reminiscent signs of such things as are only sometimes not evident and indicative signs of things which are by nature never evident. In the case of reminiscent or empirical signs constant experience sets up a connection between the sign and what it signifies. In the case of indicative signs, we reason to something which is such that, unless it existed, the sign would not exist: for example, sweating is an indicative sign of invisible pores in the skin, and certain motions of the body indicate the presence of the soul. The Sceptic Sextus Empiricus granted the cogency of reminiscent signs as a basis for opinion, but rejected indicative signs. Against Sextus, Gassendi argued on behalf of indicative signs that the proof of pores in the skin appeals only to principles founded on experience. Locke structured his treatment of probability around the same distinction between beliefs based on correlations falling *within* experience and inferences going *beyond* experience. With respect to the latter he agreed with Gassendi, arguing that hypotheses about what lies "beyond the discovery of the senses" can properly be based on a "wary reasoning from Analogy."[9]

Trust in the senses and the doctrine of signs came together in the principle that sensory appearances are always true indicative signs. The Epicurean thought seems to have been that, even if the same thing presents different appearances in circumstances in which it has not itself changed, or appears different to different observers at the same time (as in the standard sceptical example of water appearing hot to one person and cold to another), the difference in appearance accurately reflects a difference in the conditions of perception and so is a true sign of the object in those conditions. If we wrongly place the difference in the object itself, it is that judgment which is false, not the appearance. One example, repeated by Gassendi, is the changing appearance of an object as it grows more distant: the appearance is not false, although a judgment that the object is itself growing smaller or changing shape would be false.[10] In the *Essay* this doctrine took the form of the principle that simple ideas are always "true," "real," and "adequate": "their Truth consists in nothing else, but in such Appearances, as are produced in us, and must be suitable to those Powers, [God] has placed in external Objects, or else they could not be produced in us."[11] The final clause echoes the Stoic characterization of a "cognitive" (or "grasping") impression as "of such a kind as could not arise from what is not," and there are other Stoic resonances in Locke's account of simple ideas.[12] Yet the general point here is the broadly Epicurean one that simple ideas are dependable "distinguishing marks" which serve their purpose whatever unknown difference lies behind the sensible distinction. For that reason they can fulfill the role of "signs" of another kind, signs in the natural language of thought which signify their unknown causes. The signs that naturally *indicate* qualities or powers naturally *stand for* them in thought.[13] This neat conjunction of epistemology and theory of representation, encapsulated in the ambivalence of the terms "sign" and "signify" in Locke's usage, lies at the heart of his general philosophy.

The principle of the truth of simple ideas derives from ancient empiricism, but also responds to the very different Cartesian trust in innate "simple notions" or "simple natures," not to speak of the Scholastic doctrine, appealed to by Arnauld in his objections to the *Meditations,* that concepts or "simple apprehensions" are all true.[14] It plays an important part in Locke's explanation of both the certainty and the limitations of sensitive knowledge: the idea of white naturally signifies the power to cause that idea, i.e. the quality whiteness, however wrong we may be in our hypotheses about what constitutes whiteness in the object. Sensitive knowledge of existence, in other words, is theory-neutral or pre-theoretical, and that is why it is secure. Moreover, the principle was readily extensible to all *powers*: by means of the idea of power the sensible change in wax can be employed as a sign both of whatever in the sun melts wax and of whatever in wax causes it to be melted. Hence, with a murmured apology, Locke could treat ideas of powers as simple ideas and knowledge of powers as effectively foundational.[15]

In one respect Locke's determination to keep the deliverances of the senses independent of reason and prior to all inference or "judgment" led him into an even more extreme position than Gassendi's. Gassendi recognized that individual deliverances of the senses may by themselves prompt judgments which need to be corrected, falling back on the not implausible thought that the senses are here correcting themselves rather than being corrected by independent reason. His account of Epicurus accordingly placed the criterion of truth in the consensus or "suffrage" of the senses.[16] It is possible that Locke regarded any such move as too great a concession to reason, a denial of the immediate, unreasoned "evidence" of sensitive knowledge. That would help to explain what might otherwise seem an amazing fact: The *Essay,* dedicated to the examination of the extent and limits of knowledge, contains no direct discussion of that most hackneyed of epistemological topics, sensory illusion. Locke did mention a standard sceptical example of something like illusion in the chapter on primary and secondary qualities, but his employment of the primary–secondary distinction to explain "how the same Water, at the same time, may produce the *Idea* of Cold by one Hand, and of Heat by the other" was in effect a denial that *either* sensation is illusory. For *each* sensation, he suggested, is an appropriately differentiated sign of what gives rise to such sensations, namely "the increase or diminution of the motion of the minute Parts of our Bodies, caused by the Corpuscles of" other bodies. Much the same point emerges from a discussion of the possibility of people with reversed sensations of color.[17] Behind these arguments lies the ancient doctrine that appearances are always true.

There is, however, a much more significant difference between Locke's mature epistemology and that of Gassendi. Epicurean philosophy seems not to have distinguished sharply between the abstraction from sense experience of concepts giving meaning to our words, and the acquisition of propositional knowledge constituting the starting-points of reasoned enquiry. As Epicurus himself put his theory of generalized images or "preconceptions," "First . . . we must grasp the things which underlie words, so that we may have them as a reference point . . . and not have everything undiscriminated for ourselves as we attempt infinite chains of proofs, or have words which are empty."[18] The preconception of *man* was identified with the knowledge that "such and such a kind of thing is a man" and was treated, in effect, as at once an empirical summation of experience, a definition, and a foundational premiss of rational proof. Accordingly Gassendi, working within a logical tradition which laid great emphasis on the distinction between concept and judgment, term and proposition, held not only that all our concepts are acquired in experience, but also that all our knowledge derives from sensory knowledge. As he put it, "all the evidence and certainty which attaches to a general proposition depends upon that which has been gained from an induction of particulars."[19]

Locke himself, whether or not in imitation of Gassendi, adopted broadly the same position in his earliest extant essay in epistemology, in what is now known as *Essays on the Law of Nature*. He there claimed that knowledge of our duty to God and our fellows lies within reach of human reason, employing concepts and *premisses* derived from sense experience. Like Epicurus, he supported the claim that we need empirical premises by an appeal to the principle that all reasoning is *ex cognitis et concessis*. Like Gassendi, he extended the claim to mathematics. Not only are such mathematical notions as those of a line, a plane, and a solid drawn from experience, but "other common principles and axioms too" are given to reason by the senses.[20] In ethics, the senses supply reason with two kinds of premiss: first, evidence of design in the world from which we can infer the existence of a Creator whose will it is our duty to obey; and, second, knowledge of various characteristics of human nature which reveal God's particular purposes in creating us, and so the content of his will for us, the law of nature. That might suggest that the law of nature is contingent, but Locke emphasized, in opposition to extreme voluntarism, that it is not arbitrarily mutable in so far as it is tied to human nature: it has a conditional necessity in that it stands or falls with human nature "quae iam est," as it now is.[21]

Locke apparently became dissatisfied with this account of knowledge and its foundations in the course of writing the so-called Draft A of the *Essay* in 1671. At first he was still able to say that the certainty of geometrical demonstration "can be no greater then that of discerning by our eyes, which the very name 'Demonstration' how highly magnified soever for its certainty doth signifye"; and that the axioms or maxims of geometry gain assent "only by the testimony and assureance of our senses."[22] At the same time he asked whether axioms might not relate "to the signification of the words them selves they being relative words." The model is essentially Epicurean: First, "by constant observation of our senses espetialy our eys," we find certain proportions to hold without exception; we then assume they hold universally, employing them in some unexplained way as "standards" of measurement embodied in the meaning of our terms.[23] In effect, Locke was here offering a choice: Axioms can be regarded either as straightforward empirical summaries, open to empirical refutation, or as quasi-definitions founded on experience, and so "barely about the signification of words." Throughout Draft A he continued to develop the thought, with particular reference to propositions about substances, that universal propositions are either, if "instructive," uncertain or, if certain, mere assertions or denials of identity with respect to our ideas, and consequently "only verbal . . . and not instructive."[24] Yet very soon mathematical propositions came to be located unequivocally in the class of propositions about ideas employed as standards, so that demonstration was now explained as "the beare shewing of things or proposeing them to our senses *or understandings* soe as to make us take notice of them" (the "understanding" being here the imagination).[25] At the same time Locke evidently had doubts about regarding them as merely verbal, more than once hinting that mathematics has a guaranteed relation to reality. This thought was expressed, for example, in an interpolated qualification of the instructive—verbal dichotomy: "Mathematicall universal propositions are both true & instructive because as those Ideas are in our mindes soe are the things without us."[26]

The assumption appears to be that a condition of the instructive certainty of mathematics is the existence of its objects, and it is claimed that that condition is necessarily fulfilled just because of the simplicity of the ideas with which mathematics deals. Yet a final "memorandum" draws a sharp contrast between particular knowledge of existence (which is dependent on the senses) and universal knowledge (which is hypothetical and "only supposes existence"), seeming to record Locke's recognition that he had more work to do.[27]

So in the shifting course of Draft A Locke moved discernibly closer to the doctrine of the *Essay* itself, in particular towards a clear decision to restrict the essential role of the senses to the acquisition of simple ideas and (apart from questions of probability) to knowledge of particular existence and coexistence. Such less extreme empiricism, however, was entirely consistent with his original and continuing purposes. For his interest in epistemology seems to have been motivated by two early concerns: first, by his dissatisfaction with arbitrary appeals to conscience and divine inspiration (not to speak of their threat to civil order); and, second, by the study of medicine and corpuscularian science. In ethics his first considered epistemological reaction was to uphold the possibility of a reasonable morality based on the light of nature, empirically conceived. In natural philosophy, however, he adopted an opposite, if similarly "empiricist" line: the senses give knowledge of no more than the sensible effects and powers of substances, while the intrinsic properties underlying these effects remain beyond the reach of our faculties. The "corpuscularian" theory is simply our best inadequate speculation. The combination of epistemological optimism in ethics with pessimism regarding the possibility of a proper "science" of nature was not, of course, in the least inconsistent. Together with his claim that careful observation and experiment can yield probabilities sufficient for the direction of action, it constituted his pious thesis that the "candle, that is set up in us," for all its limitations, "shines bright enough for all our purposes."[28] Certainly it answered to his actual targets, on the one hand religious dogmatists and enthusiasts immune to what Locke saw as the reasonable argument of the natural law tradition, and on the other hand scientific dogmatists who trusted too much in reason's power to penetrate to the essences of things.

The chief theoretical problem facing Locke as an epistemologist was that of developing an account of the two sorts of science, moral and natural, which would explain very clearly why the one is possible for us while the other is not. From the first an analogy between ethics and the indubitably available science of mathematics was a promising line of approach. Yet his original quasi-Gassendist view of mathematics as a science with empirical axioms was a predictable loser, and the felt need for an explanation of the *necessity* of mathematics was surely Locke's motive for the experimental departures of Draft A.[29] In consequence the analogy between mathematics and ethics was actually weakened. If mathematics is a priori, what about ethics? In 1671 he was already attracted by the thought that moral notions, unlike ideas of substances, are constructed by us without reference to reality, and are therefore clearly knowable. Yet that left or even exacerbated the problem of how we can know whether they correspond to natural law, in Locke's terms the real problem of the foundations of ethics. As he himself pointed out, that is not a question that the senses can answer. In Draft B the problem was noted and set aside.[30]

It was eventually solved by a number of changes to the accounts both of mathematics and of ethics which restored the analogy between them to its full force. Mathematics was no longer taken to have existential import,[31] and its subject-matter was accordingly reclassified as arbitrarily constructible *complex* ideas, ideas of simple modes, comparable to the mixed modes which comprise the subject-matter of ethics.[32] Locke now dealt with the problem of its informativeness by developing a distinction between trifling knowledge of *identity* and informative knowledge of *relation,* the acknowledged ancestor of Kant's distinction between analytic and synthetic a priori judgment.[33] A corollary of these changes was a much sharper, but still firmly imagist, account of abstraction, owing something (as it seems) to Hobbes.

Already presaged in Draft A was an ordering of the degrees of certainty more like Mersenne's than Gassendi's. While maintaining the independent authority of the senses almost more rigorously than Gassendi himself, the *Essay* assigned to them no more than the third degree of knowledge, after intuition and demonstration.[34] Locke did not, however, adopt Mersenne's respect for maxims, and indeed, since axioms had lost their role as empirical premises even in Draft A, the principle that "all Reasonings are *ex praecognitis, et praeconcessis*" was effectively abandoned.[35] In fact the *Essay* deliberately seems to tread a careful path between Mersenne's and Gassendi's views about maxims and the relation between general and particular certainty. For Mersenne the proposition that the body is larger than a finger draws certainty from the prior certainty of the general maxim that the whole is greater than a part. For Gassendi, the latter is certain only in so far as supporting judgments like the former are certain. For Locke, both are equally self-evident, and his rider, that "if one of these have need to be confirmed to him by the other, the general has more need to be let into his Mind by the particular, than the particular by the general,"[36] is not Gassendi's inductivism, but the point that the immediate objects of universal intuition are particulars abstractly considered. We need to see the relation in the particular case before us (e.g. a geometrical diagram), in order to universalize the perception to all cases relevantly like that case.

Locke approximated his conception of morality to his reformed model of an a priori science chiefly by extending and elaborating a thought already hovering in the *Essays on the Law of Nature*: The moral law is necessarily binding on all rational creatures capable of pleasure and pain. What he added to this thought in the *Essay* was the clear statement that the law is independent of any other natural characteristics of human beings: "Were there a Monkey, or any other Creature to be found, that had the use of Reason . . . he would no doubt be subject to Law." One advantage of this emphasis, whether or not it was a motive for it, was a stronger defence against the extreme voluntarism of revelationists than had been afforded by Locke's earlier model, according to which the law is rooted in nothing more secure than an empirically known, mutable human nature. The idea of "the *moral Man*," Locke now said, is like the idea of a mode, an "immoveable unchangeable *Idea*," a postulate of the hypothetical science which is independent of contingent facts.[37] At the same time our own subjection to law, as satisfying this idea, is known intuitively with every thought we have, while the existence of the divine lawgiver is strictly demonstrable.

It should not be supposed that these changes related only to the a priori sciences of mathematics and ethics, since they constituted a clarification or development of Locke's conception of science in general. Since all universal knowledge is hypothetical,[38] empirical premisses are unnecessary to *any* science with respect to its status as knowledge or *scientia*. Although he rejected the Cartesian understanding of geometry as explication of the essence of matter, the general model of the fully intelligible, demonstrative science suited both his mechanist sympathies and his scepticism about natural essences very well indeed. The ideal mechanics could be supposed to have a quasi-geometrical form with intuitively evident foundations, hooking on to reality through the medium of empirical existential propositions rather than by means of contingent premises or axioms of the science itself. In other words, the propositions of natural science, if we could ever achieve such a thing, would be hypothetically necessary in just the same way as those of ethics and mathematics.[39] Yet, whereas in the case of the latter hypothetical necessity is all that is aimed for by the science (and the two existential propositions necessary for the conclusion that ethics applies to *us* are known by intuition and demonstration), it would be useless to build a purported natural science unless we knew experientially that things exist with essences answering to our ideas.[40] Employing this model, Locke could argue, on the one hand, that our sensitive knowledge of existence is at too coarse a level for the purpose; and, on the other hand, that the corpuscularians' failure to achieve geometrical intelligibility in their speculative explanations is itself enough to show that their hypotheses have failed to capture the essences or natures of material things. It was thoughts like these which underlay his arguments about substance, to which it is now time to turn.

II. The Logic of Substance

To understand Locke's claim that "of Substance, we have no idea of what it is, but only a confused, obscure one of what it does," it is again useful to look at earlier empiricist argument. Gassendi offers an obvious precedent. In the Second Meditation Descartes had argued that it is by means of the intellect, not the senses or imagination, that we conceive of wax as "something extended, flexible and mutable," underlying the variety of changing appearances which we perceive as it melts. Elsewhere he had claimed that further intellectual reflection allows us to identify extension as the principal attribute, or essence, of matter.[41] Gassendi's response was to agree with "what everyone commonly asserts, *viz.* that the concept of the wax or of its substance can be abstracted from the concepts of its accidents," but to deny that this means "that the substance or nature of the wax is itself distinctly conceived." "Admittedly," Gassendi remarked, "you perceive that the wax or its substance must be something over and above such [sensible] forms; but what this something is you do not perceive. . . . The alleged naked, or rather hidden, substance is something that we can neither ourselves conceive nor explain to others." According to Gassendi's argument here, the positive content of our ideas of material substances is wholly provided by the senses, and "the mind is not . . . distinct from the imaginative faculty." Hence essence always escapes us. Much the same goes for our idea of the mind or "thinking thing": "Who doubts that you are thinking?" he asked. "What we are unclear about . . . is that inner substance of yours whose property is to think."[42] Consequently, Descartes "can be compared to a blind man who, on feeling heat and being told that it comes from the sun, thinks that he has a clear and distinct idea of the sun in that, if anyone asks him what the sun is, he can reply: "It is a heating thing.' "[43]

It seems to me that whoever seriously reflects on Gassendi's meaning and motivation, and on the connections between his argument and Locke's, will be unlikely to adhere to that (to my mind) perverse interpretation of the latter, still ferociously defended in some quarters,[44] according to which the general idea of substance is for Locke the idea of a pure logical subject underlying all properties, known or unknown, and for that reason unknowable in principle.

One part of Locke's position, indeed, was common to all the "New Philosophers," dogmatic or anti-dogmatic. That was the anti-Aristotelian point that the multiplicity of sensible qualities and powers through which we know any substantial thing is not a multiplicity in the thing itself, but a multiplicity of ways in which the thing affects the senses or sensibly interacts with other things. Hobbes called it "a diversity of seeming," defining an "accident" as "concipiendi corporis modum," a way of conceiving of body (or a body). The model echoes Epicurus' account of attributes,[45] and is present throughout Locke's *Essay*, even in passages which may seem to have little to do with substance. Here is a famous sentence: "Though the Qualities that affect our Senses, are, in the things themselves, so united and blended, that there is no separation, no distance between them; yet 'tis plain, the *Ideas* they produce in the Mind, enter by the Senses simple and unmixed."[46]

Such an explanation of the relation between the one substance and its many accidents was a common element in attacks on Scholastic "real accidents," in particular on the debased account of the substance–accident relation involved in the doctrine of transubstantiation. Kenelm Digby attributed the Scholastic notion to a naïve confusion:

> what is but one entire thing in it self, seemeth to be many distinct things in my understanding: whereby . . . I shall be in danger . . . to give actuall Beings to the quantity, figure, colour, smell, tast, and other accidents of

the apple, each of them distinct one from another, as also from the substance which they clothe; because I find the notions of them really distinguished (as if they were different Entities) in my mind.[47]

In one passage in the *Essay* Locke attacked the pretensions of the
traditional doctrine of substance and accident in much the same terms
as Digby, emphasizing the mistake of taking the one–many relationship
to be a real relationship between really distinct beings: "They who first
ran into the Notion of *Accidents,* as a sort of real Beings, that needed
something to inhere in, were forced to find out the word *Substance,*
to support them."[48] But the chapter "Of Our Complex *Idea* of Substances" opens with the obverse point. Because of the presumable
unity of the thing, we fail to recognize the multiplicity in our idea of it:
"We are apt afterward to talk of and consider as one simple *Idea,* [that]
which indeed is a complication of many *Ideas* together."[49] The immediate target here is again Aristotelian, but this time it is the notion that
we can achieve simple conceptions of substances correspondent to
their real simplicity or unity. Those who think that their would-be scientific definitions capture unitary essences are misled. Just because in
ordinary experience of coexisting sensible qualities we naturally (and,
as Locke spelled out to Stillingfleet, reasonably and inescapably[50]) take
ourselves to be perceiving a unitary thing, we are liable to mistake our
complex idea of it for a simple one. If the doctrine of real accidents
mistakes ideal for real multiplicity, Aristotelian claims to know essences
mistake real for ideal unity.

This first section of *Essay,* Book II, chapter xxiii has been a main
source of the more exotically inappropriate interpretations of Locke on
substance. What seems not to have been adequately noticed is that
Locke was describing an alleged process of the mind through four
clearly distinct stages. First, there is sense perception of "a great number" of sensible qualities; second, "the mind takes notice also" that
some coexisting qualities go "constantly" together; third, the presumption that such recurrently grouped qualities belong to "one thing,"
i.e. one and the same kind of thing, leads us to combine them, for
convenience, in a single idea under a single name; fourth, "by inadver-
tency we are apt afterward to talk of and consider" this complex idea
"as one simple idea." We take this idea to correspond to the "*Substratum,* wherein [these simple *Ideas*] do exist, and from which they do
result, which therefore we call *Substance.*"

The term "we," it is clear, here includes the Aristotelians, as usual accused of merely formalizing the coarse or sloppy thinking of ordinary people. A footnote to the fifth edition, inspired by Locke if not actually written by him, warns us that this passage is not an account of the idea of substance in general, but an explanation of how the (general) names applied to "Individuals of distinct Species of Substances" have been taken to be simple names standing for simple ideas.[51] The reference is to Aristotelian theory of definition. According to a commonplace distinction, a "nominal" definition of man, such as "featherless, two-footed, broad-nailed thing," picks out men by means of a set of mutually independent features, whereas the "simple," "real" definition, "rational animal," unpacks a unitary essence.[52] Locke wanted to say that all candidate definitions of essences are in fact nominal, and of the first form. It should therefore be no surprise that the four stages of his explanation of the Aristotelian mistake correspond in close detail to the four stages which Aristotle himself had distinguished in the achievement of the principles of scientific knowledge.

Aristotle's four stages, as set out in a famous passage,[53] can be read as follows: first, the perception of any object (of whatever category), second, "experience," or the memory of repeated perceptions of similar objects; third, the formation of a universal concept or thought; and, fourth, the understanding which comes with a scientific definition. In the case of substances, we first perceive, and then lay up the memory of, recurrent or repeated similarities between individuals. Third, we form a universal notion of the same species present on all these perceptual occasions. Finally, sustained observation and reflection enables us to pick out the genus and specific difference and so to arrive at a definition which will explain the concomitance of the "properties" of the species, the cause of their union. Locke's commentary is to the effect that the concept formed at the third stage and associated with the specific name in fact remains complex and sensory, while the fourth stage is nothing but the process by which the existence of the single name, together with the natural and proper assumption of a common, recurring substratum or explanatory nature behind the recurrent experience, creates the illusion that our complex idea is simple. Locke has rewritten the Aristotelian account of the apprehension of natural principles as the psychological explanation of a vain delusion.

The argument of the rest of Book II, chapter xxiii develops the claim that no idea formed on the basis of experience ever in any case captures the unity of the thing itself. The latter is never represented to the enquirer by anything more than a place-marker, the idea of substance in general, embodying "only a Supposition of he knows not what support" of the sensible qualities "commonly called Accidents." The corpuscularian hypothesis that colour and weight inhere in "the solid extended parts" leaves us with the problem of what solid extended substance is.[54] For the unity of matter so defined remains mysterious to us. Here the question of the "cause of the union"[55] of the qualities and powers of a body becomes entwined with the explanation of its physical or material unity: We do not know "what the substance is of that solid thing . . . [i.e.] how the solid parts of Body are united, or cohere together to make Extension." Corpuscularian explanations of cohesion by "the external pressure of the Aether" fail to explain "the cohesion of the parts of the Corpuscles of the Aether it self."[56] It is evident that we lack a "clear and distinct *Idea* of the *Substance* of Matter," and the same goes for "the *Substance* of Spirit."[57]

I will not now try to map all the ramifications of Locke's theory of substance, but I would like to consider a late development of his argument which has been particularly associated with the view that for Locke "substance" is a pure logical subject, unknowable in principle. After repeating that our ideas of the sorts of substances always include, together with ideas of qualities and powers, "the confused *Idea* of *something* to which they belong, and in which they subsist," he commented:

> and therefore when we speak of any sort of Substance, we say it is a *thing* having such or such Qualities, as body is a *thing* that is extended, figured, and capable of Motion; a Spirit a *thing* capable of thinking; and so Hardness, Friability, and Power to drawn Iron, we say, are Qualities to be found in a Loadstone. These, and the like fashions of speaking intimate, that the Substance is supposed always *something* besides the Extension, Figure, Solidity, Motion, Thinking, or other observable *Ideas,* though we know not what it is.[58]

Locke was here bringing his explanation of the substance–accident relationship to bear on language. To put the same point another way, he was appealing to language in support of his explanation. The existence of the distinction in language between things and their qualities, and in particular the existence of primitive noun-predicates whose definitions reflect that distinction, is taken to constitute an implicit confession of our ignorance of what is really there behind the "observable" qualities and powers: in other words, ignorance of its real nature or essence.

I think that the difficulty that many commentators have had in reading Locke in this way stems largely from the thought that he *must* have realized that, even if (say) solidity had been the essence of matter, and we knew it, "matter" would still have been a noun-predicate definable as *thing (or substance) which is solid.* If Locke is trying to explain primitive noun-predicates and the logical primacy of the category of substance in terms of our ignorance, it may be thought, he must surely have had in mind an ignorance that is not merely contingent and remediable. Leibniz commented, "If you distinguish two things in a substance—the attributes or predicates, and their common subject—it is no wonder that you cannot conceive anything special in this subject." He accuses Locke of demanding "a way of knowing which the object does not admit of." Does this, perhaps, say it all?[59]

Other passages in the *Essay,* however, make it clear that Locke proposed his epistemological explanation of the ontological category of substance with full acceptance of its implications: if we did know the true essence of any substance, our account of it would *not* take subject–predicate form. Since essence and substance are one and the same, there would be no call for a noun-predicate distinct from the adjectival noun which names the essence. For example, if Cartesian analysis of our idea of body could reveal that its essence is extension, the two words would be interchangeable: "We can never mistake in putting the Essence of any thing for the Thing it self. Let us then in Discourse, put *Extension* for *Body*. . . . He that should say, that one Extension, by impulse, moves another extension, would, by the bare Expression, sufficiently shew the absurdity of such a Notion." On the other hand, "to say, an extended solid thing moves, or impels another, is all one, and as intelligible, as to say, *Body* moves, or impels."[60] The whole argument implies that the reason why "extension" can stand as neither subject nor object of "impels" is not because it is an adjectival or abstract noun, but because it is the wrong adjectival noun. If *x*-ness were what extension is not, the essence of body, then to say that one *x*-ness impelled another *would* make sense. The same argument, Locke continued, can be brought against the doctrine that reason is the essential property of man: "No one will say, That Rationality is capable of Conversation, because it makes not the whole Essence, to which we give the Name Man."

To understand how Locke could advance such an argument, and to recognize its historic force, we need to appreciate how he was neatly turning Cartesian logic against Cartesian pretensions to science. Descartes had himself warned against distinguishing between a substance and its principal attribute in a prominent passage: "Thought and extension can be regarded as constituting the natures of intelligent substance and corporeal substance; they must then be considered as nothing else but thinking substance itself and extended substance itself—that is, as mind and body."[61] The distinction between thought or extension and the thinking or extended substance is, on Descartes's account, a merely conceptual distinction, a piece of abstraction.[62] To think of the substance as something other or more than its nature is to make a confused division of the substance from itself. Yet this claim left an opening for those who rejected Descartes's dogmatic premiss to put his argument in reverse. Since we *can* intelligibly make just those distinctions he condemned, between extension and the thing which is extended, thought and the thing which thinks, doesn't that show that they are not, after all, cases of dividing a substance from itself? On the contrary, it was the Cartesian tendency to employ "extension" and "matter" interchangeably which appeared to Locke to fall into nonsense. Malebranche, for example, argued that extension is a substance or "being," since it is not a mode of anything as roundness is a mode of extension.[63] Locke remarked sniffily, very likely with Malebranche in mind as well as Descartes's argument against a vacuum, "That *Body* and *Extension,* in common use, stand for two distinct *Ideas,* is plain to any one that will but reflect a little. For were their Signification precisely the same, it would be as proper, and as intelligible to say, *the Body of an Extension,* as *the Extension of a Body*; and yet there are those who find it necessary to confound their signification."[64]

Malebranche's argument appealed to the standard Cartesian claim, repeated in their own terms by other corpuscularians such as Hobbes, that the ontological relationship between substance and accident, unintelligible on the Aristotelian account, becomes perspicuous when it is identified as the relation between determinable attribute and determinate mode. There is no mystery about the relation between extension and a particular shape, as there would be between the shape and the colour of a thing if we took colour to be irreducible to geometrical accidents.[65] In other words, substance and accidents form an intelligible unity on the corpuscularian account of matter. That is just what Locke was denying.

Malebranche stated that the crucial question is "whether matter does not have still other attributes, different from extension," so that "extension itself might not be essential to matter, and might presuppose something else that would be its subject and principle." He argued that the distinction between extension and its subject is a merely conceptual distinction employing the general idea of being:

> And what is said of [something else's] being the *subject* and *principle* of extension is said gratuitously and without a clear conception of what is being said, i.e. without there being any idea of it other than a general idea from logic, like principle and subject. As a result a new *subject* and a new *principle* of this subject of extension could in turn be imagined, and so on to infinity, because the mind represents general ideas of subject and principle to itself as it pleases.[66]

The immediate context of this criticism was an attack on Aristotelian matter. Because Aristotelian matter is conceived of as *subject* to extension, it is thought of as a being which is distinct from extension. Yet nothing clear can be said about this merely "logical entity" just because it is abstracted from any attributes through which it might be conceived. It was polemical misrepresentation on Malebranche's part to suggest that the Aristotelians envisaged matter's having definite attributes underlying extension, but the immediately relevant point is simply this: Malebranche's claim that the concept of a subject of extension is a "disordered abstraction," an abuse of "the vague idea of being in general," represented the subject-predicate sentence "Matter is extended" as misleading, if not ill formed, as if the tautology ought rather to be expressed in the form of an identity, "Matter is extension." It is therefore easy to see why Locke, who *did* want to postulate an unknown essence underlying extension, should have insisted that "Body is extended" is evidently *not* a gratuitous solecism, but the way we all have to talk, determined by the distinct ideas we have. It would appear, at any rate, to have been after his reading of Malebranche in the early 1680s that he introduced elements into his argument not present in the drafts of 1671: not only the direct appeals to language under discussion, but the term "idea of substance in general," later explained to Stillingfleet as "the general idea of something, or being."[67]

Another Cartesian argument concerned with the alleged mistake of dividing a substance from itself had been advanced in the Port Royal *Logic*. In their explanation of predication and nominalization, its authors distinguished three kinds of objects of thought: things, modified things, and modes of things. The full theory need not concern us, but a part of it was that primitive noun-predicates directly signify things, adjectives directly signify modified things (or things as modified), while adjectival or "abstract" nouns directly signify modes. They then denounced the practice of employing "abstract" forms of primitive noun-predicates, *humanitas* from *homo, animalitas* from *animal,* and so forth. It arises, they argued, because we generally know and name things through their modifications, as modified things, so that we become accustomed to dividing our ideas of them into subject and mode (as we might distinguish, in our idea of a ball, the idea of a body from the idea of its roundness). The habit once acquired, *homo* comes often to be "considered as the subject of humanity, *habens humanitatem,* and so to be a modified thing." This mistake treats "the essential attribute, which is the thing itself," as a mode, and as "in a subject." Hence the Scholastic solecisms "humanitas," "corporeitas," and "ratio." "Reason" may seem an odd member of this list, but is clear enough why a Cartesian should include it, and that "extension" would have the same right to be there.[68]

The Port Royal argument differs from Malebranche's in an interesting way. Although both deplore the division of a substance from its essence, i.e. from itself, Malebranche seems to have regretted the misleading character of primitive noun-predicates, and to have favoured the abstract noun "extension" over "matter," whereas Arnauld and Nicole took the reverse view. For them, the proper role of primitive noun-predicates is to name substantial things, and of abstract nouns to name modes. Locke's response to the issue is also interesting. On the one hand, he held not just that some, but that all, substantial things are known *qua* "modified things," so that the division of our ideas of them into subject and mode (in Arnauld's sense of "mode") is always legitimate. In effect he was suggesting that it would never occur to us to divide a substance from its true essence, if ever we had knowledge of such a thing. The terms "extension" and "reason" are on his view, of course, entirely legitimate, and their legitimacy demonstrates that they are not true essences. On the other hand, he followed Arnauld in recognizing the illegitimacy of such abstract terms as are created by attempting to renominalize a primitive noun-predicate. His explanation of that illegitimacy, however, given in the fascinating, neglected chapter "Of Abstract and Concrete Terms," is quite the opposite of Arnauld's and hinges on the bold claim that the proper function of abstract terms is to name known essences. Just because we know the mind-dependent real essences of non-substances, ordinary language abounds with such words as "whiteness," "justice," and "equality." On

the other hand, our not ordinarily employing such terms as "animal-
ness" or "manness" constitutes "the confession of all Mankind, that
they have no *Ideas* of the real Essences of Substances. . . . And indeed,
it was only the Doctrine of *substantial Forms,* and the confidence of
mistaken Pretenders to a knowledge that they had not, which first
coined, and then introduced *Animalitas,* and *Humanitas,* and the
like."[69]

Locke's logico-linguistic arguments, then, arose naturally and plausi-
bly enough in the context of Aristotelian and Cartesian logic as an ingenious way of advancing his kind of scepticism about essences. Leibniz's
criticisms raised no new issues. Nor was the Lockean doctrine a passing
aberration. It made a deep impression on much eighteenth-century
logic and permanently influenced the course of philosophy.[70] Kant
himself drew on it, arguing *both* (with Locke) that the possibility of
dividing subject from attribute indicates that the latter does not constitute the ultimate nature of the former, *and* (with Malebranche and
Leibniz) that we can in principle continue dividing subject from attribute indefinitely.

> Pure reason demands that for every predicate of a thing we should look
> for its appropriate subject, and for this, which is necessarily in turn only a
> predicate, its subject and so on to infinity (or as far as we can reach). But
> it follows from this that nothing which we can reach ought to be taken as
> a final subject, and that the substantial itself could never be thought by
> our understanding, however deeply it penetrated and even if the whole
> of nature were disclosed to it.[71]

By means of the premiss that we could always legitimately generate the
concept of an underlying subject, *however much we knew,* Kant
turned Locke's idea of substance in general into something he never
intended, the pure concept of a logical subject which exists in us solely
as an intimation of a "thing in itself" which is in principle unknowable.
For later idealists, it became an intimation of the Absolute, the ultimate
subject of all predication.

III. Conclusion

To stress Locke's influence on later philosophy—even on Kant—is not
quite the same as to establish his excellence. The standard English esti-
mation of the greatest English philosopher is perhaps illustrated by the

comment, made in a public discussion of his philosophy in which I recently took part, that no other philosopher "has had a greater influence in proportion to his merits." Such faint praise, I feel, is entirely inappropriate. That examination of Locke's arguments in relation to their context which reveals their meaning and point also reveals the theoretical ingenuity, quality of judgment, and pertinacity in the search for consistency and comprehensiveness which is characteristic of the very greatest philosophers—all of whom have used and responded to the tradition within which they have worked. The question no doubt arises whether Locke's contributions to seventeenth-century debates, despite their high quality, are irremediably dated. Speaking as an unregenerate realist, I would suggest that philosophical thought is now in dire need of the rich context of recognized explicanda and suggestive (if, just as they stand, untenable) explanations supplied by the *Essay*.

The present imperfect sketch of the skeleton of Locke's general philosophy has left out a number of important bones, if not whole limbs. I hope, nevertheless, that it will be seen how its two halves, one centred on the mind of the knower, the other on the objects of knowledge, fit together and presuppose each other. Both are structured round two related divisions. The first division is between, on the one hand, a priori, abstract science concerned with ideal, constructed objects and, on the other hand, enquiry into the real world of naturally unitary, given objects, enquiry which cannot for us achieve the status of "science." The second division is a division of levels between, on the one hand, the level of coarse experiential or pre-theoretical knowledge of natural things and, on the other hand, the level of speculative hypothesis or theory about the ultimate nature of those things. This second division is presupposed in Locke's conception of the authority and limitations of sensitive knowledge. It also corresponds to his distinction between the nominal and the real essences of substances, the former constituting the objects of natural history, the latter, the unattainable objects of natural science.

It is easy to assume that this epistemology is utterly outdated, partly because the barriers Locke perceived to lie in the way of natural science seem to have been bypassed, partly because his perception of them was in any case based on a misguided geometrical ideal of what a science should be, and partly just because we hear so much didactic rhetoric from relativist conceptualists against both divisions, between the a priori and the empirical and between experience and theory (not to speak of foundations of knowledge), that it is easy to assume that there must be something wrong with them. How could so many, so voluble, so confident writers be completely wrong?

Now I do not suppose that Locke's conception of "sensitive knowledge," neatly hinging as it does on a purely causal understanding of the relation between sign and significatum, satisfactorily defines the scope of perceptual knowledge. It leaves us, implausibly and incoherently, with no more than perceptual knowledge of a world of powers. Nor do I find tenable the conception of infallible knowledge-delivering faculties which Locke took over, in common with other philosophers of his time, from the ancient debates over the existence of criteria of truth. But I do suppose that, unless the senses naturally and normally presented the world to us at a conscious level, and we naturally and normally accepted their deliverances, we would have no knowledge at all; and I am no more impressed than most opticians by the curious modern thought that what we see or otherwise perceive by the senses is a direct function of our theories, scientific or "folk." Moreover, we need to recognize that the unfashionable notion of "evidence," purged of its implications of infallibility, still has valuable work to do in characterizing that central and primary kind of knowledge, typified by ordinary perceptual knowledge, which we possess when belief is engendered in circumstances of full awareness of its source and basis. In the context of perception we normally not only acquire beliefs, but do so in such a way that there is no mystery to us how and why we have come to have just those beliefs. We believe what the senses make evident to us. Without an understanding of "evidence" in this sense, we shall never achieve a satisfactory philosophical account of what knowledge is. Fortunately it looks as if philosophers will be nudged in this direction by psychology, which has begun to take a fresh interest in the role of consciousness in cognition.

Furthermore, while I do not suppose that Locke's distinction between constructed modes and natural substances satisfactorily captures and explains the undoubted difference between geometry or political theory on the one hand and chemistry or biology on the other, his assumption does seem right that a horse is a naturally unified thing as a gallop or a procession is not, and that this is connected with the role of primitive noun-predicates in our language. For such predicates give names to natural, material individuals whose individuality is prior to their individuation by us or by "our concepts." I do not accept Locke's claim that the role of such noun-predicates serves as a confession of our ignorance of natural essences, but at least one feature of that claim strikes me as extremely suggestive. The New Philosophy tore traditional ontology and logic apart just because it proposed that science requires knowledge, not of the essences of those material objects which natural language treats as the fundamental objects of predication, horses, oak trees, and the like, but of the essence of such an abstract or hypothetical entity as corpuscularian matter. Most philosophers felt the need to adapt the notion of substance to fit the new physics. Consequently, the theory of substance tended to lose its direct connection with the logic of natural language, while the metaphysics or ontology of science remained to an extent trammelled with inappropriate logical baggage. Locke, on the other hand, kept his explanation of the category of substance to the level which is relevant to an understanding of natural language: not the level at which reality might become fully intelligible to us, but the level at which it actually impinges on us in experience.

I could go on, but my point is simply that Locke is one of the great dead from whom, for all the differences, philosophers still have much to learn. He knew where he was going and he argued and theorized in an informed, intelligent, ingenious and powerful way about issues which have long been unfashionable, and to which we should return.

Notes

This chapter was written in response to a request for a broad discussion of Locke's general philosophy, and necessarily overlaps material in my more recently published monograph, *Locke,* 2 vols. (London, 1991). Nevertheless, since some of that material is here expanded (e.g. the discussion of Draft A and the Hellenistic parallels), and some compressed, while all has been taken from its various contexts and reordered, I hope that the present chapter will help to clarify (my view of) Locke's theory.

1. Thomas Hobbes, *Leviathan* (London, 1651), I. ix. "Absolute" by contrast with the hypothetical sentences which constitute science.

2. *Essay,* IV. xi. 2. The phrase occurs in Draft A, in the original version of this passage (*Drafts,* i. 20 f.).

3. A. Arnauld and P. Nicole, *La Logique, ou L'art de penser,* ed. P. Clair and F. Girbal (Paris, 1965), IV. xii. Cf. IV. i.

4. *Essay,* IV. xx. 10. The thought was an early one: see *Drafts,* i. 71.

5. *Essay,* IV. xi. 2.

6. Cited in A. A. Long and D. N. Sedley (eds.), *The Hellenistic Philosophers* (Cambridge, 1987), i. 237. The passage is from *De Placitis Philosophorum,* in Stephanus' edn. of Plutarch. As well as the similarity, there is a difference, in

that Chrysippus' "impression" not only gives notice of its cause, but reveals the intrinsic character of its cause.

7. *Essay,* IV. xi. 3.

8. Lucretius, *De Rerum Natura,* Book IV, lines 474 ff.: "at id ipsum/ quaeram, cum in rebus veri nil, viderit ante/unde sciat quid sit scire et nescire vicissim/notitiem veri neque sensus posse refelli/ . . . an ab sensu falso ratio orta valebit/dicere eos contra, quae tota ab sensibus orta est?/ qui nisi sunt veri, ratio quoque falsa fit omnis" (cited by Long and Sedley, *The Hellenistic Philosophers,* i. 78–9. The argument is recorded in Gassendi's *Syntagma Epicuri Philosphiae,* which was plagiarized in Thomas Stanley's *History of Philosophy* of 1655. Of these, Locke owned Lucretius and only a later (1687) edn. of Stanley.

9. Pierre Gassendi, *Opera Omnia* (Lyons, 1658), i. 79–86; *Essay,* IV. xvi. 12.

10. Lucretius, *De Rerum Natura,* Book IV, lines 499–500; Gassendi, *Opera Omnia,* i. 79–86. Gassendi's source is Sextus Empiricus, *Against the Professors,* 7. 206–10, cited in Long and Sedley, *The Hellenistic Philosophers, i. 81.*

11. *Essay,* II. xxxii. 14.

12. Locke's account of "clear and distinct" simple ideas corresponds to the other main features of a Stoic cognitive impression, that it "arises from what is and is stamped and impressed exactly in accordance with what is": as Locke puts it, "our *simple Ideas* are *clear,* when they are such as the Objects themselves, from whence they were taken, did or might, in a well-ordered Sensation or Perception, present them" (II. xxix. 2). The expression "clear and distinct" is, of course, Cartesian, but it echoes equivalent Stoic expressions, as Descartes was doubtless well aware. Cf. Long and Sedley, *The Hellenistic Philosophers,* i. 241–53, ii. 243–54.

13. Cf. *Essay,* IV. v. 2–5, IV. xxi. 4.

14. Cf. *The Philosophical Writings of Descartes,* trans. J. Cottingham, R. Stoothoff, and D. Murdoch (Cambridge, 1985), i. 44–7, ii. 145 f. (AT X 419–23 and VII 206). In Draft A Locke accepts even with respect to complex ideas of substances the Scholastic argument that a false concept of *x* is impossible because it would not be a concept of *x* but of something else (*Drafts,* i. 18). In the *Essay* he affirms its traditional, more correctly Aristotelian rival, the principle that "our ideas . . . cannot properly and simply in themselves be said to be true or false" (II. xxxii. 1). In the sense in which ideas can loosely be said to be true in relation to reality, not all ideas are true, although all simple ideas are true.

15. Cf. *Essay,* II. xxi. 3, II. xxiii. 7–9.

16. Gassendi, *Opera Omnia,* iii. 7.

17. *Essay,* II. viii. 21; II. xxxii, 15–16. For fuller discussion of both these topics, see Ayers, *Locke,* i. 166–7 and 207 ff.

18. Cited by Long and Sedley, *The Hellenistic Philosophers,* i. 87 f. See the editors' note on these passages.

19. Pierre Gassendi, *Institutio Logica,* ed. H. Jones (Assen, 1981), 61.

20. *Law of Nature,* 146 ff.

21. Ibid. 150–8, 190–202.

42

Michael R. Ayers

22. *Drafts*, i. 22–3.

23. Ibid. 22 f. Cf. Long and Sedley, *The Hellenistic Philosophers*, i. 87–8.

24. Cf. *Drafts*, i. 55: "Indeed all Universall propositions are either Certain and then they are only verball but are not instructive. Or else are Instructive & then are not Certain."

25. Ibid. 50. But the preference for this explanation of mathematical truths as "truths of eternall verity" is fixed as early as pp. 26–7. For explicit reference to imagination, see p. 28: "any mathematical figure imagind in our mindes."

26. Ibid. 57. On p. 26 the certainty of mathematics is attributed to "the cleare knowledge of our owne Ideas, & the certainty that quantity and number existing have the same propertys and relations that their Ideas have one to another." Cf. pp. 25 and 28.

27. Ibid. 82. Cf. the disclaimer on p. 75 (strictly true, but as glossed false), "That I never said that the truth of all propositions was to be made out to us by the senses for this was to leave noe roome for reason at all, which I think by a right traceing of those Ideas which it hath received from Sense or Sensation may come to knowledge of many propositions which our senses could never have discovered." Locke *had* said that axioms, unless merely verbal, were known only through the senses.

28. *Essay*, I. i. 5. See e.g. IV. xii. 11.

29. Cf. *Drafts*, i. 26: "proportions of numbers & extensions . . . are soe ex necessitate rei."

30. Ibid. 41–2 and 269–70.

31. Cf. *Essay*, IV. iv. 8.

32. Ibid. II. xiii–xvi.

33. Ibid. IV. i. 5 and 7, IV. viii. 8. Cf. Kant, *Prolegomena to Any Future Metaphysics*, sect. 3.

34. *Essay*, IV. ii. 14. Cf. *Drafts*, i. 45: "All such affirmations and negations [of universal identities] are made . . . as the clearest knowledge we can have which indeed is internal and mentall demonstration as certain and evident and perhaps more then the external" ("as . . . can have" interpolated). Contrast the earlier emphasis on the senses, p. 43: "all a man can certainly know of things existing without him is only particular propositions, for which he hath demonstration by his senses the best ground of science he can have or expect and what soe comes to his understanding, he receives as certain knowledge and demonstration."

35. *Essay*, IV. vii. 8.

36. Ibid. IV. vii. 11. The example of the body and a finger is discussed at IV. xii. 3. Cf. Marin Mersenne, *La Verité des sciences contre les sceptiques ou Pyrrhoniens* (Paris, 1652), 177 (cited by Susan James, "Certain and Less Certain Knowledge," *Proceedings of the Aristotelian Society*, 87 [1987], 227–42: 232); Gassendi, *Institution Logica*, 61. For the principle that "the immediate Object of all our Reasoning and Knowledge, is nothing but particulars," cf. *Essay*, IV. xvii. 8.

37. *Essay*, III. xi. 16.

38. Cf. ibid. IV. xi. 14.

39. Cf. ibid. IV. vi. 11: If we knew real essences, "to know the Properties of

Gold, it would be no more necessary that *Gold* should exist, and that we should make experiments upon it, than it is necessary for the knowing the Properties of a Triangle, that a Triangle should exist in any Matter, the *Idea* in our Minds would serve for the one as well as the other."

40. Cf. ibid. II. i. 10, II. xxx. 5, IV. xii. 12, etc.

41. Descartes, *Philosophical Writings,* ii. 20–I (AT VII 30 ff.). Cf. p. 54 and i. 227 (AT VII 78 and IXB 46).

42. Ibid. ii. 189–93.

43. Ibid. 234–5.

44. Most recently, as far as I know, by Jonathan Bennett, in "Substratum," *History of Philosophy Quarterly,* 4 (1987), an article which he elsewhere describes as showing that "when Ayers gets down to details regarding Locke on 'substratum,' his main work is done for him not by special attention to the historical background, but by inattention to what Locke actually wrote" (in P. Hare [ed.], *Doing Philosophy Historically* [Buffalo, NY, 1988], 68).

45. Hobbes, *Leviathan,* III. xxxiv; *De Corpore,* II. viii. 2 (*Latin Works,* ed. W. Molesworth [London, 1839], i). For Epicurus the attributes of body are individually picked out and spoken of in consequence of the way the mind perceives or focuses on the whole (*Letter to Herodotus,* 68–73, cited in Long and Sedley, *The Hellenistic Philosophers,* I. 34, ii. 27).

46. *Essay,* II. ii. I.

47. Kenelm Digby, *Two Treatises: Of Bodies and of Man's Soule* (London, 1645), 3.

48. *Essay,* II. xiii. 20.

49. Ibid. II. xxiii. I.

50. Cf. *Works,* iv. 18–19.

51. "This section, which was intended only to shew how the Individuals of distinct Species of Substances came to be looked on as simple *Ideas* [i.e., presumably, simple objects of thought, objects of simple conceptions], and so to have simple Names, . . . hath been mistaken for an Account of the *Idea* of Substance in general" (*Essay,* 295 n.). Sect. 14, giving the example "swan," repeats the message in terms also to be found in the drafts: "These *Ideas* of Substances, though they are commonly called simple Apprehensions, and the Names of them simple Terms; yet in effect, are complex and compounded." The connection is not straightforward, but Locke seems to have been assimilating the most available Aristotelian notion of simplicity (which involves the contrast between "simple" concepts or terms and "complex" propositions) to the different (although arguably related) conception according to which scientific definitions of essences are "simple" for other reasons.

52. Cf. *Essay,* III. x. 17: "Thus . . . we say, that *Animal rationale* is, and *Animal implume bipes latis unguibus* is not a good definition of a Man." "We" again means Aristotelian orthodoxy.

53. Aristotle, *Posterior Analytics,* B. 19. Cf. *Metaphysics* A. I.

54. *Essay,* II. xxiii. 2.

55. Cf. ibid. II. xxiii. 6: "several Combinations of simple *Ideas,* co-existing in such, though unknown, Cause of their Union, as makes the whole subsist of itself."

56. Ibid. II. xxiii. 23.
57. Ibid. II. xxiii. 5. While II. xxiii concentrates on the point that the materialists are therefore no better off than immaterialists, the argument is consonant with the obverse point, notoriously made at IV. iii. 6.
58. Ibid. II. xxiii.
59. Gottfried Leibniz, *New Essays on the Human Understanding*, II. xxii. 2, trans. P. Remnant and J. Bennett (Cambridge, 1981), 218 (pagination following edn. of A. Robinet and H. Schepers). Bennett claims (in Hare [ed.], *Doing Philosophy Historically*, 68) that his "interpretation of Locke's 'substratum' texts is exactly the same as Leibniz's," but Leibniz's remarks, unlike Bennett's, are consonant with his understanding the disagreement to be over the question whether we have "clear and distinct notions" of body and spirit in a Cartesian sense: i.e. knowledge of their essences. To see this, just suppose that the present interpretation of Locke's thesis is correct, and that Leibniz so understood Locke. To present his rival explanation of substance–attribute logic, Leibniz would have needed to claim that the subject–predicate form of definitions is merely formal, reflecting, not ignorance of anything, but the possibility of abstracting the formal concept of substance from our idea of any particular substance. This formal concept is not an obscure and confused thought of something behind observable qualities, but is clear and distinct in that it can be employed in abstract metaphysical demonstrations ("Yet this conception of substance, for all its apparent thinness, is less empty and sterile than it is thought to be. Several consequences arise from it . . . of greatest importance to philosophy"). To complain that "we have no clear idea of substance in general" is therefore to fail to recognize the nature of the substance–attribute abstraction ("you have already set aside all the attributes through which details could be conceived") and to "demand a way of knowing which the [purely formal] object does not admit of." This is pretty much how Leibniz does argue. It is true that we do not get accurate and sympathetic exposition of Locke's claims (any more than we do of, say, his accounts of "reflection" and identity, or his rejection of innate principles), but that does not mean that Leibniz really took Locke explicitly to hold the strange theory that beneath *essence* there lies a further and unknowable unknown called substance. It just means that Leibniz was a polemical writer.
60. *Essay*, III. vi. 21.
61. Descartes, *Principles*, I. 63, in *Philosophical Writings*, i. 215.
62. Despite what Descartes says here, it has been suggested (e.g. by Nicholas Jolley, *Leibniz and Locke: A Study of the "New Essays on Understanding"* [Oxford, 1984], 78–9) that Descartes might at least sometimes have thought of the substance as something over and above even its essential attributes, as when he wrote, "We do not have immediate knowledge of substances . . . We know them only by perceiving certain forms or attributes which must inhere in something if they are to exist; and we call the thing in which they inhere a 'substance' " (*Philosophical Writings*, ii. 156 [AT VII 222]; cf. p. 114 [AT VII 161]; p. 124 [AT VII 176]; René Descartes, *Conversation with Burman*, trans. J. Cottingham [Oxford, 1976], p. xxv). But what Descartes seems to have in mind in these passages is something like the view advanced by Epicurus and

Hobbes, that attributes in the general sense (i.e. attributes and modes in the technical Cartesian sense) are not things but, as it were, aspects of things, ways of conceiving of them. The substance cannot be known "directly," if that means its being known otherwise than via an attribute, a way of conceiving of it. The substance is what can be conceived or known in all these ways: it cannot be reduced to them, but is not something beyond them. Its unity is grasped by grasping the unity of its attributes (i.e., the necessary connections between Cartesian attributes, and the attribute–mode relation), not by abstracting it from those attributes as if they were distinct from it (cf. *Conversation with Burman*, pp. xxii; *Philosophical Writings*, ii. 44 ff. [AT X 418 and 421]; pp. 296 ff. [AT VIIIB 347–51]; ii. 277 [AT IXA 216]).

63. Nicholas Malebranche, *The Search after Truth*, trans. T. M. Lennon and P. J. Olscamp (Columbus, OH., 1980), III. ii. 8.

64. *Essay*, III. x. 6. In Draft A Locke chided Descartes for arbitrarily using the names "extension," "body," and "space" for the same idea, but the significance of the grammatical difference between them was not there an issue. Cf. *Drafts*, i. 45–6.

65. Cf. Descartes, *Principles*, I. 61. For the possibility of clearly conceiving how modes of quantity exist in objects, and the impossibility of so conceiving of colours, see ibid. I. 70 (cf. Hobbes, *De Corpore*, II. viii. 3).

66. Malebranche, *The Search after Truth*, III. ii. 8.

67. *Works*, iv. 19. The notion of substance was linked with the ideas (or idea) of "Entity Being Something Existing" in Draft A (*Drafts*, I. 19–20), but that argument, dropped in Draft B, had quite a different form, turning on the claim that an idea of being cannot be separated from the ideas of particular sensible qualities and powers.

68. Arnauld and Nicole, *La Logique*, I. ii.

69. *Essay*, III. viii. 2.

70. A notable example of a Lockean treatment of substance in logical theory was in William Duncan's popular *Elements of Logic* of 1748 (London).

71. Kant, *Prolegomena to Any Future Metaphysics*, sect. 46.

3

Locke, Law, and the Laws of Nature

G. A. J. Rogers

Central to Locke's account of moral and political philosophy is the ancient notion of the moral law. Not only is his earliest sustained philosophy focused on this subject,[1] but it cannot be doubted that the moral law is central to the whole rationale of the argument of his mature political writings. Nor is the concept confined to the political writings as such. Although the phrase *law of nature* is often found in the two *Treatises of Government*, it is also much used in the *Reasonableness of Christianity*. In short it is a key concept for Locke's religious, moral, and political philosophy. It is not therefore surprising that it has received considerable attention from Locke scholars. Despite such attention there remain certain puzzles and difficulties in understanding Locke's position. One specific problem relates to the logical status of the law of nature: are the moral laws necessary or contingent? Sometimes Locke's remarks seem to point in one direction, sometimes in another. What exactly was Locke's position, and given that we can discover it, why did he hold the view that he did?

That is one problem in the exegesis of Locke that will concern us. But I wish to illuminate it by reference to another. The second problem will immediately be seen to have certain features in common with the first. But to many it also appears to be far removed. It relates to Locke's views on the discoveries of science. According to a widely received view, what scientists attempt to do is to discover the laws of nature. Locke certainly believed that that was one important task of the natural philosopher. But what for Locke were the laws of nature? Were the laws of nature as discovered by the scientists necessary or contingent? Clearly the same or similar questions may be asked about the laws of nature as may be asked about natural or moral law. And, as we shall see, many of the same or similar problems arise for both within Locke's writings. It might not, then, be thought too optimistic to suppose that his treatment of the one issue may throw light on the other. Whether all the difficulties in interpreting Locke will be resolved by this comparison is much more problematic.

Fully to appreciate Locke's position we must recognise that Locke was himself aware of the strong overlap between the problems to which we are addressed. The nature of the moral law and the status of the discoveries of science were intimately connected in his mind, as they were in the minds of others, through their common ancestry in the question of the relationship between God and his universe. The theological implications, then, of our questions, were, to put it no stronger, never out of sight, and it is only through an awareness of the interactions between epistemological, moral, and theological viewpoints can we approach a proper understanding of Locke's account.

Locke and the Status of the Law of Nature

It is customary to distinguish between a rationalist or realist and a voluntarist position with regard to the law of nature.[2] The rationalist holds that it is possible to know many major moral truths by recourse to reason. It is often thought central to this view that true moral propositions are logically necessary, and false ones are either implicit or explicit contradictions. On such a view the law of nature could not change. Moral truths were both immutable and also comprehensible by rational men. Further, the natural order and the moral order would be one.

An implication of this view was to encourage a belief in some sort of commitment to innate moral knowledge. Since there are many human activities which are taken to be natural (the love of parents for offspring, and vice versa, for example) then these are also to be thought of as morally right conduct or morally worthy feelings. Conversely, unnatural actions, (for example the rejection of the child by the mother) would be known to be unnatural and therefore morally wrong.

Locke, of course, remained all his life wedded to some form of natural law theory. But he was also strongly committed to the rejection of the doctrine of innate ideas. Equally important was his espousal of the voluntarist position with regard to the origin of the law of nature. Its source was the will of God. But the will of God could not itself be other than rational. These different strands in Locke's thought are often thought to lead him to an impossible position. On the one hand he claims that a demonstrative science of ethics is possible. On the other he claims that all knowledge is derived from experience, and that no man has an innate knowledge of right and wrong.

Some of the difficulties in Locke's account of ethics as put forward in the *Essay Concerning Human Understanding* were highlighted by Thomas Burnet in his anonymously published *Remarks upon an "Essay Concerning Human Understanding"* (1697). One of Burnet's criticisms went right to the heart of a central problem in Locke's moral theory and his theology. Burnet wrote:

> You allow, I think, *moral good and evil* to be such antecedently to all human laws: but you suppose them to be such (if I understand you right) by the divine law. To know your mind farther, give me leave to ask, What is the reason or ground of that divine law? Whether the arbitrary will of God, the good of men, or the intrinsick nature of the things themselves.[3]

Burnet's argument was powerful and Locke produced no adequate response. His testy reply merely evaded the crucial issues.[4]

There was certainly good basis for Burnet's problem in the text of the *Essay*. Locke's well-known claim that morality is capable of demonstration, which seems to imply that the certainty and truth of many moral propositions are quite independent of the existence of God, stands in contrast to yet another claim that without God there can be no morality. Thus Locke argues that

> *moral knowledge* is as capable of real certainty, as mathematicks. For certainty being but the perception of the agreement, or disagreement of our *ideas*; and demonstration nothing but the perception of such agreement, by the intervention of other *ideas*, or mediums, our *moral ideas*, as well as mathematical, being archetypes themselves, and so adequate, and complete *ideas*, all the agreement, or disagreement, which we shall find in them, will produce real knowledge, as well as in mathematical figures.[5]

This appears to be a clear commitment to the autonomy of ethics. However, at other places Locke makes ethics entirely dependent on the existence of God. Thus is his discussion of the proposition. *It is the duty of parents to preserve their children.* Locke argues that "what a duty is, cannot be understood without a law; nor a law be known, or supposed without a law-maker, or without reward and punishment."[6] The position was made even more clearly in his unpublished paper "Of Ethics in General" in which Locke writes that "without showing a law that commands or forbids them, moral goodness will be but an empty sound."[7] Locke concludes this paper with the following unambiguous paragraph:

> To establish morality, therefore, upon its proper basis, and such foundations as may carry an obligation with them, we must first prove a law, which always supposes a law-maker: one that has a superiority and right to ordain, and also a power to reward and punish according to the tenor of the law established by him. This sovereign law-maker, who has set rules and bounds to the actions of men, is God, their Maker, whose existence we have already proved.[8] The next thing then to show is, that there are certain rules, certain dictates, which is his will all men should conform their actions to, and that this will of his is sufficiently promulgated and made know to all mankind.[9]

From these and similar remarks,[10] it would appear that Locke held that the true morality could only be known if we knew what exactly it was that God had commanded as axioms of a deductive ethics. It would then be possible to deduce certain conclusions or theorems from these, and thus produce a demonstrative science of ethics. There are several relevant sources here. One such is a passage in the *Essay* in which Locke considers the implications for a deductive ethics of God having himself fixed the definitions of moral concepts. He writes:

> That where GOD, or any other law-maker, hath defined any moral names, there they have made the essence of that species to which that name belongs: and there it is not safe to apply or use them otherwise.[11]

But, surely, we must conclude, God has, must have, fixed the essence of moral names, and surely Locke could not seriously have doubted this. The epistemological problem was how to discover what God's definitions were.

Locke was undoubtedly attracted to the possibility of a deductive system of ethics from self-evident axioms. When pressed by his friend William Molyneux to produce a demonstrative ethics, as hinted in the *Essay*, Locke replied:

> Though by the view I had of moral ideas, whilst I was considering that subject, I thought I saw that morality might be demonstratively made out; yet whether I am able to so make it out, is another question. Every one could not have demonstrated what Mr. Newton's book hath shown to be demonstrable; but to show my readiness to obey your commands, I shall not decline the first leisure I can get, to employ some thoughts that way.[12]

Two comments on this reply are relevant. Although Locke never accomplished the task he here undertook there is some manuscript evidence that he did in fact begin it. The results are hardly exciting, nothing to suggest that Locke could ever have become the Newton of the moral sciences, but the notes suggest that Locke was serious in his intentions.[13]

The second comment is that the explicit linking by Locke of his programme for ethics with Newton's *Principia,* which had "cultivated mathematics as far as it relates to natural philosophy"[14] perhaps suggests that he saw more than an analogy between the moral and the natural sciences, the law of nature and the laws of nature. It was a comparison Locke had made as early as about 1660. The law of nature—the moral law—he had said in his lectures, may not be known to all men, because it requires us to make proper use of our faculties to arrive at knowledge of it, just as "it does not follow that whoever is in possession of mental faculties turns out a geometer or knows thoroughly the science of arithmetic."[15] Locke himself uses the phrase 'law of nature' to refer to Newton's discovery of universal gravitation. In his *Elements of Natural Philosophy* he wrote: "It appears, as far as human observation reaches, to be a settled law of Nature, that all bodies have a tendency, attraction, or gravitation towards one another."[16] We shall return shortly to explore further the basis of this similarity.

But there is deeper problem in Locke's programme for a deductive system of ethics, which brings us full circle to the tensions within Locke's moral theory between the rationalist and the voluntarist positions. Locke claimed in the *Essay* that morality was capable of being demonstrated from self-evident propositions, and this is often taken to imply a complete commitment to the rationalist position. But this is not so obvious if the whole paragraph of the most favoured quotation is considered, for then it is clear that Locke believes that such demonstration is contingent on our having knowledge of the existence of God. This does not show that Locke was not a rationalist. But it does show that he was consistent in believing that a necessary condition for any moral law was the existence of a law-giver, whether or not the law-giver was himself constrained by logic as to what laws he might ennact. The relevant passage is:

> The idea of a supreme Being, infinite in power, goodness, and wisdom, whose workmanship we are and on whom we depend, and the idea of ourselves as understanding rational beings, being such as are clear in us, would, I suppose, if duly considered and pursued, afford such foundations of our duty and rules of action as might place morality amongst the sciences capable of demonstration: wherein I doubt not but from self-evident propositions, by necessary consequences as incontestable as those in mathematics, the measures of right and wrong might be made out to anyone that will apply himself with the same indifferency and attention to the one as he does to the other of these sciences.[17]

It is worth underlining the fact that a central feature of Locke's ethics was the belief that without a law-giver, with the power to reward and punish, there could not in the true sense be any morality. (It was the major reason why his religious toleration stopped short of the atheist.) But granted that the existence of God held this position within his moral theory, it followed that the truth of any supposedly self-evident moral propositions were contingent on the truth of the theist's claim. And here it is relevant to remember that Locke does not consider God's existence to be itself a self-evident or a necessary truth, or, perhaps more accurately, Locke held that we cannot prove the existence of God *a priori,* and the clear implication is that we can never know that the proposition *God exists* is anything other than a contingent one. From this it follows that Locke's commitment to a deductive ethics cannot be held to place him unambiguously in the rationalist camp.

Philip Abrams, in an excellent discussion, has drawn clear attention to the way in which Locke saw the existence of God as central to the moral law, and points out that in *The Reasonableness of Christianity* Locke is quite explicitly and totally commited to the centrality of God's authority as a law-giver, and abandons any attempt to justify obedience to the moral law on purely rationalist lines.[18] Abrams sees Locke as being pushed from "his ideal position, the rationalist argument, to a more effective operational one, the argument from will" because he recognised the force of the epistemological point that nobody had ever been able to give that law in its entirety. That this was for Locke an important consideration is no doubt correct, but there were other intellectual pressures pushing Locke in that direction. I wish to suggest that it was also pressure from his understanding of the new science of nature which would discourage Locke from adopting the rationalist position which is often attributed to him.[19]

Locke and the Laws of Nature

Although Locke rarely uses the words *laws of nature* to refer to the regularities to be discovered in the physical world, it has rightly been observed that a very high proportion of the *Essay* relates directly or indirectly to the possibility of man's ability to obtain knowledge of nature.[20] Despite the achievements of Boyle and Newton, he was not optimistic that a comprehensive science of nature is possible.

There were several important reasons why Locke believed that our knowledge of nature was likely to be limited, and we shall not here explore them all, or in depth, but we shall look at two relevantly important ones. The first was a consequence of our inadequate ideas of the objects which we see around us. An adequate idea was, for Locke, one which perfectly represented its archetype.[21] Without such adequate ideas we could not obtain to the general truths or laws of nature.

Locke went on to explain the problem with some examples which reveal how strongly he was committed to mechanical explanations of the properties and powers of bodies. Thus he wrote, "did we know the mechanical affections of the particles of . . . hemlock . . . as a watchmaker does those of a watch, whereby it performs its operations, and of a file which by rubbing on them will alter the figure of any of the wheels, we should be able to tell before hand that . . . hemlock (will) kill . . . as well as a watchmaker can . . . that some small part of it being rubb'd by a file, the machine would quite lose its motion, and the watch go no more."[22] But although the watchmaker knows that, say, if the mainspring breaks then the watch will not work, such knowledge is not *demonstrative* knowledge in the sense required to suggest that Locke is in this passage considering the possibility of a deductive system of physics.

It is the second argument of Locke's that I wish to consider which most clearly takes us into his reasons for rejecting the possibility of a deductive natural philosophy. Knowledge was, for Locke, the recognition of a connection between ideas. Unfortunately we can find few discoverable connections between our ideas of substances. There is "no conceivable connexion between any impulse of any sort of body, and any perception of a colour or smell, which we find in our minds."²³ The "constant and regular connexion, in the ordinary course of things" which we discover by experience is "not discoverable in the *ideas* themselves, which appearing to have no necessary dependence one on another, we can attribute their connexion to nothing else but the arbitrary determination of that all-wise Agent, who has made them to be, and to operate as they do, in a way wholly above our weak understandings to conceive."²⁴ So, though we may be certain that there is a law which governs such regularities, a proper understanding of that law, a knowledge of it in the sense in which Locke defined knowledge, is beyond us. Our "experimental knowledge" never is likely to reach to "philosophical knowledge" and we are therefore forced to ascribe the regularities or laws to "the arbitrary will and good pleasure of the wise Architect." It is "a lost labour" to expect to obtain a "perfect *science* of natural bodies."²⁵

But, although we can have no such grand expectations, it is far from clear that Locke believed that no such science exists. Although because of our mediocrity we have no knowledge of the essences of substances, it does not follow that such essences do not exist. The mistake is not to suppose that there are essences, but to suppose that we can know them. On this view we see that Locke is not committed ascribing to God an arbitrariness in his behaviour, in the ways of the world. Rather, it is that because we cannot know, in the philosophical sense of seeing the necessary connections which exist between the ideas in God's mind, we have no alternative but to view them as arbitrary, except, no doubt, in the very general sense in which we know that all of God's actions are constantly directed towards the general good.

Here, I believe, we may discern emerging some signs of symmetry between Locke's moral theory and his philosophy of science. For most men morality will consist in subscribing to a set of moral propositions, some of which are self-evidently true, many of which are known to be true only because of revelation. In theory it would be possible to show that all true moral propositions are either self-evident, or deductible from self-evident truths. But in practice no man has ever achieved this. All have their ultimate authority as having been authorised by God, without whom they would lack any categorical imperative force. In a similar way the general truths about the nature of the physical world cannot be known by deduction from self-evident principles. But this is not because such a system is in principle impossible. It merely reflects our initial lack of knowledge about the nature and essence of the objects of God's creation.

There is not only an epistemological symmetry between the law of nature and the laws of nature, there is also one with respect to ontology. With regard to the law of nature there is God, God's laws, and the creatures required to obey them, namely rational agents such as man. Similarly, with regard to the laws of nature there is God, God's laws, and the entities required to obey them, namely the substances of the physical world. But, obviously enough, the force of *required* in these two parallel accounts is totally different. Although the theological implications of this difference are clearly of great moment, they will not impinge on the issues raised in this paper to any marked extent.

The Unity of Locke's Thought

A central claim of my argument is that we must appreciate the unity of Locke's thinking on matters relating to the law of nature and the laws of nature. That Locke saw such a close relation himself is testified by the frequent juxtaposition of the two topics in the *Essay*. At the end of the *Essay* Locke distinguished a three-fold division of the sciences into natural philosophy, moral philosophy, and logic.[26] The first two were a consequence of God's will, and the third bound God and his creation. Further, God was himself a legitimate subject for consideration under the heads of both natural philosophy and of ethics.[27]

The importance of a common method in natural philosophy and ethics is illustrated by Locke's typically disparaging dismissal of the importance of maxims for obtaining knowledge. He makes a specific contrast between the method of mathematics on the one hand, and the method of ethics and natural philosophy on the other. His claim is what whilst it may (though it may not) be appropriate to begin with general maxims in mathematics, the same cannot be said for the other areas of human enquiry. If you do, he says, "I know not what may pass for truth in morality, what may not be introduced and proved in natural philosophy."[28] In another passage Locke emphasises that the same degree of certainty can attach to our mathematical, moral, religious, and empirical knowledge. Equally surely, if we fail to use our faculties correctly we may not reach certainty in any of these areas:

> He . . . that hath the *idea* of an intelligent, but frail and weak being, made by and depending on another, who is eternal, omnipotent, perfectly

wise and good, will as certainly know that man is to honour, fear, and obey God, as that the sun shines when he sees it . . . as he is certain to find, that *three, four,* and *seven,* are less than fifteen, if he will consider and compute those numbers.[29]

In the posthumously published, but considerably influential, *Of the Conduct of the Understanding* Locke again links moral and scientific knowledge, in the section on 'fundamental verities.' He wrote:

There are fundamental truths that lie at the bottom, the basis upon which a great many others rest, and in which they have their consistency. These are teeming truths, rich in store, with which they furnish the mind, and, like the lights of heaven, are not only beautiful and entertaining in themselves, but give light and evidence to other things, that without them could not be seen or known. Such is that admirable discovery of Mr. Newton, that all bodies gravitate to one another, which may be counted as the basis of natural philosophy; which, of what use it is to the understanding of the great frame of our solar system, he has to the astonishment of the learned world shewn: and how much farther it would guide us in other things, if rightly pursued, is not yet known. Our Saviour's great rule that "we should love our neighbour as ourselves," is such a fundamental truth for the regulating human society; that, I think by that alone, one might without difficulty, determine all the cases and doubts in social morality.[30]

Enough has been said, I believe, to show that Locke saw knowledge of nature and knowledge of morality as being very closely linked. It was a belief which stretches across his productive intellectual life. In the early lectures on the law of nature we find that he makes a quite explicit connection between the moral and physical order.

Even at this early stage in his thought, when we might expect Locke to be most rationalist, the primary criterion for a law is it being "the decree of a superior will, wherein the formal cause of a law appears to consist."[31] It is probably impossible to overestimate the primacy of Locke's theism for his whole account of the natural and moral order.

There is a further major claim made in the *Essays on the Law of Nature* which is central to the reading of Locke advanced here. It is Locke's arguments for the perpetual binding force of the law of nature. The law of nature is both perpetual and universal, and these characteristics are a consequence of the nature of man. Locke's argument is this: it could not be that some men are subject to this law "for this is not a private or positive law created according to circumstances and for an immediate convenience; rather it is a fixed and permanent rule of morals, which reason herself pronounces, and which persists, being a fact so firmly rooted in the soil of human nature. Hence human nature must needs be changed before this law can be either altered or anulled."[32] It is clear from this that Locke is not claiming that the law of nature is permanent and universal because it is in an unconditional sense logically necessary, but because once it is granted that man has a certain nature and God requires us to honour that nature, then certain moral rules follow. He explained it like this:

This law does not depend on an unstable and changeable will, but on the external order of things. For it seems to me that certain essential features of things are immutable, and certain duties arise out of necessity and cannot be other than they are. And this is not because nature or God (as I should say more correctly) could not have created man differently. Rather, the cause is that, since man has been made such as he is, equipped with reason and his other faculties and destined for this mode of life, there necessarily result from his inborn constitution some definite duties for him, which cannot be other than they are.[33]

At this early stage in his career, too, Locke is drawn to the analogy with mathematics: the passage continues:

In fact it seems to me to follow just as necessarily from the nature of man that, if he is a man, that he is bound to love and worship God and also to fulfil other things appropriate to the rational nature, i.e. to observe the law of nature, as it follows from the nature of a triangle that, if it is a triangle, its three angles are equal to two right angles, although perhaps very many men are so lazy and so thoughtless that for want of attention they are ignorant of both these truths.

What exactly these claims of Locke imply for the possibility of a demonstrative ethics and a demonstrative science of nature we shall explore more fully below. What does need to be emphasised here, however, is that Locke's conception of a deductive ethics is hardly as mysterious as it is sometime depicted.

Locke and Demonstration

In the light of all this what exactly did Locke believe about the possibility of demonstration in the natural and moral sciences? Let us begin with what Locke would understand by a demonstration. To demonstrate a proposition, in the appropriate sense, would for Locke be to show that the proposition was true by showing that it followed logically from a proposition already known to be true, either because it had been shown already to be true or because it was self-evidently true. But it is vitally important to recognise that a self-evident proposition was not the same as a logically necessary proposition. A demonstration, therefore, did not have to begin from logically necessary propositions. All that was necessary was that they were known to be true. Further, since the primary notion for Locke is not that of words, but that of ideas, the crucial stages in the argument are always the showing that one *idea* contains another.

Let us now apply these points to Locke's twin claims about the possibilities of the demonstration of the law of nature and the laws of nature. I shall begin with the latter.

The way that the world is, according to Locke, is because God has caused certain ideas of His to become substantiated. In the physical world it is highly probable that God began by creating various atoms with powers directly related to their constitution. The properties of an object arise ineluctably from the properties of its constituent parts, just as, say, the power of a sphere to roll on a flat surface arises from its very nature, in a way in which a cube could have no such power. If, then, we knew the fundamental natures of objects, knew the basic properties of the constituents of the universe, then we would be in a position to deduce the properties which gross bodies made of those constituents would have. But, of course, Locke held, we do not know, nor are ever likely to know, the real essences of objects, and therefore we shall never be able to demonstrate the real connections which exist. Thus, he concluded his chapter on universal propositions:

> General propositions, of what kind soever, are then only capable of certainty, when the terms used in them, stand for such ideas whose agreement or disagreement, as there expressed, is capable to be discovered by us. And we are then certain of their truth or falsehood, when we perceive the ideas the terms stand for, to agree or not agree, according as they are affirmed or denied one of another. Whence we may take notice that general certainty is to be found but in our ideas. Whenever we go to seek it elsewhere in experiment, or observations without us, our knowledge goes not beyond particulars. 'Tis the contemplation of our own abstract ideas, that alone is able to afford us general knowledge.[34]

Of course if we had knowledge of the general ideas in the mind of God, which we would know to be certainly true, then we would at least have a certain basis for a science of nature. It would, however, also be necessary for us to have the capacity to see the relationships between the relevant ideas, something which we may not be able to do, any more than we can do it in all cases of mathematical deduction.

It is important to remember that such hypothetical and highly theoretical possibilities do not for Locke hold out the possibility of coming to know logically necessary truths about God's creation. Although it is true that if God has had a certain idea and it is manifested in some aspect of his creation, in the form of some particular substance, then no doubt there are certain things which follow. But God had a completely free choice as to which of his ideas are in fact instantiated in nature. The hypothetical possibility of a demonstrative natural science, therefore, is in no way a commitment to a Leibnizian position in which all true propositions are analytic.[35]

Let us now turn to the issue of ethics. Although, as we have seen, Locke often talks of the possibility of a deductive system of ethics there is no reason to believe that such a system must begin from analytic truths. Although Locke talks of the demonstrations in ethics beginning from self-evident premises, self-evidence is not equivalent to 'trifling,' as the proposition "I exist" illustrates. But there is another reason for not reading Locke as if he subscribed to a theory of moral law which made all moral propositions tautologies, dependent on the ideas in our own minds. It is that Locke distinguishes between moral systems and the true morality. Moral systems, on this view, would be any coherent deductive ethics. The true morality would be that system which in fact matched the moral law ordained by God. There are several places where Locke makes this distinction. Thus, in discussing the importance of proving the existence of God, Locke remarks that God's existence is "so fundamental a truth and of that consequence that all religion and genuine morality depend thereon."[36]

In other words, genuine morality cannot be separated from the law ordained by God. The point was made earlier in a remark we have already quoted, that "where God or any other law-maker hath defined any moral names, there they have made the essence of that species to which that name belongs, and there it is not safe to apply or use them otherwise."[37]

It no more follows, however, that because God has ordained a law, that the truths of morality are analytic, than it did in the case of the laws of nature. The eternal law is eternal, contingent on the world remaining as it is and the will of God continuing as it does, and not because of some internal necessity. Thus Locke could remark that when a man chooses wrongly as to what it is in his interest or which will bring him happiness, the moral order and nature of things should not be changed to align his mistaken choice with his expectations: "the eternal law and nature of things must not be altered to comply with his ill-ordered choice."[38] This could only raise itself as a possibility if the laws are contingent, not necessary, truths. Morality is acting according to the law of nature, and God has ordained such laws as are fitting to our nature. But our nature might have been different and the laws then too would have been different, at least in some respects. Neither in matters relating to the laws of nature or the law of nature was Locke's commitment to the theoretical possibility of demonstration coupled with any commitment to any sort of hard-line and unconditional necessity.

Notes

1. *The Essays on the Law of Nature.* Locke does not have a collective title for these essays, but they have been so labelled by their editor W. von Leyden: *Essays on the Law of Nature. The Latin text with a translation, introduction and notes, together with transcripts of Locke's shorthand in his journal for 1676.* (Oxford 1954). On the title see p. V, footnote. Von Leyden's excellent introduction, and especially his discussion of the sources of Locke's view on the law of nature, has enabled me to keep discussion of this topic to a minimum here.

2. For discussions of this distinction see especially Otto Gierke: *Political Theories of the Middle Ages,* translated, with an introduction, by F. W. Maitland (Cambridge, 1913); Morris Ginsberg: "The Concept of Juridicial and Scientific Law," *Politia* IV (1939): 15; M. B. Foster: "The Christian Doctrine of Creation and the Rise of Modern Natural Science," *Mind* XLIII (1934); M. B. Foster: "Christian Theology and Modern Science of Nature II," *Mind* XLV (1936); Joseph Needham: "Human Laws and Laws of Nature in China and the West," Parts I and II, *Journal of the History of Ideas* XII (1951); Francis Oakley, "Christian Theology and the Newtonian Science: The Rise of the Concept of the Laws of Nature," *Church History* 30 (1961); Francis Oakley: "Medieval Theories of Natural Law: William of Ockham and the Significance of the Voluntarist Tradition," *Natural Law Forum* 6 (1961).

3. Op. cit. p. 6. In this, and other quotes from contemporary sources, I have in part modernised capitals, italics, and punctuation.

4. Locke replied to Burnet's criticisms at the end of his *Second Reply* to Stillingfleet.

5. *Essay Concerning Human Understanding*, IV, IV. 7. Quotations are taken from the Clarendon Edition of the Works of John Locke, *Essay Concerning Human Understanding*, edited by Peter H. Nidditch (Oxford, 1975), unless otherwise stated, with some modernisations. Other relevant references to morality and demonstration in the *Essay* occur at III XI 16–18; IV III 18–20; IV, IV 1–10; IV, X 7; IV, XII 11; IV, XXI 3.

6. I, III, 12.

7. Published in Lord King's *The Life and Letters of John Locke, with extracts from his Journals and Commonplace Books* (new edition, London, 1858), pp. 311–312. This paper was probably intended as a draft chapter for the *Essay*.

8. A reference to *Essay* IV, X, "Of our Knowledge of the Existence of a God."

9. King, *op. cit.*, p. 313.

10. See, for example, *Essay* II, XXVIIII 5–8; *Locke's Essay An Early Draft*, edited by R. I. Aaron and Jocelyn Gibb (Oxford, 1936) (Draft A), p. 39, § 26; *An Essay Concerning the Understanding, Knowledge, Opinion, and Assent*, edited by Benjamin Rand (Cambridge, Mass.: 1931) (Draft B), pp. 302–3, § 160.

11. IV, IV, 10.

12. Locke to Molyneux, Sept. 20, 1692. Locke: *Works*, 7th edition (1768) Vol. IV, pp. 270–271.

13. These notes include the following: "Morality is the rule of man's acting for the attaining happiness—

For the end and aim of all men being happiness alone nothing could be a rule or a law to them whose observation did not lead to happiness and whose break did draw misery after it

Def. Happiness and misery consist in pleasure and pain Good is what gives or increases pleasure or takes away or diminishes pain and evil or the contrary

Axiom 1 All men desire the enjoyment of happiness and the absence of misery and that only and always.

Ax. Men act only for what they desire . . .

Man made not himself nor any other man

Man made not the world which he found made at his birth,

therefore any man at his birth can have no right to anything in the world more than an other Men must therefore either enjoy all things in common or by compact . . ." Bodleian Library MS Locke c. 28f. 139. These notes suggest that Locke wished to base morality on axioms which would perhaps be allowed to be self-evident. But he was probably also unsure how self-evident they would be taken to be.

14. Newton wrote in the Preface to the first edition of the *Principia*, "I have in this treatise cultivated mathematics as far as it relates to philosophy."

15. Von Leyden, pp. 134–135.

16. *Works*, IV, p. 581.

17. IV, III 18. But see also IV, XII 8 where there is no reference to a lawmaker.

18. In his Introduction to his edition of *John Locke: Two Tracts on Government* (Cambridge, 1967), pp. 88–90. Abrams does not consider the argument offered above as a reason for Locke's doubts about the rationalist programme.

19. Locke's philosophy of science has been the subject of increased interest. Valuable discussions in recent years have included those by Gerd Buchdahl (*Metaphysics and the Philosophy of Science: The Classical Origins Descartes to Kant* [Oxford, 1969], Ch. 4, R. S. Woolhouse (*Locke's Philosophy of Science and Knowledge* [Oxford, 1971], *passim*), and John W. Yolton (*Locke and the Compass of Human Understanding* [Cambridge, 1970], *passim*).

20. Cf. Yolton, *Locke and the Compass of Human Understanding*, p. 2.

21. Cf. *Essay* II, XXXI, 1.

22. IV, III, 25.

23. IV, III, 28.

24. Ibid.

25. Ibid.

26. IV, XXI, 1. On this division see Yolton, (op. cit., Note 24), p. 1ff.

27. Locke makes it clear that God is a legitimate subject of enquiry under his first science in IV, XXI, 2. That God is directly relevant to the second it was not necessary to state.

28. IV, XII, 4.

29. IV, XIII, 3.

30. *Works,* IV, p. 190.

31. Ibid., pp. 111–113.

32. Ibid., Locke's seventh lecture, p. 199.

33. Ibid.

34. IV, VI, 16.

35. Leibniz wrote: "My idea of a true proposition is such that every predicate, necessary or contingent, past, present, or future, is included in the subject." Quoted in Hide Ishiguro: *Leibniz's Philosophy of Logic and Language* (London, 1972), p. 120.

36. IV, X, 7.

37. IV, IV, 10.

38. II, XXI, 56.

4

Locke on Identity: Matter, Life, and Consciousness

Edwin McCann

Locke's general theory of identity has received relatively little attention on its own. The first eight sections of the *Essay's* chapter "Of Identity and Diversity"[1] are usually treated, if they are discussed at all, as merely prefatory to the theory of personal identity. This gets things backwards. The extended discussion of personal identity in that chapter is meant to illustrate the general theory, as well as to show that the identity of persons can be accommodated within it.[2] In this paper I aim at redressing the balance. I will describe Locke's general theory of identity, showing that it is a unified and consistent theory that is able to handle such troublesome cases of identity as that of plants, animals, and persons within a mechanist framework. I will then argue that this appreciation of Locke's theory shows the most widely held recent interpretation of Locke's theory of personal identity to be mistaken.

To understand Locke's views on identity we must recognize that the problem of identity to which he is responding is a quite special one. One of the main aims of the *Essay* was to buttress the new Mechanical Philosophy[3] against its rivals, particularly the Scholastic variants of Aristotelianism which were still so influential in the English universities. The mechanists chiefly objected to the Scholastic doctrine of forms and qualities. The Scholastics taught, to put it very roughly, that each natural object has a substantial form which, as the principle of its unity and operations, unites the matter of which it is composed into a single individual thing (*unum per se*), constitutes it a member of its species, and thus provides the conditions of its continuing identity. As regards qualities, they held, again roughly, that an object's accidental qualities

63

are real (though dependent) beings which are the efficient causes of their characteristic effects, as the redness in a body is the cause of the sensations of redness it induces in us. In what follows we'll be concerned only with forms and their role in individuation, but we should keep in mind that the doctrine of substantial forms is part of a total package which the mechanists rejected in its entirety.

Substantial forms draw the enmity of the mechanist for two reasons. First, forms act as formal causes, and in reference to final causes (in the fourfold Aristotelian scheme of causes); hence any full explanation of the unity, operations, or powers of natural objects must inevitably incorporate teleological considerations. Second, and much more important, these forms are real or actual constituents of natural bodies, in that they provide the causal or metaphysical basis of their individual identity and/or their characteristic powers and operations. In Scholastic jargon, the substantial form is an actuality, and indeed the first actuality of the composite of matter and form which constitutes a natural body. This means at the very least that it is something over and above the matter of which the body is made, which, together with its primary qualities or 'mechanical affections' (Boyle's phrase), is the only real constituent of a body that the mechanists countenanced. The issue will become clearer if we chart the role forms were held to play in the individuation of substances.

Scholastic discussions of the principle of individuation were not so much concerned with formulating a set of abstract necessary and sufficient conditions for being an individual thing (the way we're apt to think of a principle of identity or individuation) as they were to specify what it is *in* an individual that gives it its identity, that is, what real constituent of it is the causal basis of its individuality.[4] Not all of the Scholastics shared the same view on this topic. For St. Thomas Aquinas, the principle of individuation for material bodies is quantified matter;[5] Durandus held, according to Suarez, that form by itself is the full and adequate principle of individuation;[6] Suarez, Fonseca, and many other late Scholastics broadly followed Scotus in holding that it is the individual existence, 'haecceity,' or 'entity' of a thing that individuates it.[7] But Thomists and Scotists alike held that form plays a fundamental role in individuation. Suarez, for example, writes:

> . . . it must be said that in a composite substance, insofar as it is such a composite, the adequate principle of individuation is this matter and this form united to each other. And between these the primary principle is

the form, which alone is sufficient for this composite, insofar as it is an individual of a particular species, to be judged the same numerically.[8]

Aquinas has similar reasons for holding that form is prior both to matter and to the composite of form and matter.[9] The basic picture is this: as the substantial form of a cow, for example, is the causal basis of its growth, respiration, nutrition, movement, and so forth, it is what unites the different material parts of the cow into one single thing and what, over time, keeps it the same cow through changes in its (accidental) qualities and wholesale, if gradual, changes of its constituent matter.

We should be careful to note that it is the basic tenet of the theory of substantial forms—that such forms are real or actual constituents of material substances in the sense explained above—that is in conflict with mechanism. Boyle's attacks on the theory of substantial forms, for example, are directed against a rather crude version of that theory, one on which substantial forms are themselves substances in their own right, able to exist apart from any matter whatsoever.[10] The views that we have been looking at are much more complicated and subtle than this, but they still conflict with mechanism. For them, forms are real beings, since the form of a thing is the causal basis of its essential properties and the principle unifying the matter of the thing; it is in this sense that they are said to be the first actuality of the form/matter composite. Construed in this way, substantial forms are just as much at variance with mechanism as they are on the cruder view on which Boyle bases his attack.

When Locke offers as a rubric for his account of identity "what is so much enquired after, the *principium Individuationis*" (II.27.3) he is placing that account squarely within the traditional framework. His problem of identity is thus the traditional one of specifying what it is in virtue of which natural objects, and particularly organisms such as plants, animals and human beings, retain their identity through change of matter. For a mechanist like Locke the problem is especially pressing, since in view of his commitment to there being no real constituents of material substances over and above matter variously figured and moved, he cannot appeal to forms or anything like them in giving an account of what makes a body or organism the same body or organism.[11]

Thus the problem; what is Locke's solution? I have claimed that he has a consistent general account of identity; I'll introduce it here, and fill it out more when we come to discuss, in the next three sections, its particular applications. The closest Locke comes to a general statement about identity is in II.27.7, a section which caps the discussion of plant, animal, and human identity (sections 4, 5, and 6 respectively) and which prefaces the ensuing discussion of personal identity, which takes up the remainder of the chapter.

> To conceive, and judge of [identity] aright, we must consider what *Idea* the word it is applied to stands for; It being one thing to be the same *Substance,* another the same *Man,* and a third the same *Person,* if *Person, Man,* and *Substance,* are three names standing for three different *Ideas*; for such as is the *Idea* belonging to that Name, such must be the *Identity.* (II.27.7)

It is the (our) idea of the kind of thing whose identity is at issue which determines its identity, and thus which accounts for its being the same thing through changes in its (accidental) qualities and particularly in its matter. There is no question, of course, of this idea's playing a causal role in organizing the thing's matter, or being a causal basis for its vital processes; it is in no sense a constituent of the thing. But as long as a spatio-temporally continuous series of masses of matter continues to satisfy the idea, we have the same thing: the same horse, or oak-tree, or whatever; and in that sense the idea keeps the thing the same. Locke tries to make this out by showing how identity differs in different types of case. I now turn to the cases.

Matter

At the start of II.27.2 Locke notes that "We have the *Ideas* but of three sorts of Substances; 1. God. 2. Finite Intelligences. 3. *Bodies.*" In the previous section Locke had laid it down as a basic principle concerning identity that it is impossible for two things of the same kind to exist in the same place at the same time, so that "we rightly conclude, that whatever exists any where at any time, excludes all of the same kind, and is there it self alone," and had drawn from this principle a derivative one to the effect that a thing *a* and a thing *b* of the same kind are identical just in case *a* and *b* have the same beginning of existence, i.e. that *a* began to exist at exactly the same place and time as did *b*.[12]

In section 2, just after listing the three sorts of substances of which we have ideas, Locke adds something new: for finite spirits and for bodies "the relation to [the determinate time and place of its beginning to exist] will always determine to each of them its Identity as long as it exists." What, exactly, is "the relation" of which Locke speaks here? It can't, on pain of circularity, be the relation of being the same thing as something that began to exist at that time and place, or any relation equivalent to this. It seems that the only possibility is that it is the relation of spatio-temporal continuity. This makes sense of the distinction drawn at the end of the section between permanent beings and the actions of those beings; it helps us see why Locke says at the start of the next section that "Existence it self" is the principle of individuation because it "determines a Being of any sort to a particular time and place incommunicable to two Beings of the same kind" (II.27.3). Furthermore, the criterion of identity for body given in that section, where Locke talks of the "continued" existence of an atom, seems to presuppose that "the relation" is one of spatio-temporal continuity, as does the derivation in section one of the principle about beginnings of existence from the general principle that two things of the same kind cannot exist in the same place at the same time. This reading is bolstered, rather than undermined, by the fact that a spirit's identity is said to be determined by 'the relation' to its beginning of existence; for Locke is insistent that spirits are spatio-temporally located (they are where the bodies that they animate are) and that they move through space.[13] Evidently, then, Locke thought spatio-temporal continuity to be the relation determining the identity of body and of spirit. He had every reason to think so, since it seems to be the only relation that is a plausible candidate in the circumstances for providing a non-circular account of identity.[14]

In discussing the identity of bodies, Locke adds a condition to the one he specifies for both finite spirits and bodies (i.e. spatio-temporal continuity); he requires for "every Particle of Matter" that there be "no Addition or Subtraction of Matter" to or from that mass of matter if it is to continue to be the same body. On this criterion, we have the same body when and only when we have masses of numerically the same matter, however differently those masses might be organized and whatever changes of place may have occurred (as long as the changes of place preserve spatio-temporal continuity). In II.27.3 he illustrates how the criterion works within the framework of the atomist hypothesis.

Locke accepted a version of the revived Democritean atomism common to Gassendi, Charleton, and Boyle. Our idea of an atom is, he accordingly says, the idea of "a continued body under one immutable

Superficies, existing in a determined time and place"—immutable due to its physical indivisibility, determinately located in consequence of its being a finite extended thing. Each atom is "the same with itself" considered at any instant of its existence, and continues the same "as long as its existence is continued: for so long it will be the same, and no other." These specifications seem empty, but they are meant to bring out the fact that atoms, as conceived of by the Gassendist followers of Democritus, are simple substances.

As bodies, or extended solid substances, atoms by their solidity exclude all other bodies or material things from the volume of space which, thanks to their extension, they at any time occupy. Since atoms are physically indivisible, they absolutely exclude all other matter from the volume of space that they occupy: having no parts, they have no empty space inside them to permit the interpenetration that is possible among larger-scale bodies. Atoms are also insusceptible of change with respect to their figure, bulk, number, and unity, again due to their physical indivisibility; among their primary qualities the only ones which are subject to change are their state of motion and their position or situation, and these changes do not threaten the integrity of the body. Thus, the continued existence of an atom is simply a matter of its continuing to occupy space, i.e. its continuing to exist: it cannot be generated or corrupted, but only created or annihilated (by divine action). For this reason, atoms count as simple substances.

The identity of a complex body or mass of matter is then given in terms of the identities of its constituent atoms:

> If two or more Atoms be joined together in the same Mass, every one of those Atoms will be the same, by the foregoing Rule: And whilst they exist united together, the Mass, consisting of the same Atoms, must be the same Mass, or the same Body, let the parts be never so differently jumbled: But if one of those Atoms be taken away, or one new one added, it is no longer the same Mass, or Body. (ii.27.3).

As Locke indicates, bodies or masses of matter, construed in this way, can undergo many sorts of alteration in respect of their qualities. Their figures and bulks can change, as well as their state of motion and situation; they can vary the arrangement of their constituent atoms (i.e. change in respect of internal and/or surface structure); and so on. As long as the parts, or constituent atoms, of the mass remain "joined together," with no addition or subtraction of any atoms, it is the same body.

Although the atomist hypothesis figures prominently in II.27.3, its main function is to simplify the illustration of the criterion for the identity of body given in II.27.2. That criterion does not itself presuppose the truth of atomism. The criterion speaks of "particles of Matter" but this phrase does not only cover atoms, since the passage allows for the possibility of "subtraction" of matter from them. Atoms provide a convenient way of specifying the numerical identity of the aggregated matter making up a complex body. The general criterion of identity for body can be applied, however, even if atomism is false: we simply identify the boundaries of a connected mass of matter, and take the matter located within these boundaries to constitute one body, which it will continue to do as long as the matter coheres together and no matter is added or taken away.

It will help clarify Locke's theory if we consider an important criticism of it. M. R. Ayers has argued[15] that Locke's account confuses two disparate conditions: the condition that there be the same stuff or matter, and the condition that there be a continuing coherent or unified parcel of matter. The latter condition, but not the former, can be satisfied by parcels which have undergone a change of constituent matter, as long as the change is gradual; as Ayers points out, bodies or masses of matter understood in this way can be numerically identical with the organisms they can in some sense be said to compose.

For Locke we could respond as follows. The conditions Ayers mentions are disparate but not incompatible, and Locke's account simply combines them. On his view, a body remains the same as long as it continues as a coherent unified whole *and* as long as it suffers no addition or subtraction of its matter. The two conditions together give a perfectly consistent and well-defined criterion, one which involves no confusion on Locke's part so long as he does not intend it as an account of sameness of stuff or matter,[16] or as a faithful analysis of our ordinary talk about bodies;[17] but I see no evidence that Locke takes it for either of these.

What was Locke's purpose in offering this account of the identity of body? It is clear that he was not trying to prepare the way for a reductive explanation of the identity-conditions of material objects generally in terms to those of parcels or masses of matter. In the last half of section 3 he stresses as much as any Scholastic ever did that the identity-conditions of plants and animals (and humans) cannot be reduced to those of parcels of matter. His further aim, however, is to undermine one of the central tenets of the Scholastic view about the nature of

material substances. It is a leading Aristotelian doctrine that matter cannot by itself (without a form, or principle of unity) constitute a genuine
substance or *bona fide* object: an *ens per se*. Locke rejects this doctrine, showing that the identity conditions for bodies can be given entirely in terms of matter, i.e. the same numerical matter constituting a
cohesive mass (where this means only: all sticking together) and thus
constituting it one single thing, a substance. There is no need of form
or any other non-material principle of unity. Indeed, on Locke's view
the (connected) parts of substances could themselves be taken to be
substances: my big toe, for example, is a body in its own right. In practice, of course, we usually speak only of the largest connected masses
(e.g., my whole body) as the body. Locke usually follows this practice,
and his conditions accommodate it perfectly well. In any case, all Locke
has to claim for his conditions is that they give a coherent and intelligible way of conceiving the identity of bodies; if they do, as I think they
do, then he has made a significant thrust against Scholastic hylomor-
phism.

One last point about the identity of body. In the next two parts of
this paper we'll be concerned with the identities of plants, animals, and
persons. Locke evidently has these identities in mind when at II.27.7,
summing up the argument of II.27.3–6, he says: " 'Tis not therefore
Unity of Substance that comprehends all sorts of Identity, or will determine it in every Case." He then proceeds to give the general criterion
of identity I quoted earlier. This can give the impression that Locke is
implying that in cases where identity is determined by unity of substance (the identity of body and of spirit) no idea is involved, in contrast with the case of plant and animal identity, for example. But unity
of material substance, no less than any other identity, depends on an
idea: the idea of body as an extended solid substance. Thus Locke's
discussion of the identity of atoms, and the derivative identity of
masses of matter (the bodies composed of these atoms), takes off from
our idea of body. It is the fact that atoms are bodies, cohesive parcels
of matter, taken together with certain other facts about them (e.g. their
indivisibility), that determines their identity-conditions, and hence
those of the larger bodies composed of them. The immutability of the
atoms and their primary qualities, and the relations between them
(whatever they are) which serve as the causal basis of the cohesion
of these atoms into large-scale bodies are, we might say, natural or
preconventional facts. Their *identity* as bodies, however, is a function
of our idea of body, which while a close gloss of the physical facts of

the matter is nevertheless *our* idea. We turn now to the identities of plants, animals, and persons.

Life

Near the end of II.27.3, as we have seen, Locke notes that the identity of a living body does not in general consist in that of a body, or mass of matter, since the matter making up such a body can be gradually exchanged for other matter without a change in the identity of the organism. This is no problem for the Aristotelian with his substantial forms, but it is, as we have seen, a pressing problem for the mechanist. Locke outlines his solution to the problem as regards the identity of plants in II.27.4, and in II.27.5 and 6 extends it to animals and human beings. In view of its importance I quote II.27.4 in full:

> We must therefore consider wherein an Oak differs from a Mass of Matter, and that seems to me to be in this; that the one is only the Cohesion of Particles of Matter any how united, the other such a disposition of them as constitutes the parts of an Oak; and such an Organization of those parts, as is fit to receive, and distribute nourishment, so as to continue, and frame the Wood, Bark, and Leaves, *etc.* of an Oak, in which consists the vegetable Life. That being then one Plant, which has such an Organization of Parts in one coherent Body, partaking of one Common Life, it continues to be the same Plant, as long as it partakes of the same Life, though that Life be communicated to new Particles of Matter vitally united to the living Plant, in a like continued Organization, conformable to that sort of Plants. For this Organization being at any one instant in any one Collection of *Matter,* is in that particular concrete distinguished from all other, and is that individual Life, which existing constantly from that moment both forwards and backwards in the same continuity of insensibly succeeding Parts united to the living Body of the Plant, it has that Identity, which makes the same Plant, and all the parts of it, parts of the same Plant, during all the time that they exist united in that continued Organization, which is fit to convey that Common Life to all the Parts so united.

Locke here identifies animal or plant 'life' with the organization of the parts of a living body. It is this organization or disposition of parts which is the causal basis of the living thing's functional or organic unity, and of its ongoing vital functions such as nutrition, respiration, growth,

etc., some of which involve the exchange of matter with the environ-
ment.

In spite of the functional similarities between Locke's 'life' and the
Peripatetics' substantial forms, there is a crucial difference. As II.27.5
makes plain, the organization of parts in which the life of a plant or
animal consists is nothing but the mechanical organization of its body.
The only difference Locke sees between the fit organization of parts
for animal life and that which make an assemblage of gears and wheels
and so forth into a watch is that in the former case the motion that sets
the parts to work comes from within, whereas in the latter case it
comes from without. Just as there is no need of a form (a principle of
horological life, as it were) to underlie and explain the function of a
watch, so there is no need for such forms as regards plants and animals:
in both cases the characteristic operations of the thing are explained in
terms of the putting-together of solid parts, suitably figured and
moved.

We might be tempted to read Locke as a straightforward reductionist, attempting to reduce substantial forms to species-typical mechanistic constitutions. The 'life' Locke talks about is, after all, species-typical:
the life of an individual horse or oak-tree is the life of *an* oak, or *a*
horse. Furthermore, Locke certainly proposes to understand this life in
terms of the organization of the parts of the thing. We should resist
this temptation, as Locke's view is a bit more complicated than that.
This ties up with larger issues concerning Locke's views on the nature
of species and, especially, their objective reality.[18]

The straightforward reductionist view has it that all members of a
common species must share a single distinctive mechanistic organization of parts; a given object is a member of the species only because,
and only for as long as, it possesses that internal constitution. This
mechanical constitution, or real essence of the species, continues the
same through all times at which a given individual plant or animal exists, and it is what keeps the organism the same even through changes
in its matter.

In Locke's view, it is the nominal essence, i.e. our abstract idea of
the species, that is the essence of the species.[19] Locke gives a general
argument for this claim at III.6.6, in the course of which he clarifies the
relation between real and nominal essence.[20] The real essence, i.e. the
mechanical constitution of the individual thing, is the causal basis of
the thing's powers and qualities. It is styled an essence, however, only

because of its relation to the nominal essence, i.e. our abstract idea of the sort to which the thing belongs:

> But *Essence,* even in this sense, *relates to a Sort,* and supposes a *Species:* For being that real Constitution, on which the Properties depend, it necessarily supposes a sort of Things, Properties belonging only to *Species,* and not to Individuals.

He gives as an example the case of gold. A particular body has, say, the qualities of being yellow, malleable, and soluble in *aqua regia*; but until we have constructed a nominal essence of gold that makes these qualities definitional of membership in the kind, none of them are *properties* (in the traditional sense). Once we have put together this definition of the species, however,

> Here are *Essences* and *Properties,* but all upon supposition of a Sort, or general abstract Idea, which it considered as immutable: but there is no individual parcel of Matter, to which any of these Qualities are so annexed, as to be *essential* to it, or inseparable from it. That which is essential, belongs to it as a Condition, whereby it is of this or that Sort: But take away the consideration of its being ranked under the name of some abstract *Idea,* and then there is nothing necessary to it, nothing inseparable from it.

Locke has a shrewd point here. The taxonomic divisions we have set up, more or less arbitrarily, are what determine the level of abstraction at which internal structure is to be described so as to arrive at an internal constitution characteristic of the species. There will, on the individual level, be a great deal of variation in the powers and qualities of members of the same species, reflecting, it is reasonable to assume, variations in their internal structure.[21] So for two things to be the same in constitution there need be no more specific structural similarities between the bodies than that they each have internal structures (however unlike) which are causally responsible for the body's having the observable characteristics which are definitive of membership in the kind.

We should not overdo the point. Locke takes care to note that the species definitions we construct are based on a long, if not very systematic, process of observing salient resemblances among objects, and it is reasonable to think these surface resemblances reflect deeper resemblances in internal constitution. Thus Locke writes at III.6.36 that

This then, in short, is the case: *Nature makes many particular Things, which do agree* one with another, in many sensible Qualities, and probably too, in their internal frame and Constitution.

It is necessary, of course, that all members of the same species have the sensible qualities contained in the nominal essence of the species; given this degree of similarity they probably will be similar in internal constitution as well. The accent, however, is on *probably*.

The same goes for an individual existing over time. For it to remain in the same species it must continue to satisfy the nominal essence of that species; given that it does continue to satisfy it, it probably will have certain very general structural features that remain constant. But there is, again, no necessity of this. If, what is perhaps unlikely, the internal constitution of a thing came to be entirely rearranged without a change in the qualities comprised in the nominal essence, it would remain in the same species throughout, and would be the same thing.[22]

For a parcel of matter to have the life of an oak-tree is then simply for it to have an appropriate organization of parts. What determines whether an organization of parts is an appropriate one is our idea, or nominal essence, of an oak-tree. Now in terms of the identity of its constituent matter, this particular parcel of matter will substantially overlap the parcels of matter that at closely preceding and succeeding times are located at or contiguous to the place it's in. This degree of spatio-temporal continuity is less stringent than that required for the continued identity of body and of spirit, and most important, it is continuity under the idea of an oak-tree. As long as this succession of parcels of matter continues to satisfy our idea of an oak-tree, there will be the same continued life and so the same oak-tree.

Locke is thus able to provide for the identity of plants and animals (including human beings) in a way which transcends the identity of the matter of which they are at any time made up but which is consistent with the mechanistic doctrines of the *Essay*. It is the life of an oak-tree or a horse that keeps it the same thing through various changes, i.e. its having parts organized in such a way that it has, and continues to have, the sensible qualities definitive of its species. This life cannot in general be reduced to the real essence the thing at any time has, or to a set of features of this real essence. Although the body's real essence or internal constitution is the causal basis of its qualities and operations, it is the nominal essence that determines what is the life of the thing. Clearly, then, the life is not a further constituent of the organism, a real entity over and above the constituent matter with its mechanical affections. It is an artifact of sorts—one grounded in long and careful observation (natural history) and so too, probably, in underlying facts about the structures of things—but for all that, an artifact, due primarily to the abstract ideas we construct.

Consciousness

Locke discusses personal identity at much greater length than any of the other cases of identity. One obvious reason for this has to do with its theological import. There were heated controversies over such Christian doctrines as the eternal punishment or reward of the person after death and the resurrection of the body on the Last Day; the issue of personal identity is clearly implicated in these larger issues.[25] Another reason, I suggest, is that the way the rational soul provides for the identity of a person is a paradigm case of a substantial form's providing for the continuing identity of a thing. For the Scholastics the soul is the form of the living human body, although able to survive its separation from the body at death and thus secure the identity of the person after death with the person before death. If Locke can account for the identity of persons without calling upon any immaterial principles of unity—souls, substantial forms—then he will have snatched the best case away from the Scholastics. And if his account of personal identity also preserves Christian doctrines concerning immortality and personal responsibility, then mechanism will be theologically that much less suspect.

My aim in this section is to show how Locke's account of personal identity fits into his general account of identity. It is obvious how it fits with the II.27.7 injunction that the identity of a thing is to be judged in accordance with an idea, for Locke explicitly notes there that the subsequent discussion of personal identity is meant to illustrate that point. It is less obvious, however, how much the account of the identity of persons carries over from that of the identity of living things. We will see how Locke exploits the similarities and the differences between persons and living things to serve both philosophical and theological ends.

Simply put, consciousness is the life of persons. Less simply put, consciousness makes for personal identity in just the way life makes for animal or vegetable identity. Early in the discussion of personal identity Locke makes this comparison:

> Different Substances, by the same consciousness (where they do partake in it) being united into one Person; as well as different Bodies, by the same Life are united into one Animal, whose *Identity* is preserved, in that change of Substances, by the unity of one continued Life. For it being the same consciousness that makes a Man be himself to himself, *personal Identity* depends on that only, whether it be annexed only to one individual Substance, or can be continued in a succession of several Substances. (II.27.10)[24]

Consciousness and life have this in common, that they can 'unite' different substances (as judged by the criteria of unity of substance for bodies and, presumably, spirits) into a single thing, a plant, animal, man, or person.[25] More than this, they unite the various substances they at different times qualify by means of ongoing processes characteristic of the kind of thing in question—vital processes such as nutrition and respiration, in the case of life, and mental processes such as deliberation, reasoning, and most important, memory, in the case of consciousness.

Famously, and in line with his II.27.7 injunction to consider the idea under which identity is to be judged, Locke opens his discussion of personal identity with an account of "what *Person* stands for" which exhibits consciousness as the key element in our idea of person. It is by virtue of his consciousness that a person has "reason and reflection, and can consider it self as it self, the same thinking thing in different times and places" (Section 9). Sameness of consciousness, accordingly, is the basis of the identity of the person.

Locke never specifies exactly what sameness of consciousness consists in, although it is clear that the ability to remember having had a certain experience or having done a certain action is sufficient for sameness of consciousness. It also is clear that sameness of consciousness is the basic relation making for personal identity, and that memory has its special role to play in personal identity only because of its connection with sameness of consciousness.[26] Thus, section 10:

> For as far as any intelligent Being can repeat the *Idea* of any past Action with the same consciousness it had of it at first, and with the same consciousness it has of any present Action; so far is it the same *personal Self.* For it is by the consciousness it has of its present Thoughts and Actions,

that it is self to it self now, and so will be the same self as far as the same
consciousness can extend to Actions past or to come.

One is conscious of one's current self by being conscious of what one
is now thinking and doing. This does not in any way involve memory,
and yet this consciousness is not only germane to personal identity, it
is its basis. This passage is of special interest in view of the talk in it of
'extending' one's current consciousness not only to past actions but to
actions "to come." Presumably he has some such thing as this in mind:
when I plan what to say in tomorrow's lecture, for example, I am seeing
the actions I am envisioning as *mine*, as *my* actions; and when I think
about my scheduled root canal the pain I anticipate is *my* pain. Memory
is no doubt an important, perhaps the most important, continuity of
consciousness, but it is not the only one. Whatever continuities are
involved in sameness of consciousness, it is this sameness of consciousness that makes for personal identity, just as continuity of life is what
makes for plant or animal identity.

While consciousness and life are analogous in many ways, there is an
important disanalogy between them. Plant and animal identity, and so
human identity as well, requires perfect continuity of life: there can be
no gaps in the successive sequence of living states of the organism
during which it is not alive. Locke talks in Sec. 4, for example, of how
the life of an individual oak-tree taken at any one time makes different
collections of matter into the same plant in virtue of the fact that it
exists "constantly from that moment both forwards and backwards in
the same continuity of insensible succeeding parts united to the living
Body of the Plant." Consciousness, on the other hand, can unite inter-
rupted stretches of experience into the same person.

In Section 10, Locke takes the interruptedness of consciousness to
set the very problem of personal identity, and he later goes on, in Sect.
16 for example, to point to the special ability consciousness has to
unite "Existences, and Actions, very remote in time, into the same Person." In the thought-experiment he presents there, where he remembers having seen the Deluge, or having done some action "a thousand
years since," and in similar examples, such as that of remembering
having done Nestor's actions at the siege of Troy (Sect. 14), he does not
suppose that our remembered experiences are part of a continuous
sequence of remembered experiences stretching between the present
time and those far-off experiences. He again appeals to the systematic
interruptions in the experiences of the day-man and the night-man in

Sect. 23, and in a similar vein, his case against the Cartesian doctrine
that a person must always be thinking consists in pointing out that we
have periods of dreamless sleep during which we are not conscious at
all, although we certainly wake up as the same persons we were before
we went to sleep.[27]

It is crucial to Locke's account of personal identity that consciousness allows for such interruptions and discontinuities. Locke's theory
is often criticized for allegedly being unable to handle cases of amnesia
and the like. Our intuitions say that I am the same person as the infant
who poured paprika in my sister's hair, although I don't remember
doing that; Locke's theory says that I am not the same person. Recent
supporters of the memory theory of personal identity have responded
to this problem by looking for a way to include unremembered experiences within the total set of a person's experiences; these solutions to
the problem are often presented as friendly amendments to Locke's
theory.[28] Locke himself, however, with his emphasis on the ability of
consciousness to "unite remote Existences into the same Person"
(Sect. 23), takes an entirely different tack. His diagnosis is that intuitions such as the one mentioned above are due to confusion. Thus in
Sect. 20 he writes:

> But yet possibly it will still be objected, suppose I wholly lose the memory
> of some parts of my Life, beyond a possibility of retrieving them, so that
> perhaps I shall never be conscious of them again; yet am I not the same
> Person, that did those Actions, had those Thoughts, that I was once con-
> scious of, though I have now forgot them? To which I answer, here we
> must take notice what the word *I* is applied to, which in this case is the
> Man only.

Locke simply denies that my infant misdeeds, for example, belong to
me as a person. I am the same man, or human being, as the infant who
did them, but not the same person.

This seems an heroic line to take, especially in light of the almost
universal tendency of recent theorists to take such intuitions at face
value and attempt to shape the theory to fit them. Locke certainly feels
the need to argue for the correctness of his diagnosis. First off, in Sect.
20, he argues that his way with the problem is not so much a revision
of our views as a consistent application of them. He gives it out as "the
Sense of Mankind in the solemnest Declaration of their Opinions," i.e.
in law, that a madman is not the same person as the same man sane;

this is shown by the fact that the madman is not held liable for what he (the same man) did when sane, or the sane man liable for what he did while mad. He finds the same view implied in ordinary ways of talking, where in cases such as this where the same man has "distinct incommunicable consciousness at different times," "we say such an one is *not himself* or is *beside himself.*" This evidence, it must be admitted, is rather slim.

Locke must have realized this, for he continues his argument in the next two sections. It's worth looking at them in some detail, as the first has not been much discussed and the second, although often discussed, has been misunderstood.

In Sect. 21 Locke offers to help us to see, what he grants is hard to conceive, that *"Socrates* the individual Man should be two Persons" by considering what is meant by "the same individual Man." He mentions three proposals: that sameness of man is just that of a soul, or immaterial thinking substance; that it is sameness of an animal (i.e., presumably, a living human body), and that it is sameness of an animal plus sameness of the soul united to that animal. He does not decide between these proposals, although he does note that the first has the uncomfortable consequence that humans born of different women and at different times could turn out to be the same man. In any case, the first proposal allows the same man to be different persons, as long as they have lived "in different Ages without the knowledge of one anothers Thoughts." As regards the second and third proposals, Locke notes that it will be impossible, on them, for Socrates in his earthly life and Socrates after his death to be the same man, since the animal in question would have died. We can't get around this, he says, by making the identity of a man to be a matter of identity of consciousness, for the following reason:

> But then they who place *Humane Identity* in consciousness only, and not in something else, must consider how they will make the Infant *Socrates* the same Man with *Socrates* after the Resurrection.

Locke must be assuming that the person Socrates, resurrected in the body, is the same man as well as the same person as Socrates before death. On Locke's account the infant Socrates, the mature Socrates, and the resurrected Socrates can be the same man, and the mature and the resurrected Socrates the same person (on the assumption that Socrates resurrected can remember having done and experienced what

mature Socrates thought and did), but neither of the latter can be the
same person as infant Socrates (assuming neither remembers his doings). But on the disastrous proposals Locke is considering, infant Socrates is not only not the same person as mature and/or resurrected
Socrates, he is not the same man as either one; at least as regards the
mature Socrates, this is extremely counterintuitive. Thus

> personal Identity can by us be placed in nothing but consciousness
> (which is that alone which makes what we call *self*) without involving us
> in great Absurdities.

With personal identity thus placed in consciousness, we have the possibility that one and the same man should be two persons.

The next section, Sect. 22, takes up the famous case of the sober
man and the drunk man. Locke holds that human judicatures, which
can punish only "with a Justice suitable to their way of Knowledge,"
can punish someone awake and sober for what he (the same man) did
while drunk or sleepwalking, even though it is possible that he is not
then conscious of having done it. The reason Locke gives for this is
that the judicatures "cannot distinguish certainly what is real, what
counterfeit" in such cases, and while "the Fact is proved against him"
(i.e. the same man did those things), "want of consciousness cannot
be proved for him."

This account occasioned one of the rare expressions of dissent from
Molyneux. He argues that Locke has assigned the wrong reason for the
Court's not accepting drunkenness as a plea, the real reason, according
to him, being that drunkenness is itself a crime.[29] Allison has argued
that Locke capitulated to Molyneux on this point,[30] but clearly he did
not. In his response Locke acknowledges that Molyneux has stated "the
common reason" for the failure of the plea of drunkenness, but, he
goes on to say,

> This reason, how good soever, cannot, I think, be used by me, as not
> reaching my case; for what has this to do with consciousness? nay it is an
> argument against me, for if a man may be punished for any crime which
> he committed when drunk, whereof he is not allowed to be conscious, it
> overturns my hypothesis.[31]

The distinction here is between drunkenness which removes consciousness, and drunkenness which does not. A few sentences further
on he writes:

But drunkenness has something peculiar in it when it destroys consciousness; and so the instances you bring justifie not the punishing of a drunken fact, that was totally and irrevocably forgotten, which the reason that I give being sufficient to do, it well enough removed the objection . . . For I ask you, if a man by intemperate drinking should get a fever, and in the frenzy of his disease (which lasted not perhaps above an hour) committed some crime, would you punish him for it? If you would not think this just, how can you think it just to punish him for any fact committed in a drunken frenzy, without a fever? Both had the same criminal cause, drunkenness, and both committed without consciousness.[32]

Plainly, Locke never wavers on his main point, which is that human judicatures punish deeds done while drunk because they cannot be sure that in a particular case the drunkenness has removed consciousness. It is Molyneux who capitulates.[33]

Locke holds consistently to the theory that sameness of consciousness makes for personal identity, and is prepared to explain away contrary intuitions. His insistence on this, even in the face of the interruptedness in the existence of persons that is its consequence, is quite understandable given his desire to provide for the possibility of resurrection and judgment at the Last Day, as called for by Christian doctrine. This concern is prominent in Sects. 26 and 27, and is the main motivation for the claim made in Scct. 26 that 'person' is a forensic term. There Locke speaks of the Great Day on which God will judge what disposition to make of us in light of our doings in life:

The Sentence shall be justified by the consciousness all Persons shall have, that they *themselves* in what Bodies soever they appear, or what substances soever that consciousness adheres to, are the same, that committed those Actions, and deserve that Punishment for them.

Locke's eagerness to allow that we can have the same person at the Day of the Judgment as one who lived in Biblical times, say, gives him good reason to dispense with any requirement that there be an uninterrupted stream of experiences uniting any two stages of the same person.[34] And as the sentence just quoted makes clear, one of the signal advantages of Locke's account of personal identity is that it allows for the resurrection of the dead in a way that requires only minimal metaphysical commitments. As Locke points out to Stillingfleet, one goes beyond the scriptures in requiring that the same body be resur-

rected, or even the same immaterial substance; on Locke's account we
need make no such suppositions.[35]

It remains for me to indicate, if only briefly, how our account tends
to undermine the currently most popular interpretation of Locke's
views on personal identity.[36] On this interpretation, the identity of a
person is constituted by the causal continuity of a 'core' or causal basis
(usually identified as a certain neural structure or organization) which
underlies and explains the psychological continuities characteristic of
persons. I see two main motivations for this interpretation: first, it enables us to bring Locke's view into line with the intuitive judgments we
allegedly make to the effect that the amnesiac is the same person with
his past self, and second, a point Wiggins emphasizes, it fits the notion
of a person into the framework of the most popular recent theories of
natural kinds, those of Kripke and Putnam. For 'person' to be the general name for a natural kind, on this view, there must be a 'real essence'
which underlies and explains the possession of the qualities contained
in the 'nominal essence' of a person.[37]

The first thing to be noted about the causal basis interpretation, as I
shall call it, is that it has very little, if any, basis in the text of the *Essay*.
The terminology of real and nominal essences, for example, does not
figure at all in the chapter, nor is there any sort of speculation on
Locke's part as to the causal mechanisms, if any, underlying the continuity of consciousness, or of plant and animal life. Such passages as
the one at II.27.27 where Locke says that we have no idea whether
the thinking thing, or self, within us "could or could not perform its
Operations of Thinking and Memory out of a Body organized as ours
is," or the one at II.27.17 where he speculates about one's consciousness becoming to be attached to one's little finger, making the finger
the whole person when it is cut off from the rest of the body, do not
fit at all well with the causal basis interpretation.

Given what we've said so far, this is not surprising. The first alleged
advantage for the view is not one that would appeal to Locke. As we
have just seen, he clearly and consistently denies that unremembered
experiences are part of a person's history. More important, though, the
view that there must be a real essence common to members of species
and definitive of the identities of the individual members is in conflict
with what we have seen to be Locke's general views on the matter.
There is no more reason to think that persons *must* have some set of
salient structural features in common, or that one person *must* have
some such structural features of his remain unchanged during his con-

tinuing life as a person, than there was to think that all plants or animals of a particular species must share an inner structural arrangement, or that it is such a structural arrangement which keeps an individual member of the species the same over time.

As in the case of plants, and animals, and men, in the case of persons it is the idea of the sort that determines the identity by determining the continuity that is required for continuing as the same thing. In the cases of plants, animals, and men, continuity of life permits of no interruption; in the case of persons, continuity of consciousness can and does obtain even when there are significant interruptions. Thus Locke's last word in the *Essay* on this subject is:

> For whatever be the composition whereof the complex *Idea* is made, whenever Existence makes it one particular thing under any denomination, the same Existence continued, preserves it the same individual under the same denomination. (II.27.29, last sentence)

The continuities ("the same existence continued") that make for the identity of the object are probably often based in a continuing internal structure the object has in common with other members of its kind. Whether they are or not, it is its continuing to satisfy our idea of the kind that suffices for the object's continuing identity. As Locke had said in II.27.7, as is the idea, so is the identity.

I have argued that Locke's theory of identity is a consistent and even subtle attempt to provide for the identities of natural objects, including plants, animals, and persons, within the framework of mechanism. It is a question, and a large one, how defensible Locke's theory is; but that it is an important part of his brief for the Mechanical Philosophy is, I hope, beyond doubt.

Notes

I acknowledge with gratitude the helpful comments of Viorica Farkas and Janet Levin on earlier drafts of this paper. I am especially grateful to Edwin Curley for stylistic suggestions and for advice concerning the Scholastic background, and to Michael Ayers and Jonathan Bennett for their extensive and very valuable sets of written comments.

1. Book II, chapter 27 of Locke's *An Essay Concerning Human Understanding*. This chapter was added to the second (1694) edition of the *Essay*. When I give only a section number, I am referring to this chapter, otherwise my references to the *Essay* are by Book, chapter, section number. Quotations

are taken from P. H. Nidditch's edition of the *Essay* (Oxford: Clarendon Press, 1975).

2. This last is an important desideratum for Locke's theory, in view of the connection between personal identity and such highly charged theological issues as immortality and the resurrection of the body. More on this later.

3. For background see E. J. Dijksterhuis, *The Mechanization of the World-Picture* (Oxford: Oxford University Press, 1961), pp. 433 ff.; Marie Boas (Hall), "The Establishment of the Mechanical Philosophy," *Osiris* 10 (1952): 412–541; R. Kargon, *Atomism in England from Hariot to Newton* (Oxford: Clarendon Press, 1966), esp. chaps. 1, 8 and 9; and Robert Westfall, *The Construction of Modern Science* (New York: John Wiley & Sons, 1971), esp. chaps. 2 and 4. While Scholastic Aristotelianism was the main alternative to mechanism, it was not the only one. Other important contenders included the followers of Paracelsus, known variously as the iatrochemists, the Spagyritic chemists, or most loosely, the alchemists, who recognized certain vital or living principles as the agents of chemical reactions; and the Cambridge Platonists (most notably Ralph Cudworth and Henry More), who espoused a world-soul as a sort of conscious demiurge carrying out God's general intentions in creating the world, and subordinate particular vital principles or "Plastick Natures" which are the proximate sources of activity in causation. These views are quite different from one another, and from Aristotelianism, but they all share a commitment to immaterial or non-mechanical principles of unity or activity as real constituents of things. In addition to the works cited above, see my "Lockean Mechanism" in A. Holland, ed., *Philosophy: Its History and Historiography* (Dordrecht: D. Reidel, 1985).

4. There is a nice discussion of this notion of a principle in Jorge J. E. Gracia's introduction to *Suarez on Individuation: Metaphysical Disputation V: Individual Unity and Its Principle* (Milwaukee: Marquette University Press, 1982), pp. 15–17.

5. See for example St. Thomas's *Commentary on the Metaphysics of Aristotle*, Bk. V, Lesson 8, Sec. 876, as translated by John P. Rowan (Chicago: Henry Regnery Co., 1961), vol. 1, p. 341:

> Those things are one in number whose matter is one. For inasmuch as matter stands under designated dimensions, it is the principle of individuation for forms. And for this reason it is from matter that a singular thing is one in number and divided from other things.

(I have slightly altered the translation.) See further fn. 8 to Gracia's introduction, op. cit. p. 25. The introduction as a whole is a very valuable short discussion of Scholastic theories of individuation.

6. *Fifth Metaphysical Disputation*, IV.1, Gracia, p. 105. Suarez there attributes this view to Averroes as well.

7. There is a very helpful survey of the history of Scholastic views on individuation in chapter one of G. Lewis (later Rodis-Lewis), *L'individualité selon Descartes* (Paris: Vrin, 1950). She writes that "None of the scholastics at the beginning of the seventh century accepted the Thomist solution by way of matter" (p. 34); some version or another of Scotism was the prevalent position.

8. *Fifth Metaphysical Disputation,* VI.15, Gracia, p. 132; cf. IV.4, Gracia, p. 107, and IV.7, Gracia, p. 109.

9. See e.g. Aquinas, *Commentary on the Metaphysics of Aristotle,* VII.2, secs. 1278–1279, Rowan, vol. 2, p. 498; cf. also V.5, secs. 825–26, Rowan, vol. 1, p. 324.

10. See Robert Boyle, *The Origin of Forms and Qualities* (Oxford, 1666), as reprinted in *The Works of Robert Boyle* (London, 1772), vol. 3, pp. 37 ff., and in M. A. Stewart, ed. *Selected Philosophical Papers of Robert Boyle* (Manchester: Manchester University Press, 1979), pp. 53 ff. Boyle himself disassociates Aristotle from the view of substantial forms that he attacks, and even distinguishes between the teachings of the Greek commentators, and the later, Latin commentators, regarding the status of forms as substances.

11. In a recent article on this topic (Harold Noonan, "Locke on Personal Identity," *Philosophy* 53 (1978): 343–51) we find the following statement: "Although Locke's notions of substance and matter are so manifestly unaristotelian, something like Aristotle's substantial form holds a prominent place in his thought, at least with respect to living creatures" (p. 344). Unless this is only making the point that Locke conceived of the problem of identity in the same way as his predecessors, it is either a gross distortion of Locke's views or an implicit charge of inconsistency. As we'll see in the second section of the paper, Locke's notion of 'life' is meant to fill the role the substantial form plays in making for the identity of organisms, but in a way totally different from the way forms do it.

12. This principle is repeated again towards the end of Section 1, and again in Section 2. It is sometimes asserted that Locke's basic criterion of identity is this, that two things (of the same kind) are identical just in case both had the same beginning of existence, i.e., began to exist in the same place at the same time. (See for example Baruch Brody, "Locke on the Identity of Persons," *American Philosophical Quarterly* 9 (1972): 327–34, pp. 327–29; Margaret Atherton, "Locke's Theory of Personal Identity," *Midwest Studies in Philosophy,* vol. 8, 1983, pp. 280–81.) Even a cursory reading of II.27.1 will reveal, however, that the principle about beginnings of existence is derived from the more general principle mentioned above. Joshua Hoffman, in his "Locke on Whether a Thing Can Have Two Beginnings of Existence," *Ratio* 22 (1980), pp. 107–8, also notices that the one principle is derived from the more general one.

13. See II.23.19–21. I owe this point and the appreciation of its relevance to the present topic to Michael Ayers. He promises a fuller development of it in writings yet to appear.

14. Hoffmann, in "Locke on Two Beginnings," argues that Locke does not commit himself to spatio-temporal continuity as a condition of the identity of a substance. Hoffman thinks that to do so would have been a mistake, since it overlooks the possibility that a body may go out of existence at one time or place and come back into existence at another time (and perhaps another place as well). He doesn't tell us, however, how to make sense of this alleged possibility. What would be the grounds for taking a body coming into existence after a period of time has elapsed during which the original body has not been

in existence to be numerically identical with the original? Locke does not anywhere suggest that we could make sense out of such a thing as regards bodies
or spirits—as we shall see, persons are a different case—and his discussion of
the difference between creation and causation at II.26.2 gives ground for thinking that he would not be as quick as Hoffman is to assume (implausibly) that
the notion of recreation makes sense.

15. "Individuals without Sortals," *Canadian Journal of Philosophy* 4
(1974): 113–48, pp. 125–27.

16. Cf. Ayers, ibid., p. 126, for cogent objections to such an account.

17. Locke's criterion is obviously too strict to match our ordinary talk, where
for example we usually count a big rock the same body even after a tiny sliver
has been knocked off.

18. For a fuller discussion see the important recent paper by M. R. Ayers,
"Locke versus Aristotle on Natural Kinds" *Journal of Philosophy* 78 (1981):
247–72. I differ from Ayers, however, in thinking that Locke's account of kinds
is pretty nearly right, even as regards contemporary scientific practice.

19. See for example III.3.13–14, III.6.2–8, 36–37.

20. See Ayers, op. cit., pp. 255–59, 261–63. A similar account of III.6.6 is
to be found in my unpublished Ph.D. dissertation, *Locke's Theory of Essence*
(University of Pennsylvania, 1975), pp. 214–18. In his first letter to Stillingfleet
(*A Letter to the Right Reverend Edward, Lord Bishop of Worcester* [London,
1697], pp. 211–12; reprinted in *The Works of John Locke* [London, 1823], vol.
4, pp. 90–91), responding to Stillingfleet's remark that "real essences are unchangeable, i.e., the internal constitutions are unchangeable," Locke writes:

Of what, I beseech your Lordship, are the *internal Constitutions unchangeable*? Not of any thing that exists, but of God alone; for they may
be changed all as easily by that hand that made them, as the internal
Frame of a Watch. What then is it that is *unchangeable*? The internal
Constitution or real Essence of a Species: Which, in plain English, is no
more but this, whilst the same specifick Name, *v.g.* of *Man, Horse,* or *Tree,*
is annexed to or made the Sign of the same abstract, complex idea, under
which I rank several Individuals, it is impossible but the real Constitution
on which that unalter'd, complex idea, or nominal Essence depends, must
be the same, *i.e.* in other Words, where we find all the same Properties,
we have Reason to conclude there is the same real, internal Constitution,
from which those Properties flow.

21. This point is made, for example, in III.6.8.

22. This last point might seem to conflict with the famous passage in which
Locke denies that there is anything essential to individuals:

There is nothing I have, is essential to me. An Accident, or Disease, may
very much alter my Colour, or Shape; a Fever, or Fall, may take away my
Reason, or Memory, or both; and an Apoplexy leave neither Sense, nor
Understanding, no nor Life. (III.6.4)

(Compare III.3.19, and the similar passage in the third letter to Stillingfleet
(*Mr. Locke's Reply to the Right Reverend the Lord Bishop of Worcester's Answer*

to His Second Letter [London, 1699], p. 358; *Works,* vol. 4, pp. 433–34), and see Ayers' discussion in "Locke versus Aristotle," pp. 258–59, 262-63.) There is no conflict, however. In the passage Locke is denying that a individual has essential properties *when it is considered apart from any abstract idea of its species.* We can take Locke to be saying that if we judge his identity as a man, he does not survive the loss of life, but judged as a body, for example, he does remain the same thing before and after death (at least for a time). His point is that there is nothing in the nature of things that requires us to judge of his identity according to the one idea or the other. This way with the passages brings up the question of whether, and if so how far, Locke was a relative identity theorist; I plan to take this up on another occasion.

23. See E. M. Curley, "Leibniz on Locke on Personal Identity," in M. Hooker, ed., *Leibniz: Critical and Interpretative Essays* (Minneapolis: University of Minnesota Press, 1982), especially pp. 305–6 and 310–14. Curley's response to those critics who hold Locke's treatment of amnesia in II.27.20 to be inconsistent with his theory is similar to the one I develop below, although I think the uses to which we put the point are different. For background, see D. P. Walker, *The Decline of Hell: Seventeenth Century Discussions of Eternal Torment* (Chicago: University of Chicago Press, 1964), and Norman T. Burns, *Christian Mortalism from Tyndale to Milton* (Cambridge, Mass.: Harvard University Press, 1972); also relevant is R. C. Tennant, "The Anglican Response to Locke's Theory of Personal Identity" *Journal of the History of Ideas* 42 (1981): 73–90. Although I have not yet seen it, I am told that Udo Thiel's *Lockes Theorie der personalen Identität* (Bonn: Bouvier, 1983) has extensive discussion of the theological background.

24. See also II.27.12:

And therefore those, who place thinking in an immaterial Substance only, . . . must shew why personal Identity cannot be preserved in the change of immaterial Substances, or variety of particular immaterial Substances, as well as animal Identity is preserved in the change of material Substances, or variety of particular Bodies.

25. There is, it must be admitted, a slight disanalogy even here. Locke takes it to be certain that life unites different parcels of matter into the same living thing; but at II.27.25 he says it is "the more probable Opinion" that consciousness is the affection of one individual immaterial substance, or spirit. (He gives no reason for thinking this probable.) He stresses throughout the chapter, however, (for example in the passage quoted in the note above) that consciousness can unite different immaterial substances into the same person, and that we cannot know for certain that each person is associated with only one such substance. The disanalogy, then, if there is one, is only *de facto.*

26. For further discussion see Margaret Atherton, "Locke's Theory," esp. Section II (pp. 275–29). Note, too, that my understanding of 'consciousness extended to things to come' seems to fit well with the discussion of deliberation and willing at II.21.29 ff.

27. See II.i.9–19. The day-man/night-man case of II.27.23 is anticipated, by the way, in the first edition of the *Essay* at II.1.11–12. For a discussion of the

differences between the first and second edition treatments of personal identity see Curley, "Leibniz and Locke," pp. 302–8.

28. See the papers by Quinton, Grice, and Perry in John Perry, ed., *Personal
Identity* (Berkeley and Los Angeles: University of California Press, 1975); see
also Perry's helpful introduction to that volume. Also Margaret Atherton, op.
cit., J. L. Mackie, *Problems from Locke* (Oxford: Clarendon Press, 1976), chap.
6; and David Wiggins, *Sameness and Substance* (Cambridge, Mass.: Harvard
University Press, 1980), chap. 6.

29. Molyneux's letter to Locke of 23 December 1693, Letter #1685 in E. S.
de Beer, ed., *The Correspondence of John Locke* (Oxford: Clarendon Press,
1979), vol. 4, p. 767.

30. Henry Allison, "Locke's Theory of Personal Identity," as reprinted in I.
C. Tipton, ed., *Locke on Human Understanding* (Oxford: Oxford University
Press, 1977), pp. 110–11.

31. Locke to Molyneux, 19 January 1694 (in this letter and #1712 the year
given by the correspondents is of course 1693/4). #1693 in de Beer, *Correspondence of Locke,* vol. 4. p. 785.

32. Ibid., pp. 785–86.

33. See Molyneux to Locke, 17 February 1694, #1712 in de Beer, *Correspondence of Locke,* vol. 5, p. 21; and Locke to Molyneux, 26 May 1694, #1744 in
ibid., p. 58. For further discussion see P. Helm, "Did Locke Capitulate to Molyneux?" *Journal of the History of Ideas* 42 (1981): 669–71. Allison and Nicholas
Jolley reply in "Locke's Pyrrhic Victory," ibid., pp. 672–74; they concede
Helm's main point, but with reservations. These appear to be based on the
assumption that Locke was trying to provide an empirically serviceable third-
person criterion for assigning responsibility for actions. There is no support in
the text for this assumption.

34. Locke discusses these issues at much greater length in the third of his
letters to Stillingfleet. He distinguishes the doctrine of the resurrection of the
dead from that of the resurrection of the (same) body, finding scriptural basis
only for the former. Locke's view is that all that is needed for theological purposes is that one's consciousness, which is what carries personal identity, become associated with some human body, perhaps a newly fashioned one, but
in any case one no particle of which need ever have been part of the body the
person had while alive. See *Mr. Locke's Reply to the Bishop of Worcester's Answer to his Second Letter,* pp. 162–210; *Works,* vol. 4, pp. 300–34. Boyle, by
the way, discussed this issue in his *Some Physico-Theological Considerations
about the Possibility of the Resurrection* (London, 1675), reprinted in *Works
of Boyle,* vol. 4, pp. 191–202; Stewart, *Selected Papers of Boyle,* pp. 193–208.

35. See e.g. *Mr. Locke's Reply to the Bishop of Worcester's Answer to His
Second Letter,* p. 210; *Works,* vol. 4, p. 334.

36. D. Wiggins, ibid., and J. L. Mackie, op. cit., pp. 199–203, offer their accounts as emendations or extensions of Locke's own views. Viorica Farkas, in
"Locke on Ideas, *Substratum,* and the Identity of Persons," unpublished Ph.D.
dissertation, UCLA 1982, chap. IV, and M. Atherton, on "Locke's Theory," pp.
287–89, ascribe this view to Locke himself.

37. See Wiggins, *Substance and Sameness,* p. 188.

5

Berkeley's Ideas of Sense

Phillip D. Cummins

In Section One of the *Principles*,[1] Berkeley divides the objects of human knowledge into three groups. They are either "ideas actually imprinted on the senses, or else such as are perceived by attending to the passions and operations of the mind, or lastly ideas formed by the help of memory and imagination, either compounding, dividing or barely representing those originally perceived in the aforesaid ways." Berkeley proceeds to specify, with respect to ideas of the first division, the qualities which are the proper objects of each of the five senses. By smell, for example, odours are perceived and by hearing, sounds. Next he states, "And as several of these are observed to accompany each other, they come to be marked by one name, and so to be reputed as one thing." After listing some of the things constituted by ideas of sense, for example, apples, stones, and books, he asserts that as they are pleasing or disagreeable, such collections excite "the passions of love, hatred, joy, grief and so forth." In the next section, ideas are contrasted to that which "knows or perceives them and exercises divers operations, as willing, imagining, remembering, about them." That which knows is not an idea. No, Berkeley insists, it is "a thing entirely distinct from them, wherein they exist, or, which is the same thing, whereby they are perceived." As if to explain, he adds, "for the existence of an idea consists in being perceived." The meaning and import of this startling claim are made clearer at the beginning of Section Three, for there Berkeley asserts

> That neither our thoughts, nor passions, nor ideas formed by the imagination, exist without the mind, is what every body will allow. And it seems

89

> no less evident that the various sensations or ideas imprinted on the
> sense, however blended or combined together (that is, whatever objects
> they compose) cannot exist otherwise than in a mind perceiving them.

No sound, no odour, in short, no sensed quality can exist unperceived.
Neither can any combination of sensed qualities, not even that immense and elaborate combination to which the word *mountain* is applied. The reason? Because, in Berkeley's phrase, "Their *esse* is
percipi."

Berkeley's immaterialism is rich and diverse. He developed an
agency theory of causation and used it to argue for God's existence.
He insisted and tried to establish that mathematics and the natural
sciences can and must be metaphysically neutral. He attempted to secure genuine perceptual knowledge in the absence of material substances and genuine perceptual knowledge of minds in the absence of
ideas of them. He offered a proof of the immateriality of the soul. For
all that, however, the core of his system is the attack on material substance. To suppose the existence of material substances (unperceiving
things capable of existing unperceived) is to open the door to scic-
ism and to do so needlessly, he argued, since the supposition itself is
either meaningless or contradictory. In attempting to prove these central positions, Berkeley reiterated and reiterated his contention that no
sensible object can exist unperceived, that their *esse* is *percipi.*

Sections 1 through 17 constitute a systematic demonstration of the
non-existence of material substance. After introducing sensibles and
other objects of awareness, contrasting them with minds, and insisting
that no sensible object can exist unperceived, Berkeley asserts in Section 7 that minds (active perceiving things) are the only substances. He
has already shown that no sensible object (combination of sensible
qualities) is a material substance, since to be a material substance is to
be capable of existing unperceived, whereas no sensible qualities or
combination of such can so exist. Their *esse* is *percipi.* In Section 7, he
adds that no sensible quality can exist in a material substance, since the
latter do not perceive. In Section 8, Berkeley rejects the alternative that
sensible objects are images and material substances archetypes. The
alternative presupposes that something imperceptible can have the
same types of qualities as a sensible object, which is absurd. Berkeley
rejects, too, the theory of primary qualities. Extension, shape, and
other known qualities offered as examples of primary qualities are sensible qualities. They are either sensed or defined in terms of sensed

qualities. Like sounds, colours, and odours, therefore, they must be perceived to exist. Hence they cannot be real properties of material substances. Nor can it be said that material substances underlie or support sensible qualities (Section 16). If 'underlie' and 'support' are not empty metaphors, they imply that material substances are extended. Since extension is a sensible quality, this position generates either instant absurdity or an infinite regress. To give content to the doctrine of material substance leads to inconsistency, but to refuse to give it content leaves only an insignificant phrase. Berkeley utilized basically the same dilemma in the *Three Dialogues* to attack the claim that material substances cause sensible objects. If one is not using "material substance" for what accurate thinkers call minds, those being genuine causes, one must specify what one means by "cause" and how material substances operate causally. But virtually all descriptions are framed with reference to sensible qualities. Because no sensible quality can exist unperceived, then, the defender of material substance is reduced to insignificance or absurdity. Once it is established that sensed qualities cannot exist unperceived, the doctrine of material substances cannot be saved from incoherence.

What exactly is expressed by and what is the force of *"Esse est percipi"*? What is the basis for the claim that no ideas of sense or combination of them can exist unperceived? There have been a multitude of conflicting answers to these questions, none of them definitive. It is convenient, at the very least, to divide them into two groups. There are, first, those which found Berkeley's rejection of unsensed sense objects on an explicit or implicit position concerning the nature of the immediate objects of sense or the structure of the process of perceiving. These can be styled *metaphysical interpretations*. To argue, for example, that the dependence of sensory objects on perceivers is a consequence of interpreting perceiving in terms of the inherence relation between accident and substance is to offer a metaphysical interpretation.[2] Second, there are those answers which emphasize the nature and limits of conceptualization, meaning, or the criteria and limits of knowledge. They may be termed *epistemological interpretations*. To maintain, for example, that Berkeley's denial of abstract ideas led him to define "existence" in terms of being perceived, an actual characteristic of objects which are known to exist, is to develop an epistemological interpretation.[3]

Thomas Reid developed a historically oriented critique of the doctrine of sensory images in his *Essays on the Intellectual Powers of Man*.

At one stage, he fashioned an interpretation—a metaphysical interpretation—of Berkeleyan ideas of sense. It is both ingenious and plausible. Reid's interpretation provided him an object for criticism, but should not for that reason be rejected. In Reid's portrait, Berkeleyan idealism is a powerful, tightly-reasoned system which reveals several critical turning points in philosophy.

According to Reid, Berkeley's system is based on the sweeping but false thesis that *sensations are the only objects of perception,* that is, that what one perceives whenever one perceives is invariably a sensation or combination of sensations.[4] Reid assigned a quite definite meaning to the term "sensation"; in his philosophy it designates a class of entities which are important elements in, though not objects of, acts of perceiving. In order to assess Reid's interpretation, the following procedure may prove effective. First, what Reid meant by 'sensation' shall be specified and clarified. Second, textual and historical evidence for Reid's interpretation of Berkeley will be examined. Third, some objections will be considered. My own judgment—hopefully not a mere bias—is that Reid did uncover the central thought pattern or one of several perhaps incompatible thought patterns in Berkeley's philosophy.

I

For Reid, first-hand knowledge of current matters of fact is acquired either by consciousness (observation of the mind and its states and activities) or by perception (observation of bodies and their properties and relations). Perceiving is non-inferential belief in the existence of a being having one or more primary or secondary qualities.[5] Some philosophers treat perception as a situation or process wherein an existent (an object) is given or made present to the perceiver and thus contrast it to belief or judging. Reid, however, held that perception is one of several basic kinds of non-inferential judgment. He rejected the supposition of an infallibly known given, denied that he discovered introspectively an inferential process in perceiving, and claimed that there are no known non-perceptual truths from which a genuine perceptual judgment can be inferred.[6] Here is Reid on perceiving:

If, therefore, we attend to that act of our mind which we call the perception of an external object of sense, we shall find in it these three things.

First, Some conception or notion of the object perceived. *Secondly,* A strong and irresistible conviction and belief of its present existence. And, *thirdly,* That this conviction and belief are immediate, and not the effect of reasoning.[7]

If one perceives a die, for example, one not only conceives of a black and white, solid, hard cube, one also affirms its existence, though not as the result of reasoning.

Reid's analysis seems to portray perception as a nonsensuous intellectual operation. This defect was remedied by his doctrine of sensations. Every act of perceiving, he held, is accompanied by or includes one or more sensations.[8] Having sensations and perceiving are dual responses to stimulation of the same psychological systems. As Reid put it,

We know, that when certain impressions are made upon our organs, nerves, and brain, certain corresponding sensations are felt, and certain objects are both conceived and believed to exist.[9]

Sensations occur constantly and never pass totally unnoticed, even when they are not attended to, that is, when they do not become subjects of beliefs or judgments. Despite their prevalence, sensations are usually misdescribed and mis-classified by philosophers. Some sensations are painful, others decidedly pleasant. To such sensations attention is directed. Consequently, they generally are distinguished from the perceptions they accompany. But with neutral (non-painful non-pleasant) sensations the case is otherwise. They do not become objects of attention. Consequently, they are easily overlooked when perception is analyzed, being either absorbed into the operation of perceiving or equated with its object.[10] For these reasons, Reid considered it important to specify what sensations are.

Two features of sensations as Reid characterized them need to be emphasized. First, in sensations, act and object are one. For Reid, mental states are acts, either volitional acts or cognitive acts. All acts of mind are intentional; that is, for each act an object can be specified. Sensations, though, are unique. In their case, and only in their case, the object intended is not wholly distinct from the act. To illustrate, Reid wrote, "When I am pained, I cannot say that the pain I feel is one thing, and that my feeling it is another thing."[11] In perceiving, say, a cube of sugar, what is perceived, that is, conceived and believed to exist, is not a part or feature of the act of perceiving. But a feeling of pain is a painful feeling. Either the occurrence of the pain is the feeling of it, or the pain is an inseparable part or feature of the feeling of pain. So, too, with all other sensations. Another feature of sensations is that most of the can be placed or located on not one but two continua, the pleasure-pain continuum and a second one involving either different degrees of some sensible qualities or different and complementary sensible qualities. For example, a sensation of touch is either pleasant, painful, or neutral and can equally be classified in terms of the hot-warm-neutral-cool-cold continuum. Another sensation may be sweet and pleasant or overly sweet and so painful. A sound can be described in auditory terms and also as painful; the pain is not a second sensation accompanying the sound; the sound itself is a painful sensation.[12]

Sensations accompany acts of perceiving, Reid claimed. The following may serve to explain what that means.

> When I grasp an ivory ball in my hand, I have a certain sensation of touch. Although this sensation be in the mind, and have no similitude to any thing material, yet, by the laws of my constitution, it is immediately followed by the conception and belief, that there is in my hand a hard smooth body of a spherical figure, and about an inch and a half in diameter. This belief is grounded neither upon reasoning nor upon experience; it is the immediate effect of my constitution.[13]

Since it is acknowledged that every perception includes or is accompanied by one or more sensations, why not equate sensations with acts of perceiving or identify sensations as the immediate objects of perception? Reid rejected both suggestions. Sensations are not acts of perceiving because they differ from them in structure. In perceiving, the object of cognition is wholly distinct from the act by which it is cognized. Such is not the case for sensation. Reid insisted,

> The form of the expression, *I feel pain,* might seem to imply that the feeling is something different from the pain felt; yet, in reality, there is no distinction. As *thinking a thought* is an expression which could signify no more than *thinking,* so *feeling a pain* signifies no more than *being pained.* What we have said is applicable to every other sensation.[14]

Sensations, thus, are not acts of perceiving. Nor are they objects of such acts. They are completely different from the material properties and the things possessing those properties which are the objects of perceiving. Though unable to articulate a definition of them, every normal adult knows what solidity is and what pain is and distinguishes the former from the latter.[15] Further, Reid argued, solidity, when conceived, is conceived as in no way implying a sentient being as its subject, while pain is invariably conceived as a state of a sentient being. Where and when pain is, there and then a sentient being is. In Reid's words,

> When I am pained, I cannot say that the pain I feel is one thing, and that my feeling it is another thing. They are one and the same thing, and cannot be disjoined, even in imagination. Pain, when it is not felt, has no existence. It can be neither greater nor less in degree or duration, nor any thing else in kind, than it is felt to be. It cannot exist by itself, nor in any subject, but in a sentient being. No quality of an inanimate insentient being can have the least resemblance to it.[16]

What holds for pains and pleasures, Reid insisted, holds for all sensations. None is an object of perception, since the latter yields direct knowledge and empirical inferences concerning insentient beings and their states, but sensations neither are insentient beings nor states of such. They exist only in sentient beings or minds.

Reid credited Berkeley with having a precise and accurate conception of sensations, that is, of meaning by "sensation" what he, Reid, meant by it. He praised Berkeley for avoiding Locke's errors, writing,

> As there can be no notion or thought but in a thinking being; so there can be no sensation but in a sentient being. It is the act, or feeling of a sentient being; its very essence consists in its being felt. Nothing can resemble a sensation, but a similar sensation in the same, or in some other mind. To think that any quality in a thing that is inanimate can resemble a sensation, is a great absurdity.[17]

Berkeley's mistake, Reid maintained, was in conflating the sensations which accompany acts of perceiving with the objects of those acts. This inevitably led to the conclusion that sensations are the sole objects of perception. Reid conceded that if this premise is granted, Berkeley's attack on material substance cannot be blocked. The premise need not, however, be granted. In fact, Reid argued, it must not be granted. He wrote,

> Suppose I am pricked with a pin; I ask, is the pain I feel, a sensation? undoubtedly it is. There can be nothing that resembles pain in any inani-

mate being. But I ask again, is the pin a sensation? To this question I find myself under a necessity of answering, that the pin is not a sensation, nor can have the least resemblance to any sensation. The pin has length and thickness, and figure, and weight. A sensation can have none of those qualities. I am not more certain that the pain I feel is a sensation, than that the pin is not a sensation; yet the pin is an object of sense; and I am as certain that I perceive its figure and hardness by my senses, as that I feel pain when pricked by it.[18]

The point of Reid's criticism is obvious. It is equally obvious that it is unwarranted unless Berkeley meant by "idea of sense" what Reid meant by "sensation." To this question we must now turn.

II

Although, strictly speaking, it is not relevant to proving that Berkeley construed ideas of sense as sensations, in Reid's sense of the term, his tendency to use the two terms interchangeably in the *Philosophical Commentaries, Principles of Human Knowledge,* and *Three Dialogues between Hylus and Philonous* is worth noting. From the first, there is this example.

> Extension itself or anything extended cannot think these being mere ideas or sensations whose essence we thoroughly know.[19]

From the *Principles,* this:

> If we had a new sense, it could only furnish us with new ideas or sensa-tions: and then we should have the same reason against their existing in an unperceiving substance, that has been already offered with relation to figure, motion, colour, and the like. Qualities, as hath been shown, are nothing else but *sensations* or *ideas,* which exist only in a mind perceiv-ing them.[20]

And from the *Three Dialogues,* this:

> The things, I say, immediately perceived, are ideas or sensations, call them which you will. But how can any idea or sensation exist in, or be produced by, any thing but a mind or spirit?[21]

The next question, which is the real question, is whether or not Berkeley construed ideas, that is, sensations, as Reid did.

A Berkeleyan idea of sense (sensation) agrees with a Reidian sensation in being incapable of existing unperceived (unfelt, unsensed). But is this common position founded on a shared conception of the nature of sensations? Of the four reasons to be given below for the affirmative, three are based on straightforward textual comparisons and the fourth is an argument from the occurrence of a rather unusual argument in Berkeley's campaign to prove the non-existence of material substances.

Berkeley, like Reid, made pleasures and pains paradigmatic of sensations (entities which cannot exist unfelt) and attempted to reduce qualities perceived by the several senses to them. The following exchange between Hylas and Philonous is a familiar example.[22]

> *Phil:* But is not the most vehement and intense degree of heat a very great pain?
> *Hylas:* No one can deny it.
> *Phil:* And is any unperceiving thing capable of pain or pleasure?
> *Hylas:* No certainly.
> *Phil:* Is your material substance a senseless being or a being endowed with sense and perception?
> *Hylas:* It is senseless without doubt.
> *Phil:* It cannot therefore be the subject of pain.
> *Hylas:* By no means.
> *Phil:* Nor consequently of the greatest heat perceived by sense, since you acknowledge this to be no small pain.
> *Hylas:* I grant it.

Berkeley's earnestness in introducing this argument is evidenced by his handling of Hylas's attempt to cancel his original concession that an intense heat is a pain. Note that in the following exchange Philonous argues that pain and pleasure cannot be felt or conceived as distinct from some type of sensible quality and so are intense degrees of those sensations. The passage reads:

> *Phil:* Upon putting your hand near the fire, do you perceive one simple uniform sensation, or two distinct sensations?
> *Hylas:* But one simple sensation.
> *Phil:* Is not the heat immediately perceived?
> *Hylas:* It is.

Phil: And the pain?

Hylas: True.

Phil: Seeing therefore they are both immediately perceived at the same time, and the fire affects you only with one simple, or uncompounded idea, it follows that this simple idea is both the intense heat immediately perceived and the pain; and consequently, that the intense heat immediately perceived, is nothing distinct from a particular sort of pain.

Hylas: It seems so.

Phil: Again, try in your thoughts, Hylas, if you can conceive a vehement sensation to be without pain, or pleasure.

Hylas: I cannot.

Phil: Or can you frame to yourself an idea of sensible pain or pleasure in general, abstracted from every particular idea of heat, cold, tastes, smells? etc.

Hylas: I do not find that I can.

Phil: Doth it not therefore follow, that sensible pain is nothing distinct from those sensations or ideas, in an intense degree.

Hylas: It is undeniable; and to speak the truth, I begin to suspect a very great heat cannot exist but in a mind perceiving it.[23]

One realizes the significance of this exchange if one recalls that in Section 8 of the *Principles,* Berkeley argued that just as ideas cannot exist unperceived, so nothing like an idea can exist unperceived, and notices that in the context of the above exchange he goes on to make the same point.

Phil: . . . Tell me, whether in two cases exactly alike, we ought not to make the same judgment?

Hylas: We ought.

Phil: When a pin pricks your finger, doth it not rend and divide the fibres of your flesh?

Hylas: It doth.

Phil: And when a coal burns your finger, doth it any more?

Hylas: It doth not.

Phil: Since therefore you neither judge the sensation itself occasioned by the pin, nor any thing like it to be in the pin, you should not, conformably to what you have now granted, judge the sensation occasioned by the fire or any thing like it, to be in the fire.[24]

Reid, as was noted above, treated feelings of pain and pleasure as para-
digms of sensations. Berkeley attempted to construe immediate objects of sense in terms of the same feelings. We have then some
evidence that Berkeley's ideas of sense were understood along the
same lines as Reid's sensations.[25]

It will be recalled that Reid was insistent that in sensations one cannot distinguish what is sensed from the sensing of it. Berkeley's ideas
of sense are no different. In the *Principles,* Section 5, he states,

> Hence as it is impossible for me to see or feel anything without an actual
> sensation of it, so it is impossible for me to conceive in my thoughts any
> sensible thing or object distinct from the sensation or perception of it.

In the *Three Dialogues,* Philonous shreds Hylas's attempt to invoke
the act-object distinction. His chief argument is the questionable one
that since there is no willing of what one senses, there is no action in
a sensation. However, he does make the following point as a supple-
ment to his main argument.

> *Phil:* Besides, since you distinguish the *active* and *passive* in every
> perception, you must do it in that of pain. But how is it possible
> that pain, be it as little active as you please, should exist in an
> unperceiving substance. In short, do but consider the point, and
> then confess ingeniously, whether light and colour, tastes, sounds,
> etc., are not all equally passions or sensations in the soul.[26]

Whether or not one accepts his arguments for the thesis, one must at
least acknowledge that Berkeley did deny the act-object distinction in
the case of sensations and did fall back on the case of pain to make
clear his own position. Here, too, his account of ideas of sense anticipates Reid's characterization of sensations. Here, too, then, Reid's interpretation is corroborated.

For Reid, the occurrence of a sensation is the occurrence of an episode in the history of a sentient being. A sensation cannot occur in an
insentient or inanimate object.[27] Thus, not only must a sensation be
felt in order to exist, it must also occur as a state of a consciousness, a
mind, a sentient thing. Once again, it is not difficult to link Berkeley
and Reid, since throughout the *Principles* and *Three Dialogues* Berkeley says of ideas of sense both that they cannot exist unperceived and
that they cannot exist in an unperceiving or insentient being.[28] In Section 9 of the *Principles,* he argued against the possibility of material

substances, as defined by the new (mechanistic) philosophers on the basis of the second, not the first, claim. His argument, that is, is not that figure, for example, cannot exist unperceived and so cannot be in or a part of an unperceived substance. Instead, Berkeley argued,

> By matter therefore we are to understand an inert, senseless substance, in which extension, figure, and motion, do actually subsist. But it is evident from what we have already shown that extension, figure and motion are only ideas existing in the mind, and that an idea can be like nothing but another idea, and that consequently neither they nor their archetypes can exist in an unperceiving substance. Hence it is plain, that the very notion of what is called *matter* or *corporeal substance,* involves a contradiction in it.[29]

Berkeley's argument is really quite peculiar. Note that if one takes the phrase "extension, figure and motion are only ideas existing in the mind" to mean "extension, figure and motion must be perceived to exist," the conclusion drawn does not follow. So long as they are perceived by another being, *X,* instances of extension, figure, and motion could exist in an unperceiving thing, *Y.* Unless, of course, they are construed as states of mind, episodes in the history of a sentient thing. In that case, to have extension is to perceive it, and that is impossible for an unperceiving thing. That this is what Berkeley intended is strongly suggested by his first demonstration of the impossibility of material substance in Section 7 of the *Principles.* There he wrote,

> From what has been said, it follows, there is not any other substance than *spirit,* or that which perceives. But for the fuller proof of this point, let it be considered the sensible qualities are colour, figure, motion, smell, taste, and such like, that is, the ideas perceived by sense. Now for an idea to exist in an unperceiving thing, is a manifest contradiction; for to have an idea is all one as to perceive: that therefore wherein colour, figure, and the like qualities exist, must perceive them; hence it is clear there can be no unthinking substance or *substratum* of those ideas.

On this view, *esse est percipi* states not just that for a sensible quality to exist it must be perceived, but also that its existence (its occurrence) is the perception of it. The occurrence of a sound is the occurrence of the hearing (the perception) of that sound. Its occurrence is the occurrence of a perceiving and of an object perceived. Its occurrence is an episode in the existence of a sentient being, that which is said to perceive the sound. Small wonder, then, that Berkeley insisted that no inanimate and unperceiving thing can have or be like a sound. The only thing like a sensation (a sound) is a sensation (a sound); the only thing that can have a sensation is a sentient thing (a mind).

If one interprets Berkeley along the lines we've recommended, one can discover historical antecedents for his doctrine of sensations without much difficulty. The "New Philosophers" generally construed colours, sounds, odours, tastes, and various tactile qualities as responses in consciousness to physical–physiological transactions. As early as the *Assayer* (1623), Galileo argued that heat is no more in the fire that causes us to feel it than a tickle is in the feather which brushes one's armpit.[30] Such diverse thinkers as Descartes, Rohault, Malebranche, Boyle, and Locke used "sensation" for immediately experienced objects, sounds, colours, and the like, which were denied extra-mental existence.[31] As scientists, they extruded from the external world whatever was not susceptible of a mechanistic explanation. The reduction of sensed qualities to the level of feelings of pleasure and pain guaranteed that extrusion. Here is Locke on the topic:

> And yet he that will consider that *the same fire* that at one distance *produces* in us the sensation of *warmth* does, at a nearer approach, produce in us the far different sensation of *pain,* ought to bethink himself what reason he has to say that his *idea of warmth,* which was produced in him by the fire, is actually in *the fire*; and his *idea of pain,* which the same fire produced in him in the same way is *not* in the fire.[32]

A. A. Luce maintains that Berkeley merely exploited these positions by purely *ad hominem* arguments to the effect that the mechanists themselves provide grounds for denying that material substances exist or are knowable.[33] But to so argue is to ignore two important truths. The first is that the sensationalistic characterization of objects of sense does not presuppose mechanism or the so-called corpuscularian philosophy of Boyle and Locke. Consequently, Berkeley could retain the former while rejecting the latter. The second is that having refuted the indirect realism—the unperceived material substances—of the new philosophers, Berkeley did not opt for naive or direct realism. He denied that material substances (unperceiving beings capable of unperceived existence) are immediate objects of sense, and he did so on the grounds that no immediate object of sense can exist unperceived. Consequently, one can hardly hold that Berkeley asserted the last solely as an *ad hominem* argument against the new philosophers.

III

Now for a few objections. First, one might be inclined to argue that my interpretation must be wrong because Berkeley would never have maintained the absurd view that extension is on a par with feelings of pleasure and pain. Such confidence may be unwarranted. Admittedly, one cannot quote Berkeley to the effect that in perceiving extension sensations of pleasure and pain are invariably felt, but he did maintain

> Extension a sensation, therefore not without the mind.

> Extension abstract from sensible qualities is no sensation, I grant, but then there is no such idea as any one may try. There is only a considering the number of points without the sort of them, & this makes more for me, since it must be in a considering thing.[34]

Moreover, he had Philonous explain why philosophers distinguished between secondary and primary qualities as follows:

> Heat and cold, tastes and smells, have something more visibly pleasing or disagreeable than the ideas of extension, figure and motion, affect us with. And it being too visibly absurd to hold, that pain and pleasure can be in an unperceiving substance, men are more easily weaned from believing the external existence of the secondary than the primary qualities. You will be satisfied there is something in this, if you recollect the difference you made between an intense and a more moderate degree of heat, allowing the one a real existence, while you denied it to the other. But after all, there is no rational ground for the distinction, for surely an indifferent sensation is as truly a *sensation,* as one more pleasing, or painful; and consequently should not be any more than they be supposed to exist in an unthinking subject.[35]

It is far from clear just how Berkeley analysed extension, since he denied that it is immediately perceived by both sight and touch and hinted that it is reducible to arrangements of minimum visibles or minimum tangibles. Because of the intricacies of Berkeley's position on the perception of distance, shape, location, and magnitude, it is perilous to dictate what he could not have meant when he insisted that extension cannot exist unperceived.

Next we must consider our interpretation in terms of Section 49 of the *Principles.* There Berkeley poses the following objection.

> [I]f extension and figure exist only in the mind, it follows that the mind is extended and figured; since extension is a mode or attribute, which (to speak with the Schools) is predicated of the subject in which it exists.

He replied,

> I answer, those qualities are in the mind only as they are perceived by it, that is, not by way of *mode* or *attribute,* but only by way of *idea*; and it no more follows, that the soul or mind is extended because extension exists in it alone, than it does that it is red or blue, because those colours are on all hands acknowledged to exist in it, and no where else.

It is clear that Berkeley denies that for him a mind's perceiving a quality is that quality's being a mode or attribute inhering in that mind. Does the interpretation at hand conflict with this stricture? I think not. According to the interpretation, an occurrence of a pain or an instance of blue is, as such, a feeling of pain or a sensing of blue. Whatever the relation between sensations and minds is—and it is far from obvious what it is—*it* is not the basis for *sensing.* Even if sensations are construed as modes or attributes, it would be correct to say that blue is in the mind by way of sensation since an occurrence of blue is a sensing of blue, i.e., a sensation.

Finally, what of Berkeley's insistence that he transformed ideas into things, not things into ideas.[36] That is, what of Luce's contention that since Berkeley insisted he did not reject bodies in rejecting material substance, he remained a mind-body dualist and, therefore, could not have intended to reduce bodies to states of mind.[37] It is undeniable and so must be conceded that Berkeley did attempt to secure the reality of bodies and our knowledge of them. But does this mean that his position precludes Reid's interpretation of his ideas of sense? It is far from obvious that it does. In the first place, the crucial step in the transformation of ideas into things is the attempt to demonstrate the impossibility of imperceptible material substances. So long as the latter are posited, the immediate objects of sense are construed as appearances. A colour seen and a sound heard are, at best, accurate copies of things. The first and crucial step in considering those sensibles as things, not images, is eliminating the objects behind the scenes. Berkeley's demonstration of the impossibility of imperceptible material substances utilizes the thesis that the immediate objects of sense cannot exist unperceived. Consequently, it is difficult to see how the transformation of ideas into things could require repudiation of that thesis. Now a second point. The contrast between the real and the imaginary is drawn among immediate objects of sense. The real is defined in terms of lawful connections among sense objects as well as their intensity, distinctness, and involuntariness.[38] All are features and relations sensations can have. The point is that an immediate object of sense, though understood as a sensation, can be part of a class of such objects which meet the requirements for being a real thing. In the third place, Berkeley did retain the mind-body distinction, but only as more-or-less equivalent to his sharp distinction between perceivers and sensibles. He jettisoned the dualism of mental substances and physical (material) substances. Sensible objects are both causally and perceptually dependent upon perceiving minds, and imperceptible matter is a philosophical fiction. This position does not preclude mind-body dualism, however, so long as knowledge of bodies can be analysed in terms of sensibles, that is, sensations. In sum, we may say that Berkeley's handling of his claim to have retained knowledge of bodies and, so, the reality of bodies does not show that for him the immediate objects of sense are not sensations. Whether Berkeley's handling of his claim is philosophically satisfactory is, of course, another and more important question.

Notes

1. The source for all quotations from and references to writings of Berkeley is *The Works of George Berkeley,* ed. by A. A. Luce and T. E. Jessop, 9 vols. (London: Nelson and Co., 1948). Whenever possible, citations will specify a particular work and section thereof; otherwise, a volume and page of the Luce and Jessop edition will be cited following the name of the writing cited or quoted.

2. This position is defended in E. B. Allaire, "Berkeley's Idealism," *Theoria* 29 (1962–63): 229–44, and Phillip D. Cummins, "Perceptual Relativity and Ideas in the Mind," *Philosophy and Phenomenological Research* 24 (1963): 202–14.

3. This, perhaps, is what W. H. Hay is suggesting in his "Berkeley's Argument from Nominalism," *Revue Internationale de Philosophie* 7, fasc. 1–2 (1953): 19–27.

4. Thomas Reid, *Essays on the Intellectual Powers of Man,* ed. by B. Brody (Cambridge, Mass.: MIT Press, 1969), II.xi, pp. 190–91. It may prove helpful to provide cross references to Thomas Reid's *Philosophical Works,* ed. by Sir William Hamilton, 2 vols., second edition (Hildescheim: Olms Verlagsbuchhandlung, 1967). In this instance, see *Works,* I, p. 289.

5. Reid, *Essays*, I.i, pp. 8–10; II.v, pp. 111–18; II.xvii, pp. 252–75. Reid, *Works*, I, pp. 222, 258–60, and 313–38.

6. This contention is argued at length in my "Reid's Realism," *Journal of the History of Philosophy* 12 (1974): 317–40.

7. Reid, *Essays*, II.v, pp. 111–12; Reid, *Works*, I, p. 258.

8. Reid, *Essays*, II.xvi, p. 242; Reid, *Works*, I, p. 310.

9. Reid, *Essays*, II.xx, p. 288; Reid, *Works*, I, p. 327.

10. Reid, *Essays*, I.i, p. 23; II.xvi, pp. 244–49. Reid, *Works*, I, pp. 229, 311–13.

11. Reid, *Essays*, I.i, p. 27; Reid, *Works*, I, p. 229. See also Reid, *Essays*, II.xi, p. 197; Reid, *Works*, I, p. 292.

12. Reid, *Essays*, II.xvi, pp. 244–47; Reid, *Works*, I, pp. 311–12.

13. Reid, *Essays*, II.xxi, p. 302; Reid, *Works*, I, p. 332.

14. Thomas Reid, *An Inquiry into the Human Mind on the Principles of Common Sense* (1764), VI.xx (in the Hamilton edition, I, p. 183).

15. Reid, *Essays*, II.xi, pp. 192–93; II.xvi, pp. 249–50; II.xvii, pp. 252–55. Reid, *Works*, I, pp. 290, 312–14.

16. Reid, *Essays*, I.i, p. 27; Reid, *Works*, I, p. 229. See also Reid, *Essays*, II.xvi, pp. 243–44, 249; Reid, *Works*, I, pp. 310, 312.

17. Reid, *Essays*, II.xi, p. 191; Reid, *Works*, I, pp. 289–90.

18. Reid, *Essays*, II.xi, pp. 192–93; Reid, *Works*, I, p. 290.

19. *Philosophical Commentaries*, Sect. 34. See also Sects. 249, 280, 286, 377, 440, and 666.

20. *Principles*, Sect. 78. See also Sects. 3–5, 18–20, 25, 32, 74, 81, 90, 136–37, 146, 148, and 149 for the use of "idea of sensation," showing the interchangeability of the two terms.

21. Berkeley, *Works*, II, p. 215. See also pp. 176–77, 187–88, 201, 203–4, 206, and 248–49.

22. *Three Dialogues*, in Berkeley, *Works*, II, p. 176.

23. *Three Dialogues*, in Berkeley, *Works*, II, pp. 176–77.

24. *Three Dialogues*, in Berkeley, *Works*, II, p. 179.

25. For some further examples, see Berkeley, *An Essay toward a New Theory of Vision*, Sect. 41; *Principles*, Sect. 41; and *Three Dialogues*, in Berkeley, *Works*, II, pp. 180, 191–92, 197, and 240–41.

26. *Three Dialogues*, in Berkeley, *Works*, II, p. 197. As my colleague, Laird Addis, pointed out to me, Berkeley does not directly consider in this context whether a sensation can be analysed into act and object. From the point at which Hylas introduces the topic, the issue is whether immediate perception can be analysed into sensation (an act of mind) and object of sense. It is clear that Berkeley would resist all attempts to analyse sensations into acts and their objects, given his implicit concession that a genuine act-object distinction would provide grounds for questioning the dependence of the object and his criteria for identifying acts. For Berkeley, perception is the occurrence of a sensation. He rejects attempts to find in perception an act (called sensation) and an object. So clearly he cannot admit to finding an act and object in sensation.

There is another interesting point to be made. It is that Reid was free to speak of sensations (states of sentient beings) as acts whose objects cannot be distinguished from them, since he did not make volition a necessary condition of activity. Berkeley did lay down that condition (see pp. 196–97). He thus could not speak of sensations as acts, as Reid later did, even though he too took sensations to be states of sentient beings.

27. Reid, *Essays,* II, xi, p. 191; *Works,* I, pp. 289–90.

28. Cf. *Principles,* Sects. 15, 41, 45, 76, 78, and 91; see also *Three Dialogues,* in Berkeley, *Works,* II, pp. 175–76, 177, 181, 191–92, 195, 197, and 237.

29. *Principles,* Sect. 9.

30. See Galileo, "A Letter to the Illustrious and Very Reverend Don Virginio Casarini," in *The Philosophy of the 16th and 17th Centuries,* ed. by R. H. Popkin (New York: The Free Press, 1966): 65–68.

31. On Descartes, see his *Le Monde,* Chs. I and II of the essay on light, *De la Lumiere*; see his *The Philosophy of Descartes,* trans. and ed. by H. A. P. Torrey (New York: Holt, 1892), pp. 207–14. For Rohault, see the entry under "sensation" in the *Dictionnaire Français,* ed. by C. P. Richelet (Geneva: Widerhold, 1680). For Boyle, see the *Oxford English Dictionary* (Oxford: Clarendon Press, 1933), entry for "sensation." For Locke, see his *Essays Concerning Human Understanding,* II.viii.16. For Malebranche, see, for example, his *De la recherche de la vérité,* VI.ii.2, and the T. Taylor translation (1700) of that chapter. Taylor used "sensation" for Malebranche's *"sentimen."*

32. Locke, *Essays Concerning Human Understanding,* II.viii.16.

33. Berkeley, *Works,* II, p. 192 n. 1.

34. *Philosophical Commentaries,* Sects. 18 and 440.

35. *Three Dialogues,* in Berkeley, *Works,* II, pp. 191–92.

36. *Principles,* Sects. 38–39.

37. A. A. Luce, *Berkeley's Immaterialism* (London: Nelson, 1945), chs. 1, 3–5.

38. *Principles,* Sects. 28–33, 36, and 40–41.

6

Did Berkeley Completely Misunderstand the Basis of the Primary-Secondary Quality Distinction in Locke?

Margaret D. Wilson

I

According to leading seventeenth-century philosophers and scientists, our sensory "ideas" of physical objects are of two importantly different types. Certain sorts of ideas, the "ideas of primary qualities," *resemble* qualities actually existing in the object. While there are some differences about what *exactly* these comprise, size, shape, motion or rest, and number are among the accepted examples. (Locke, notoriously, includes "solidity"; he sometimes mentioned position. Gravity, as we will see below, was sometimes included later.) On the other hand, the "ideas of secondary qualities" do not resemble any quality really existing in the object, although they are systematically produced by the interactions of the objects' primary qualities with percipients. Ideas or sensations of colors, odors, tastes, sounds, and temperature (hot and cold) are among the traditional "ideas of secondary qualities."[1]

Berkeley is the best known early critic of this distinction—although, as we shall see, he did have predecessors. In the early twentieth century, the distinction was vigorously attacked by Whitehead, who considered it a prominent manifestation of the "fallacy of misplaced concreteness"—which, he claimed, has "ruined" modern philosophy.[2] More recently, D. J. O'Connor, after critically expounding Locke's doctrine of qualities, dismisses it with the comment:

Clearly all this is a great muddle. The doctrine of primary and secondary qualities is, in truth, nothing but some scientific truths dangerously elevated into a philosophical doctrine.[3]

But since O'Connor's article was published in 1964, the primary-secondary quality distinction has increasingly been treated with respect, especially by philosophers sympathetic to "scientific realism." In terms of historical criticism, this development has been accompanied by an increasingly sympathetic construal of Locke's philosophy in general, and a tendency to dismiss Berkeley as having had a very poor understanding of Locke's position. The following views, in particular, have been espoused by a number of writers. (1) Locke's distinction should be viewed as principally grounded in the explanatory success of Boylean atomism. (2) Berkeley erroneously and misleadingly construed the distinction as one supposed to rest on ordinary experience of macroscopic objects. More specifically (some have held), Berkeley misinterpreted the "arguments" of the *Essay Concerning Human Understanding*, bk. II, chap. viii, sects. 16–21—having to do with illusion and the relativity of perception—as Locke's main foundation for the distinction, and therefore falsely supposed that he could refute the distinction by showing that primary-quality perceptions are also subject to relativity considerations. But in fact the issue of perceptual relativity plays no such central role in Locke's thought. (The reasoning of *Essay*, II, viii, 16–21 should be read either as some incidental "bad arguments" for the distinction, or simply as an attempt to bring out the explanatory power of the Boylean conception of body.) (3) Berkeley is responsible, through his stress on relativity considerations, and epistemological issues generally, for a long subsequent history of misinterpreting Locke as relying on such considerations. He is correspondingly responsible for the widespread failure to recognize the truth stated above under (1). (4) When Locke's distinction is correctly reinterpreted as resting on a tacit appeal to the "explanatory success" of contemporary science, it is a much stronger position than traditionally believed. (In fact, at least one prominent philosopher has firmly endorsed Locke's position, with only minor qualifications, relating mainly to scientific progress since Locke's time.)[4]

I fully agree with the view that Locke's distinction was heavily influenced by Boylean science. However, I do not think there is strong reason to suppose that Berkeley seriously "misrepresented" or "misinterpreted" Locke in this connection, is "wholly unfair" to him, read him "carelessly," or produced arguments against Locke that are "wholly [or "simply"] beside the point," as various critics allege.[5] As Barry Stroud has recently noted, this conception of Berkeley, "like the old view of Locke, is a purely fictional chapter in the history of philosophy."[6] Stroud persuasively demonstrates this claim by a careful examination of the arguments of the *Principles* and the *Dialogues,* in relation to the primary-secondary quality distinction. Stroud stresses throughout that Berkeley is primarily concerned with what he sees as his predecessors' "faulty notion of existence"—specifically, their assumption that something unperceived and unperceiving could exist.[7] It is this assumption that Berkeley sees as their major error, rather than mistakes about the relativity of primary quality perceptions, or the epistemological appearance-reality distinction generally.

In the present essay I will defend a point of view that is similar to Stroud's, but with a somewhat different approach.[8] I will focus on the claims of three commentators—Mandelbaum, Alexander, and Mackie—who hold that Berkeley falsely believed Locke's primary-secondary quality distinction to rest on facts about ordinary perception. After quoting some passages from their writings, I will argue that there is in reality very little basis for attributing this interpretation of Locke to Berkeley. I will suggest, however, that there *is* something of a puzzle about the role of relativity arguments in the history of the primary-secondary quality distinction. (As we will see, the puzzle in question goes back beyond Berkeley; I am unable to resolve it.) I will then show that there is ample evidence that Berkeley was aware that Locke's distinction was supposed to derive major support from arguments from scientific (or corpuscularian) explanation. He in fact deals with such arguments repeatedly, searchingly, and—at least in part—astutely. I will also sketch the variety of considerations by which he tries to meet them.

It is so easy to show that Berkeley was aware of the supposed corpuscularian grounding of the distinction that what really requires explanation is the fact that he has so long been accused of missing it. In conclusion I will point out that two of the three critics indeed seem to acknowledge obliquely that Berkeley is far from simply ignoring the alleged scientific basis of Locke's distinction. But—perhaps out of sympathy for Locke's philosophy?—they do not sufficiently consider the implications of these concessions for their other charges against Berkeley.

While this is strictly an interpretive essay, I would like to mention in passing that I am in some respects quite sympathetic to Berkeley's position on the subject under discussion. That is, I share his view that the primary-secondary quality distinction is an affront to common sense, and I am not convinced that a satisfactory version of the argument from explanation has so far been brought forward to establish it.[9]

II

A key passage from Mandelbaum's influential essay on "Locke's Realism" reads as follows:

> The upshot of our argument . . . is that the basis on which Locke established his theory of the primary qualities was his atomism; it was not his aim to attempt to establish the nature of physical objects by examining the sensible ideas which we had of them. Thus instead of viewing Locke's doctrine of the primary and secondary qualities as a doctrine which rests on an analysis of differences among our ideas, his doctrine is to be understood as a theory of physical entities, and of the manner in which our ideas are caused. To this extent the Berkeleian criticism of Locke's distinction between primary and secondary qualities is wholly beside the point, for it rests on an assumption which Locke did not share—that all distinctions concerning the nature of objects must be based upon, and verified by, distinctions discernible within the immediate contents of consciousness.[10]

Mandelbaum does not explain exactly what he means by "distinctions discernible within the immediate contents of consciousness." However, in a footnote he cites *Essay*, II, viii, 21 as the only passage in Locke where it might seem that the theory of primary and secondary qualities is being supported by such a distinction. (This is the passage in which Locke observed that the corpuscularian theory of warmth in our hands as merely a motion of animal spirits enables us to understand how the same water can feel warm to one hand and cold to another, "Whereas it is impossible that the same Water, if those *Ideas* were really in it, should at the same time be both Hot and Cold."[11] He goes on to indicate that "figure" does not present the same problem, "that never producing the *Idea* of a square by one Hand which has produced the Idea of a Globe by another.") Mandelbaum remarks that the passage is primarily concerned with the causal story of the origin of ideas of secondary qualities, and he suggests that "the contention that we are not deceived by tactile impressions of shape plays no significant part in the discussion."¹²

Rather similarly, Peter Alexander writes in the introduction to "Boyle and Locke on Primary and Secondary Qualities":

> Locke has been seriously misrepresented in various respects ever since Berkeley set critics off on the wrong foot. I wish to discuss just one central view the misunderstanding of which has been particularly gross, namely, the distinction between primary and secondary qualities and, especially the alleged arguments for this distinction in *Essay* II, viii, 16–21. Robert Boyle is often mentioned in connection with Locke but the extent and importance of his influence on Locke has seldom been realized. [Alexander here cites Mandelbaum as one of two "honourable exceptions."] If the arguments of II, viii were intended, following Berkeley, to *establish* the distinction between primary and secondary qualities then Locke was both foolish and incompetent; a study of Boyle can help us to see that he was neither of these things by making it clear what he was driving at.¹³

And, finally, some excerpts from Chap. I of John Mackie's book, *Problems from Locke*:

> But Locke [after well arguing that the corpuscularian science can explain the "illusion" of lukewarm water feeling cold to one hand and hot to the other] throws in, for contrast, the remark that "figure"—that is, shape—"never produce[s] the idea of a square by one hand [and] of a globe by another." Though literally correct, this is unfortunate because it has led careless readers from Berkeley onwards to think that Locke is founding the primary/secondary distinction on the claim that secondary qualities are subject to sensory illusion while primary qualities are not. It is then easy for Berkeley to reply that illusions also occur with respect to primary qualities like shape, size, and motion, and hence that there can be no distinction between the two groups of qualities. . . . But of course Locke's argument does not rest on any such claim . . .; it is rather that the corpuscular theory is confirmed as a scientific hypothesis by its success in explaining various illusions in detail.¹⁴

The textual support offered for these negative characterizations of Berkeley's understanding of Locke is surely, by anyone's standards, singularly meager. Neither Mandelbaum nor Alexander cites any texts at all, while Mackie refers us (in the paragraph after the one partially quoted) to "especially . . . the First Dialogue." What, then, do they have in mind? Following up Mackie's clue, let us turn first to that Dialogue. One feature of Berkeley's strategy there does afford at least *prima facie* support for the charge against him.

In the first part of the Dialogue, Philonous has argued in a variety of ways (*not* just through notions of relativity or illusion) that sensible colors, sounds, heat and cold, tastes and odors exist "only in the mind." Hylas, reluctantly persuaded of this conclusion, suddenly bethinks himself of the distinction between primary and secondary qualities. "Philosophers," he points out, assert that all of the properties so far covered in the Dialogue "are only so many sensations or ideas existing nowhere but in the mind." The primary qualities, however— "Extension, Figure, Solidity, Gravity,[15] Motion, and Rest"—"they hold exist really in bodies." Hylas concludes his speech as follows: "For my part, I have been a long time sensible there was such an opinion current among philosophers, but was never thoroughly convinced of its truth until now."[16] Philonous then introduces the next phase of the argument for immaterialism in the following terms: "But what if the same arguments which are brought against Secondary Qualities will hold good against [extensions and figures] also?"[17] He then proceeds to argue that perceptions of extension are relative to the condition and situation of the percipient. This discussion includes a passage that does indeed recall the argument of *Essay,* II, viii, 21:

> *Phil:* Was it not admitted as a good argument [cited in our previous discussion] that neither heat nor cold was in the water, because it seemed warm to one hand and cold to the other?
>
> *Hyl:* It was.
>
> *Phil:* It is not the very same reasoning to conclude, there is no extension or figure in an object, because to one eye it shall seem little, smooth and round, when at the same time it appears to the other great, uneven, and angular?[18]

In response to Hylas' expression of skepticism as to whether this ever happens, Philonous goes on to cite the instance of the microscope.

Now, does this passage, together with Philonous' subsequent development of relativity arguments for motion and solidity, show that Berkeley seriously overestimated the importance of relativity considerations for Locke? This seems to me a rather extravagant supposition, for several reasons. First (and least important), surely there really is a suggestion in *Essay,* II, viii, 21 that relativity considerations show that hot and cold as we perceive them are not really in the water; and *some* contrast is suggested in this respect between hot-and-cold and figure. Second, as Michael Ayers has pointed out, the fact that there is an "association" of Philonous' reasoning with Locke's brief remarks about relativity scarcely shows that Berkeley *sees Locke* as resting the distinction between subjective ideas and real qualities on considerations of relativity or the possibility of illusion.[19] And, finally, the argument of the First Dialogue is clearly not presented in the form of *ad hominem* reasoning at all. That is, the overt strategy is not simply to take a premiss from the opposition—that relativity considerations establish the subjectivity of the "secondary qualities"—and show that anyone who holds *that* can logically be forced into immaterialism. Rather, Berkeley first has Philonous systematically *persuade* Hylas (through relativity and other considerations) that colors, odors, etc., are mere ideas in the mind. Following Ayers, then, I would deny that Berkeley's treatment of relativity arguments in the First Dialogue tends to convict him of a misunderstanding or "careless reading" of Locke.[20]

It might be suggested, however, that the *Principles* actually provide more direct proof than do the *Dialogues* that Berkeley saw Locke and his followers as resting the primary-secondary quality distinction on considerations of perceptual relativity. For we do find in *Principles*, I, sect. 14 the following statement:

> I shall farther add, that, after the same manner as modern philosophers prove certain sensible qualities to have not existence in Matter, or without the mind, the same things may be likewise proved of all other sensible qualities whatsoever. Thus, for instance, it is said that heat and cold are affections only of the mind, and not at all patterns of real beings, existing in the corporeal substances which excite them; for that the same body which appears cold to one hand seems warm to another.[21]

He goes on to claim that the same relativity considerations hold in the cases of extension and motion. It is true, as Ayers points out, that Berkeley immediately goes on (in sect. 15) to observe that this reasoning does not establish the mind-dependence of *either* class of qualities:

> Though it must be confessed this method of arguing does not so much prove that there is no extension or colour in an outward object, as that we do not know by sense which is the true extension or colour of the object.[22]

The passage does, however, provide direct evidence that Berkeley thought that "modern philosophers" drew on relativity arguments to establish the subjectivity of secondary qualities. It appears to imply that he thought they had not noticed that perception of primary qualities, too, could be affected by the position or condition of the percipient. What does this tell us about his reading of Locke?

The first point to observe is that the idea that relativity considerations extend to primary as well as secondary qualities did not originate with Berkeley—nor did the use of this point as a criticism of the view that perceptions of primary qualities possess superior objectivity. The passage quoted above from Berkeley's *Principles* has an extremely close parallel in section G of the article "Zeno of Elea" in Bayle's *Dictionary*, published years before.[23] The likelihood that Berkeley adopted this part of his reasoning from Bayle was apparently first demonstrated by Richard Popkin in 1951, and has frequently been noted in subsequent writings by Popkin and others.[24] Bayle is criticizing "the 'new' philosophers." The following passage is representative:

> All the means of suspending judgment that overthrow the reality of corporeal qualities also overthrow the reality of extension. Since the same bodies are sweet to some men and bitter to others, one is right in inferring that they are neither sweet nor bitter in themselves and absolutely speaking. The 'new" philosophers, although they are not skeptics, have so well understood the bases of suspension of judgment with regard to sounds, smells, heat, cold, hardness, softness, heaviness and lightness, tastes, colors, and the like, that they teach that all these qualities are perceptions of our soul and that they do not exist at all in the objects of our senses. Why should we not say the same thing about extension? . . . [N]otice carefully that the same body appears to us to be small or large, according to the place from which it is viewed; and let us have no doubts that a body that seems very small to us appears very large to a fly.[25]

Now, against whom, exactly, does Bayle suppose that such reasoning is effective? In another article Bayle credits Simon Foucher with influencing his views on the indefensibility of the primary-secondary quality distinction.[26] He specifically cites Foucher's *Critique de la Recherche de la Verité*, an attack on Malebranche published in 1675.[27] This would take the criticism of the primary-secondary quality distinction back to fifteen years *before* the publication of Locke's *Essay*. While Foucher does argue that the primary-secondary distinction is indefensible, however, he does not, as far as I can find, focus on the issue of the comparable relativity and variability of primary qualities.[28] It is perhaps logical that he should not, since Malebranche himself makes much of the relativity of perceptions of extension in the *Recherche*![29] Bayle himself notes that such arguments are found in Malebranche and the *Port Royal Logic,* among other sources.[30] It is therefore presently unclear to me just whom Bayle thought he was refuting in the passage quoted, and just what he thought their error was. (Not noticing that perceptions of primary qualities are variable? Not drawing the right conclusion from the observation?)—There certainly seems to be no good reason to suppose he had in mind specifically *Essay,* II, viii, 16–21. The same difficulties then come up at one remove about Berkeley's closely comparable reasoning (and even wording) in *Principles,* sects. 14–15. That is, there may have been "modern" or "new" philosophers who fit the role that Bayle and Berkeley cast them in more closely than Locke— and Bayle and Berkeley may have had them in mind. Or there may not have been, in which case Berkeley will have taken over from Bayle a piece of reasoning without a proper target. In contrast to this rather murky situation, however, it is possible to show clearly that Berkeley (if not Bayle) fully appreciated the importance of the alleged success of corpuscularian explanations as a basis for the primary-secondary quality distinction. Let us now turn to this task.

III

It is an interesting fact that Mandelbaum, Alexander, and Mackie, in arguing that the explanatory success of corpuscularianism is the main basis for Locke's distinction, particularly cite the ability of this science to explain the production of ideas in us, including the ideas of secondary qualities. But this is, as it happens, a topic with which Berkeley deals repeatedly and emphatically. For instance, at the very beginning of the Second Dialogue, Hylas first admits that he can see no false steps in the reasonings of the previous day. But, he says,

> when these are out of my thoughts, there seems, on the other hand, something so satisfactory, so natural and intelligible, in the modern way of explaining things that, I profess, I know not how to reject it [31]

The conversation proceeds as follows:

Phil: I know not what you mean.
Hyl: I mean the way of accounting for our sensations or ideas.

Phil: How is that?

Hyl: It is supposed the soul makes her residence in some part of the brain, from which the nerves take their rise, and are thence extended to all parts of the body; and that outward objects, by the different impressions they make on the organs of sense, communicate certain vibrative motions to the nerves; and these being filled with spirits propagate them to the brain or seat of the soul, which, according to the various impressions or traces thereby made in the brain is variously affected with ideas.

Phil: And call you this an explication of the manner whereby we are affected with ideas?[32]

In objecting to this reasoning, Philonous first points out that by the previous day's reasoning the brain is just one sensible object among others, and hence itself exists "only in the mind." How could one idea or sensible thing reasonably be supposed to cause all the others? But, he continues, Hylas' position is intrinsically inacceptable, even apart from conclusions previously arrived at.

Phil: . . . for after all, this way of explaining things, as you called it, could never have satisfied any reasonable man. What connexion is there between a motion in the nerves, and the sensations of sound or colour in the mind? Or how is it possible these should be the effect of that?[33]

As this passage shows conclusively, Berkeley was perfectly aware that the primary-secondary quality distinction was supposed to derive support from the alleged ability of contemporary science to explain perception in terms of materialist mechanism—and hence of primary qualities. His response is straightforward: the purported "explanation" is a sham. In presenting this response he invokes the notion that the production of ideas by states of matter is not "possible." Such an a priori stricture on causal relations would be considered untenable by many philosophers today. It was, however, accepted by Locke, who argued at length that states of matter cannot "naturally" produce "Sence, Perception, and Knowledge."[34] Far from missing Locke's point, Berkeley has come down on a crucial weakness—and problem of consistency—in the Lockean system.[35]

Berkeley raises this issue repeatedly.[36] However, he also deals in other ways with the notion that the contemporary concept of external matter characterized (just) by primary qualities is justified by its "explanatory success." Some of his arguments draw on problematic—even idiosyncratic—views about causal relations. For present purposes there is no need to analyze the relevant passages in detail. I will merely summarize the main considerations he advances.

(1) From the contention that only spirits are active, Berkeley argues that extension, motion, etc.—or unthinking matter characterized by these qualities—cannot be causes of anything. Hence they cannot "explain" the production of any effect.[37]

(2) Even apart from the impossibility of understanding how a motion of matter could produce an idea, or how an "inert" entity could be a cause, contemporary materialism is far from explanatorily adequate. Have the materialists, Berkeley demands,

> by all their strained thoughts and extravagant suppositions . . . been able to reach the mechanical production of any one animal or vegetable body? . . . Have they accounted, by physical principles, for the aptitude and contrivance, even of the most inconsiderable parts of the universe?[38]

(3) The explanatory successes that the new science has had can readily be accommodated within the immaterialist philosophy. They have to do mainly with uncovering regularities and "analogies" in nature. Nothing but confusion results when it is thought that these regularities are leading to the discovery of productive material causes (e.g., "gravitational attraction"). Rather they should be conceived as part of an increasingly comprehensive theory of ideal "signs" to significata. The underlying ground of *this* relation is the causality of the infinite spirit, orderly producer of these ideas or sensible objects that constitute nature.[39]

These contentions range, clearly, from prodigious metaphysics to simple common sense. Taken together, however, they hardly indicate unawareness of the explanatory claims of contemporary mechanism—or of the philosophical significance attributed to these claims.

Two final points should be added, in concluding this discussion of Berkeley. First, the specific considerations against arguments from "explanatory success" for the Boylean concept of matter are offered despite the fact that Berkeley (in the *Principles,* anyway) believes that he can demonstrate the *unintelligibility* of the notion before the issue of its "explanatory power"—which surely is in some sense posterior—is even raised. Second, it would be wrong to suppose (as Mandelbaum sometimes seems to)[40] that Berkeley neglects the prevailing view that qualities of material bodies are supposed to derive from their inner real essences or constitutive corpuscles. He clearly states and disputes this Lockean conception in more than one passage.[41]

IV

In conclusion, I want to acknowledge that both Mandelbaum and Alexander show some recognition that Berkeley's attack on Locke was not wholly a matter of misinterpretation. In the case of Mandelbaum, the recognition is extremely oblique and in several ways puzzling. Mandelbaum points out that Berkeley did not merely overlook the fact that Locke'sphilosophy was founded on scientific considerations; rather he consciously "sought to free philosophic questions from any direct dependence upon science."[42] From this observation Mandelbaum somehow moves to the conclusion that it is *accordingly* "misleading" to interpret Locke in the light of Berkeley's criticisms. He also seems to think that Berkeley's efforts "to free philosophic questions from any direct dependence upon science" entail his reading the *Essay* "as an epistemological treatise devoid of a scientific substructure."[43] But none of this really follows, unless it be supposed that Berkeley's attempt to free philosophy from dependence on science was somehow a mere blind turning away from the earlier "tradition" without any direct confrontation with its assumptions. Perhaps this inference is tied in with Mandelbaum's undefended claim that Berkeley simply assumes that all distinctions among ideas must be drawn within the contents of ordinary experience of macroscopic objects. In any case, I hope to have shown that Berkeley did understand these "scientific" aspects of Locke's position that Mandelbaum is concerned to stress—and still had reason to regard the position as incoherent.

At the end of his article, Alexander does allow that "perhaps the most difficult objection for Locke to meet," with respect to the primary-secondary quality distinction, "is an argument about causality put by Berkeley."[44] It appears at first that Alexander means (surprisingly) Berkeley's argument that everything except spirit is "inert" and hence causally inefficacious. But the whole passage gives the impression that "the most difficult objection" that Alexander has in mind is really Berkeley's observation, expounded at some length above, "that no philosopher even pretends to explain 'how matter should operate on a spirit.' "

In my opinion, this has to be a crucial point of contention between Berkeley and Locke's present-day apologists, with respect to the primary-secondary quality distinction.[45] Berkeley, I have argued, *rejected* the argument from the explanatory success of mechanistic physics; he did not merely ignore it. And I have also claimed that, insofar as Berkeley was pointing out an inconsistency in the philosophy he opposed, his position is solidly grounded. It is apparently open to the contemporary philosopher, concerned with philosophical truth as well as Locke exegesis to deny that there is, after all, any special problem about causal relations between the mental and the physical, and hence about "explaining" perceptions in physical terms. (In this, I stress again, he would have to disagree with *both* Berkeley and Locke.) Mandelbaum and Mackie do not address this point; they do not seem to see it.[46] Alexander does at least partly see it. But rather than reject the eighteenth-century assumption that there is some special problem about mind-body interaction, he attempts to help Locke out of the difficulty by invoking an unexplained distinction between scientific and philosophical issues:

> Locke believes, as does Boyle, that the facts of experience force dualism upon us; the consequent problem is not scientific but philosophical and is therefore not particularly involved in the distinction between primary and secondary qualities.[47]

But surely the whole drift of Berkeley's attack on Locke's distinction is that the "facts of experience" do *not* force dualism upon us—so the philosophical inconsistency that Locke falls into can be avoided. Berkeley thinks that his immaterialism lets us accommodate the facts of experience without *having* a problem—whether "philosophical" or "scientific"—about how matter could possibly produce ideas in the mind. Alexander has not only conceded to Berkeley a relevant, if not powerful, objection to Locke's system.[48] He has unintentionally pointed to one of the strongest positive features of Berkeley's anti-Lockean metaphysics.

Notes

1. See John Locke, *Essay Concerning Human Understanding,* bk. II, chap. viii. Descartes, Galileo, and Boyle are among the other prominent exponents of the distinction.

2. A. N. Whitehead, *Science and the Modern World* (1925; repr. New York: The Free Press, 1967), chap. 3.

3. "Locke," in D. J. O'Connor, ed., *A Critical History of Western Philosophy* (New York: The Free Press, 1964), p. 211.

4. J. L. Mackie, *Problems From Locke* (Oxford: Clarendon Press, 1976), chap. 2. Other sources for the views cited (with less explicit philosophical endorsement of Locke's distinction) are found in the works of Mandelbaum and Alexander, cited below. At the beginning of the paper cited in n. 6, Barry Stroud gives many references to works advancing the "old" interpretation of Locke.

5. All of these comments are from Mackie, Alexander, and Mandelbaum. Some of them occur in the passages I cite from their works at the beginning of pt. II.

6. "Berkeley v. Locke on Primary Qualities," *Philosophy* 55 (April 1980): 150. See also Daniel Garber, "Locke, Berkeley, and Corpuscular Scepticism," *Berkeley: Critical and Interpretive Essays,* Colin M. Turbayne, ed. (Minneapolis: University of Minnesota Press, 1982), pp. 174–94.

7. Stroud, "Berkeley v. Locke," pp. 150–51 and passim.

8. To the best of my knowledge, my views about the interpretation of Berkeley developed in complete independence from Stroud's. I did not become aware of the similarities between our ideas on this matter until I came across the published version of his paper, after an earlier version of the present article had been submitted for publication. I must acknowledge, however, that I had in my possession all the while a manuscript version of his essay, which constituted part of a much longer paper on Locke and Berkeley that he sent me years ago. Apparently, I had never read the section on Berkeley, and had indeed misremembered the paper as being wholly on Locke. (My oversight came to light as a result of recent correspondence with Stroud.)

I have extensively revised pt. I of the present essay to take account of Stroud's prior work. For reasons of structure and exposition, it has proved impractical to remove all overlap from later sections, however. In particular, my treatment of Berkeley on relativity arguments is in several respects close to Stroud's. Stroud also touches briefly on Bayle's precedence to Berkeley, which I discuss in more detail, and on the issue of materialist explanation.

9. I critically discuss Mackie's exposition of the argument in "The Primary-Secondary Quality Distinction: Against Two Recent Defenses," 1979, unpublished.

10. Maurice Mandelbaum, "Locke's Realism," in *Philosophy, Science, and Sense Perception* (Baltimore: Johns Hopkins Press, 1974), pp. 27–28; see also p. 20.

11. John Locke, *An Essay Concerning Human Understanding,* ed. Peter H. Nidditch (Oxford: Clarendon Press, 1960; repr. 1975), p. 139.

12. Mandelbaum, "Locke's Realism," p. 28, n. 52.

13. In I. C. Tipton, ed., *Locke on Human Understanding* (Oxford: Oxford University Press, 1977), p. 62; see also p. 73. (Originally published in *Ratio* 16 [1974].)

14. *Problems from Locke,* pp. 22–23; cf. p. 24.

15. The inclusion of gravity constitutes an important departure from Locke:

cf. Margaret D. Wilson, "Superadded Properties: The Limits of Mechanism in Locke," *American Philosphical Quarterly* 14 (April 1979): 148–49. On the other hand, Berkeley does not always include gravity in the list of primary qualities: cf. *A Treatise Concerning the Principles of Human Knowledge*, I, sect. 9. (In A. A. Luce and T. E. Jessop, eds., *The Works of George Berkeley, Bishop of Cloyne*, 9 vols. [London: Thomas Nelson and Sons, 1948–57], vol. II, p. 44. This edition hereafter referred to as *Works*.)

16. *Works*, II, pp. 187–88.

17. Ibid., p. 188..

18. Ibid., p. 189.

19. "Substance, Reality, and the Great Dead Philosophers," *American Philosophical Quarterly* 7 (January 1970): 43. Ayers is disputing a rather different allegation of Berkeleyan misunderstanding—that of Jonathan Bennett—but some of his remarks are relevant to the present context as well.

20. Ayers points out that Berkeley's deployment of relativity arguments in the First Dialogue can well be read as the outcome of "his own quasi-sceptical reflections on the fact that the state, position, etc. of the perceiver help to determine how *any* aspect of the world is perceived." However, as I explain below, there is considerable reason to believe that the "quasi-sceptical reflections" in question were strongly influenced by Bayle.

21. *Works*, II, pp. 46–47. In *Principles*, sect. 14–15, Berkeley specifically mentions relativity considerations as applying to color and taste, as well as hot and cold, among the secondary qualities, and extension, figure, and motion among the primary qualities.

22. Ibid., p. 47. A similar point is made by Bayle in the section of "Zeno" cited in the next note.

23. Pierre Bayle, *Dictionnaire historique et critique*, nov. éd., tome XV (Paris: Desoer, 1820), pp. 44–45; *Historical and Critical Dictionary*, ed. Richard H. Popkin (Indianapolis: Bobbs-Merrill, 1965), pp. 364–66. Subsequent references are to Popkin's edition. The *Dictionary* was originally published in 1697.

24. Richard H. Popkin, "Berkeley and Pyrrhonism," *Review of Metaphysics* 5 (1951–52): 223–46. See also his notes to his edition of Bayle's *Dictionary*, s.v. "Pyrrho" and "Zeno of Elea." See also Richard A. Watson, *The Downfall of Cartesianism, 1673–1712* (The Hague: Martinus Nijhoff, 1966), p. 3; and his *Introduction* to Simon Foucher, *Critique de la Recherche de la Verité* (New York and London: Johnson Reprint Corporation, 1969), p. xxix. I am grateful to Phillip Cummins for calling my attention to Bayle's (and Foucher's) relevance to the present inquiry.

25. *Dictionary*, pp. 364–65.

26. s.v. "Pyrrho," ibid., p. 197.

27. Reprinted 1969: see n. 24. See esp. pp. 76–80 of this work. Foucher's influence on Bayle has been noted by Popkin and Watson in the works cited above. Watson's *Downfall of Cartesianism* contains an especially detailed discussion of Foucher and his relationship to Malebranche, Bayle, Berkeley, and others. See also Phillip Cummins, "Perceptual Relativity and Ideas in the Mind," *Philosophy and Phenomenological Research* 24 (December 1963): 202–14.

Cummins notes Bayle's seemingly erroneous emphasis on the issue of perceptual relativity and provides an interesting analysis of his (and of Foucher's) conception of the issue.

28. Popkin indicates that he does: cf. Popkin, "Skepticism," in Paul Edwards, ed., *The Encyclopedia of Philosophy,* vol. 7 (New York: Macmillan and The Free Press, 1967), p. 454. He does not give an exact reference, however. Watson, in his detailed discussion of Foucher's anti-Malebranche works, does not seem to point to the presence of an "equal variability" argument in Foucher. (I have personally had access to only the first of Foucher's critical works.)

29. *Recherche de la verité,* bk. I, chap. vi, sect. 1, in Nicholas Malebranche, *Oeuvres complètes,* ed. A. Robinet, vol. I (Paris: J. Vrin, 1958), pp. 79ff. However, Malebranche does claim that judgments about bodies' primary qualities involve truths about proportions and relations, while judgments about secondary qualities are more wholly erroneous: cf. Watson, *Downfall,* p. 44.

30. Bayle, *Dictionary,* s.v. "Zeno," nn. 66 and 67, pp. 365–66.

31. *Works,* II, p. 208.

32. Ibid., pp. 208–9.

33. Ibid., p. 210.

34. Cf. Wilson, "Superadded Properties," pp. 144–48; and Stroud, "Berkeley v. Locke," p. 158.

35. Foucher had already observed this inconsistency—and some related ones—in the dualist, realist philosophies of his day, and had dwelt on it emphatically and at length. As noted above, however, his targets were post-Cartesian continental philosophers, especially Malebranche. Foucher's critical arguments and their influence on Berkeley and others have been meticulously detailed by Watson in *Downfall.*

In "Berkeley on the Limits of Mechanistic Explanation" (Turbayne, op. cit., pp. 95–107, Nancy L. Maull also stresses Berkeley's use of this line of argument, and mentions its *ad hominem* relevance. Unfortunately, I did not learn of Maull's essay until the present paper had been submitted for publication. While there are a number of points of contact between our approaches, I disagree strongly with Maull's conclusion that we can now see that Berkeley's criticism of contemporary materialist philosophy was "ultimately ineffectual and irrelevant." That is, I do not believe that Berkeley's criticism has been shown to reflect a merely dogmatic distinction between the mental and the physical (as she seems to imply), or that it has been discredited by the subsequent development of psychophysiology.

36. See *Principles,* I, sect. 50 (*Works,* II, p. 62):

> You will say there have been a great many things explained by matter and motion: take away these, and you destroy the whole corpuscular philosophy, and undermine those mechanical principles which have been applied with so much success to account for the phenomena. . . . To this I answer, that there is not any one phenomenon explained on that supposition, which may not as well be explained without it. . . . To explain the phenomena, is all one as to shew, why upon such and such occasions we are affected with such and such ideas. But how matter should operate on a

spirit, or produce any idea in it, is what no philosopher will pretend to explain.

See also *Philosophical Commentaries,* sect. 476, ed. A. A. Luce (London: Thomas Nelson and Sons, 1944), p. 161.

37. Cf. *Principles,* I, sect. 25, and I, sect. 102, *Works,* II, pp. 51–52, 85.

38. Third Dialogue, ibid., p. 257.

39. *Principles,* I, sects. 58ff. and 103, ibid., pp. 65ff., 86. Compare *Philosophical Commentaries,* sects. 71 and 403, in Luce, ed., pp. 19 and 131. (See also Stroud, "Berkeley v. Locke," pp. 158–59.) As the first of the two passages from the *Commentaries* suggests, Berkeley felt that the mechanists were faced with certain problems in merely understanding *physical* causality, problems that his system avoided. Probably he had in mind, for instance, some of Locke's statements about the incomprehensibility of cohesion on materialist principles: cf. Wilson, "Superadded Properties," p. 149.

40. Cf. Mandelbaum, "Locke's Realism," p. 3.

41. *Principles,* I, sect. 65 and 102, *Works,* II, pp. 69, 85; *Philosophical Commentaries,* sect. 533, in Luce, ed., p. 185. See also Garber's detailed discussion, this volume.

42. "Locke's Realism," p. 3.

43. Ibid.

44. Alexander, "Boyle and Locke," in Tipton, ed., p. 75.

45. At least those discussed in this paper. Jonathan Bennett's defense of the distinction does not focus on the issue of explanatory adequacy, and to this extent avoids completely any problem about body-mind causation: cf. his *Locke, Berkeley, Hume: Central Themes* (Oxford: Oxford University Press, 1971).

46. As becomes clear in a later chapter, Mackie does see a problem about "reducing" phenomenal properties or sensations to states of matter: see *Problems from Locke,* pp. 167ff.

47. "Locke and Boyle," p. 76.

48. Alexander also concedes at the end of his article that he has not "dealt adequately with Berkeley's conclusion from his various arguments that the idea of matter is unintelligible." It seems, then, that Alexander concedes in conclusion that there is *a good deal* that is relevant, if not powerful, in Berkeley's attack on Locke's distinction, and the "idea of matter" that is tied to it.

7

Berkeleian Idealism and Impossible Performances

George Pappas

Berkeleian idealism minimally consists of three theses that, on the face of it, are independent of one another, namely: (1) each perceiving entity, whether finite or infinite, is a spirit; (2) each perceived entity, whether simple or complex, exists if and only if (or perhaps when and only when) it is perceived; and (3) everything that exists is particular—that is, there are no universals *in re* or in the mind of any perceiver or anywhere else. Perhaps, under a certain interpretation, Berkeley took the nominalist thesis expressed in (3) to entail or at least strongly to support (2). I touch on that possibility, albeit briefly, below. My primary concern in this essay is with thesis 2.

Scholarly attention regarding thesis 2, the *esse est percipi* thesis, has been considerable, but I think we may safely say that three primary questions have been addressed. First, how shall we interpret the thesis? Berkeley's actual texts support more than one reading, and the differences between readings are not trivial. Second, is the thesis supposed to be some sort of necessary truth? Most commentators have thought the answer to this question is yes, and this not without reason, for Berkeley writes as if he so regarded the thesis. Third, what exactly are the arguments Berkeley proposes in behalf of the thesis? There have been almost as many answers to this last question as there have been writers on the subject. In this essay I do not break with this grand tradition; I propose a new account of what I think is afoot with Berkeley's central argument for the *esse est percipi* thesis. The account to be given has certain affinities with the performative account of Descartes' cogito that Hintikka has discussed,[1] so I call the account to be provided here the performance analysis of Berkeley's master argument for *esse est percipi*. The roots of the present account, though, are not in Hintikka but rather in an interpretation once presented by Marc-Wogau.[2]

Thesis 2, What?

Thesis 2 speaks of perceived entities, and for Berkeley, one might say, all perceived entities are ideas. So a natural reading of thesis 2 would be this:

A. Each idea exists if and only if it is perceived.

Of course, if *A* is true, then any idea cluster is also an entity that exists if and only if it is perceived, since every idea in every idea cluster is perceived, given *A*, and surely a sufficient condition for perceiving a cluster of entities is that one perceive every element in the cluster. Thus, *A* readily gives way to a more specific claim:

B. Each idea and each idea cluster exists if and only if it is perceived.

Statement *A*, and by implication *B*, are suggested by various passages in the *Principles*. For example, Berkeley tells us that a spirit or mind is not "any one of my ideas, but a thing entirely distinct from them, wherein they exist, or, which is the same thing, whereby they are perceived, for the existence of an idea consists in being perceived" (PR 2). Related comments occur at many other places in the *Principles* (e.g., see PR 7, 45, 48) making it seem that *A* and thus *B* are natural readings of the text.

However, there are reasons to resist taking *A* or *B* as the meaning of thesis 2. One is that from the *Three Dialogues* especially, but also from places in the *Principles,* it is clear that Berkeley is talking about what he calls sensible qualities and sensible objects, that is, perceivable qualities such as colors, sounds, and shapes, and ordinary macro-objects such as trees and tables. In the second of the *Three Dialogues,* Philonous, speaking for Berkeley, says, "To me it is evident, for the reasons you [Hylas] allow of, that sensible things cannot exist otherwise than in a mind or spirit" (D 212). Throughout this book Berkeley uses the term 'sensible thing' variably, to denote either sensible qualities or sensible objects or both; and existing in a mind is, for Berkeley, the same thing as being perceived by a mind. Or, consider this passage: "Some truths there are so near and obvious to the mind that a man need only open his eyes to see them. Such I take this important one to be, to wit, that all the choir of heaven and furniture of the earth which compose this mighty frame of the world, have not any subsistence without a mind, that there being is to be perceived or known" (PR 6). These passages, and others like them, indicate that neither *A* nor *B* is an accurate reading of thesis 2.

Quite independent of the texts, another reason for rejecting *A* and *B* is, to put it paradoxically, that each is so *obviously* true. Of course the *esse* of an *idea* is *percipi*. Such a claim would have been regarded as true, merely in virtue of the meanings of the constituent terms, by nearly every philosopher in Berkeley's period, including all those Berkeley cites as materialists. No one would have found such a claim disputable or controversial. Yet Berkeley took himself to be making an important discovery in coming on the truth of thesis 2; and we know that thesis 2 was and ever has been controversial at best.

Let us think of a sensible-quality cluster either as any group of two or more sensible qualities that happen to be perceived simultaneously, typically by means of the same sense modality, such as two different colors adjoining one another, or as two or more sensible qualities that are linked together whether or not simultaneously perceived, such as the particular shape and color of some object. Then we may formulate thesis 2 more accurately as

C. Each sensible quality, sensible-quality cluster, and sensible object is an entity that exists if and only if it is perceived.

Notice that *C* is far from truistic; unlike *A* and *B*, it is debatable at best. Indeed, on the face of it, *C* seems clearly false. So, for this very reason, *C* is better suited to serve as expressing the thesis Berkeley thought he was discovering, the "simple though amazing truth" that each nonperceiving entity exists if and only if it is perceived.

Statement *C* makes no mention of possible perception; instead, the *esse* of each sensible thing is reckoned as actually being perceived. There are passages, however, where Berkeley speaks of possible or hypothetical perception, for instance, in the *Philosophical Commentaries,* where he says:

> Existence is percipi or percipere (or velle i.e. agere) the horse is in the stable, the Books are in the study as before. (PC 429, 429a)

Bodies taken for powers do exist w^n not perceiv'd but this existence is
not actual. W^n I say a power exists no more is meant than that if in y^3 light
I open my eyes & look that way I shall see it i.e. y^3 body &c. (PC 293a)

Passages such as these suggest that *C,* too, is in need of amendment,
so that what follows the biconditional is a disjunction, giving us

D. Each sensible quality, sensible-quality cluster, and sensible object
   is an entity that exists if and only if either it is perceived or it
   would be perceived if such-and-such conditions were to obtain.

The expression 'such-and-such conditions,' of course, denotes various
things, for example, someone's looking in a certain direction or audito-
rially attending at a certain time.

Although *D* does comport with some texts, I doubt if it is Berkeley's
considered view. The reason has to do with God and God's perceptions. Berkeley holds that all sensible qualities not being perceived by
some finite perceiver are nonetheless at all times perceived by God.
For example, Philonous says, "[I]s there therefore no difference between saying, *there is a God, therefore he perceives all things*: and
saying, *sensible things do really exist: and if they really exist they are
necessarily perceived by an infinite mind: therefore there is an infinite mind, or God"* (D 212; emphasis in original). Here the first view
expressed is what some of Berkeley's opponents are supposed to hold,
whereas the second is Berkeley's own. In fact, here Berkeley endorses
the stronger thesis that every sensible thing not perceived by God at
all times it exists; a fortiori, each existing sensible thing perceived by a
finite being is still perceived by God.

We should, then, side with *C* rather than *D* as expressive of the import of thesis 2. Passages in which *D* seems indicated are relatively few
and mostly in the early *Philosophical Commentaries* entries; references to God and his perceptions are many and spread through the
mature works. Moreover, we know on independent grounds that the
existence and perceptual activity of God is of critical importance in
Berkeley's philosophy; so his insistence that God perceives all sensible
things at all times, something Berkeley repeats several times, is also apt
to be a matter he took to be of central significance.[3]

Semantic Status of *C*

Thesis 2, here taken as given by *C,* is usually reckoned a necessary
truth, at least as Berkeley saw the matter, for Berkeley almost says as

much. For example, he seemingly tells us that the denial of *C* is a contradiction. He writes, "[T]o what purpose is it to dilate on that which may be demonstrated with the utmost evidence in a line or two, to anyone that is capable of the least reflection? It is but looking into your own thoughts, and so trying whether you can conceive it possible for a sound, or figure, or motion, or color, to exist without the mind, or unperceived. This essay trial may make you see, that what you contend for is a downright contradiction" (PR 22). In the *Dialogues* the sentiment is repeated: "[I]t is absolutely impossible, and a plain contradiction to suppose any unthinking being should exist without being perceived by a mind" (D 244). Elsewhere Berkeley speaks not of contradictions but rather of repugnancies, but his point seems to be the same. He says: "But why should we trouble ourselves any farther, in discussing this material *substratum* or support of figure and motion, and other sensible qualities? Does it not suppose they have an existence without the mind? And is not this a direct repugnancy, and altogether inconceivable?" (PR 17; emphasis in original). Other passages are not so clear. There are places where Berkeley seems to hedge a bit and to maintain that the denial of *C* is *either* a contradiction *or* meaningless. Consider PR 24, which I here quote in full.

> It is very obvious, upon the least inquiry into our own thoughts, to know whether it be possible for us to understand what is meant, by the *absolute existence of sensible objects in themselves, or without the mind.* To me it is evident those words mark out either a direct contradiction, or else nothing at all. And to convince others of this, I know no readier or fairer way, than to entreat they would calmly attend to their own thoughts: and if by this attention, the emptiness or repugnancy of those expressions does appear, surely nothing more is requisite for their conviction. It is on this therefore that I insist, to wit, that the absolute existence of unthinking things are words without a meaning, or which include a contradiction. This is what I repeat and inculcate, and earnestly recommend to the attentive thoughts of the reader. (emphasis in original)

This passage, it should be noted, comes immediately after Berkeley has presented his most well-known and notorious argument for *C*. This is the so-called master argument, to be discussed below, in which Berkeley argues that no one can conceive a sensible object existing unperceived, so that no such object exists unperceived. In other words, he is summing up what he thinks he has established by the argument of the preceding section. This, it seems to me, is some evidence that

Berkeley is at least not sure that the denial of C is a contradiction, and it also goes some way toward showing that it is an open question whether Berkeley regarded thesis 2 as a necessary truth.

The foregoing passage is not the only place where Berkeley treats the denial of C as meaningless. In considering and responding to an objection to C he makes the same point, claiming that a person who finds that he cannot conceive a sensible thing existing unperceived"will acknowledge it is unreasonable for him to stand up in defence of he knows not what, and pretend to charge on me as an absurdity, the not assenting to those propositions which at bottom have no meaning in them" (PR 45). It is true that Berkeley sometimes says that the denial of C is impossible, that is, that the existence of an unperceived sensible thing is an impossibility. However, lest we think that he thereby took C to be a necessary truth, we should note how Berkeley talks about the impossibility of matter.

At the end of the second dialogue Berkeley has Philonous acknowledge that the impossibility of matter's existence is not based on its being somehow contradictory. Philonous continues:

> Now in that which you call the obscure indefinite sense of the word *matter,* it is plain, by your own confession, there was included no idea at all, no sense except an unknown sense, which is the same as none. You are not therefore to expect that I should prove a repugnancy between ideas where there are no ideas; or the impossibility of Matter taken in an *unknown* sense, that is no sense at all. My business was only to show, you meant *nothing*; and this you were brought to own. So that in all your various senses, you have been shown either to mean nothing at all, or if anything, an absurdity. And if this be not sufficient to prove the impossibility of a thing, I desire you will let me know what is. (D 225–26; emphasis in original)

As this passage makes clear, Berkeley is prepared to infer the impossibility of a sensible thing's existing unperceived from the fact that the denial of C is meaningless or empty. However, such an impossibility would not be any sort of logical or conceptual impossibility. For the meaninglessness in question would derive not from the demonstrated repugnancy between ideas but rather from the fact that there is no idea of an existing unperceived sensible thing.

Of course, the last-quoted passage speaks of matter, and not of unperceived sensible things. But I assume that Berkeley would draw the same inference regarding the latter as with the former provided the same point about meaninglessness holds.

Even if the lack of meaning is the correct way to construe the denial of *C* for Berkeley, one might wonder how that fact can be used in support of *C*. After all, as we recall from discussions of the verifiability theory of meaning a few decades ago, if a proposition is meaningless, then so is its denial. Thus, *C* would be meaningless provided that its denial was—hardly a comforting result for Berkeley. I return to this question later, following a discussion of Berkeley's arguments for *C*. For now I take it that some evidence has been provided for the claim that *C* is not, for Berkeley, a necessary truth if the denial of any necessary truth is or implies a contradiction.

The Arguments for *C*

I believe that Berkeley has three distinct arguments in behalf of thesis 2, or *C*. The first is presented in a capsule and unsatisfactory way in the first dozen sections of the *Principles* and is repeated in a more satisfactory way in the *Three Dialogues*. The two points that drive the argument are (1) that each sensible quality is an idea and (2) that each physical object is a collection of sensible qualities. From these a species of phenomenalism follows, namely, that each sensible object is a collection of ideas. Then, from the truism that no idea exists when not perceived, it is supposed to follow that no sensible thing or physical object exists when not perceived, nor does any sensible quality so exist. By reasoning given earlier, it would also follow that no sensible-quality cluster exists when not perceived, so that *C* would be established.

The claim that each sensible object is a collection of sensible qualities is defended on the grounds that there is no material substance in which such qualities might inhere. The *Principles* version of the argument is not satisfactory, because its first premise (that each sensible quality is an idea) is not at all argued for, but instead is assumed from the very start. That premise, surely, is no truism, yet Berkeley opens the *Principles* by baldly asserting it without justification. He must have realized that this was a serious problem, for he devotes the bulk of the first dialogue to an elaborate argument for this very premise. There he uses a variety of perceptual relativity and other arguments to show of each sort of sensible quality (sound, taste, color, figure, motion, and so on) that it is an idea.

There is much of interest in this argument, and a great deal can be said about its various elements. I will limit myself to a few observations. First, neither of its main premises, those that I say drive the argument, is a necessary truth. Moreover, very little that is essential to the arguments for those respective premises qualifies as a necessary truth. Consider the relativity arguments used in support of the first premise, that every sensible quality is an idea. Premises to the effect that objects appear different under different conditions are contingently true, if true at all. Or consider the case for the second premise, that each sensible object is a collection of sensible qualities. This is defended partly on the grounds that there are no material substances, and I showed earlier that when Berkeley claims that such entities are impossible, he means only that the concept of matter is meaningless, not that it is contradictory. These considerations strongly indicate that even if sound, this first argument does not establish the necessity of C. Thus, we should not construe Berkeley as committed to the necessity of C, or thesis 2, on the basis of this argument.[4]

Another often overlooked argument for C depends on the rejection of abstract ideas. Specifically, there is some evidence that Berkeley accepted the claim that if there are no abstract general ideas, then the *esse est percipi* thesis is true. We know that in the introduction to the *Principles* Berkeley attacks the claim that such ideas exist; this is couched in the form of an attack on some doctrines attributed to Locke. Thus, we would have the following simple argument (the no-abstraction argument):

(1) If there are no abstract general ideas, then the *esse est percipi* thesis [i.e., thesis 2 in the form of C] is true.
(2) There are no abstract general ideas.
(3) Hence, the *esse est percipi* thesis is true.

Whether Berkeley actually presents this argument, as I think, depends on whether he actually asserts or otherwise endorses its first premise. I have presented evidence for this claim elsewhere, and so will not rehearse it here.[5] In some ways more interesting is how Berkeley did (or could) defend this premise. I believe the arguments for it rest on comments Berkeley makes about conceivability, especially this: "Can there be a nicer strain of abstraction than to distinguish the existence of sensible objects from their being perceived, so as to conceive them existing unperceived?" (PR 5). One point made in this passage seems to be this:

>(1a) One can conceive a sensible object existing unperceived only if one can conceive an abstract idea.

But we also know from the master argument (to be discussed below) that Berkeley accepts the claim that

>(1b) if one cannot conceive a sensible object existing unperceived, then the *esse est percipi* thesis (= *C*) is true.

It is clear that

>(1c) if there are no abstract ideas, then one cannot conceive of an abstract idea.

Given what I here refer to as a *de re* reading of the term 'conceives,' these three statements imply the first premise of the no-abstraction argument. And it is clear that a *de re* reading is appropriate, since Berkeley speaks always of conceiving actual objects unperceived, not of conceiving that some sensible object in fact exists unperceived.

De re conception of the sort I have in mind can be clarified by contrasting it with *de re* belief. In the latter case, we say that a person believes of some entity E that it is F (has the property F). Thus, John may believe of the man on the corner that he is a spy. We could have a perfectly analogous notion of *de re* conception. John may conceive of the differential equation vexing him at the moment that it is of type T. And this notion of *de re* conception would be, perhaps, the normal way of thinking of the matter, on a par with *de re* belief. But it is not what Berkeley makes use of, because for him there is no predication included within the *de re* conceiving. Instead, one conceives the thing itself. The analogy would be with nonpropositional direct perception of an object, as when we say, "John perceives O." In such a case, the perceptual verb takes a grammatical direct object as complement. The same holds for the sort of *de re* conceiving made use of by Berkeley. Let us call this nonpropositional *de re* conception *pure*: whatever is the character of one's mental state when one conceives a cup-on-a-table, rather than conceiving *that* there is a cup on a table, or when one conceives a white cup, rather than conceiving that a cup is white.

There is, then, Berkeleian support for the first premise of the no-abstraction argument. And there is certainly support for the second premise as well. I will not review here the arguments against abstract ideas in the introduction to the *Principles* except to say that Berkeley distinguishes different kinds of abstract ideas, and only some of them are held to be entities whose existence would be logically impossible. In particular, the sort of abstract idea relevant to the truth of premise 1 is the abstract idea of existence; it is this sort of idea that is relevant, moreover, to the truth of (1a). It is, thus, the sort of abstract idea Berkeley must minimally reject in premise 2 of the no-abstraction argument. However, although Berkeley finds such an abstract idea the most incomprehensible of all abstract ideas (PR 81), he presents no argument to show that such an idea cannot exist. So, again, the no-abstraction argument would not commit Berkeley to the conclusion that *C*, the *esse est percipi* thesis, is a necessary truth.

The third argument Berkeley presents for *C* is the so-called master argument of PR 22–23 and the first dialogue. This argument, too, makes important use of the notion of conceivability. Berkeley is willing to allow that if one *can* conceive a sensible object existing unperceived, then the *esse est percipi* thesis, or *C*, is false. He notes that this sort of conception cannot be achieved or carried out, and so he concludes that the *esse est percipi* thesis is true. Here is the *Principles* version of the argument:

> I am content to put the whole upon this issue; if you can but conceive it possible for one extended movable substance, or in general, for any one idea or anything like an idea, to exist otherwise than in a mind perceiving it, I shall readily give up the cause: And as for all that *compages* of external bodies which you contend for, I shall grant you its existence, though you cannot give me any reason why you believe it exists, or assign any use to it when it is supposed to exist. I say the bare possibility of your opinion's being true, shall pass for an argument that it is so. (PR 220)

This passage sets up a part of the argument; it is continued in the next section.

> But say you, surely there is nothing easier than to imagine trees, for instance, in a park, or books existing in a closet, and no body by to perceive them. I answer, you may so, there is no difficulty in it: but what is all this, I beseech you, more than framing in your mind certain ideas which you call *books* and *trees*, and at the same time omitting to frame the idea of

anyone that may perceive them? But do not you your self perceive or think of them all the while? This therefore is nothing to the purpose: it only shows you have the power of imagining or forming ideas in your mind; but it doth not shew you can conceive it possible, the objects of your thought may exist without the mind: to make out this, it is necessary that you conceive them existing unconceived or unthought of, which is a manifest repugnancy. When we do our utmost to conceive the existence of external bodies, we are all the while only contemplating our own ideas. But the mind taking no notice of itself, is deluded to think it can and does conceive bodies existing unthought of or without the mind; though at the same time they are apprehended by or exist in it self. (PR 23)

In the first of these passages, Berkeley speaks of conceiving a possibility: conceiving the possibility of a sensible object existing unperceived. If one can do this conceiving, he tells us, he will grant the falsity of the *esse est percipi* thesis. But, he says in the second passage, we cannot do this conceiving, because to accomplish it we would have to conceive an unperceived but existing sensible object, and this is a manifest repugnancy. We can represent what he is saying in a simple argument:

Master Argument, First Version

(1) If one can conceive the possibility of a sensible object existing unperceived, then the *esse est percipi* thesis is false.
(2) One can conceive the possibility of a sensible object existing unperceived only if one can conceive a sensible object existing unperceived.
(3) But one cannot conceive a sensible object existing unperceived.
(4) Hence, one cannot conceive the possibility of a sensible object existing unperceived.

Notice that one cannot pass directly from (4) to an affirmation of the *esse est percipi* thesis, since doing so commits an elementary blunder: (4) is the denial of the antecedent of premise 1. However, the argument can be continued if Berkeley accepts the principle that what is inconceivable is impossible, as it seems he does.[6] Thus:

(5) If something is inconceivable, then it is impossible.
(6) Hence, a sensible object existing unperceived is impossible (from 1, 4, and 5).

From (6) it follows that it is not possible that a sensible object exists unperceived, in which case the *esse est percipi* thesis comes out as a necessary truth.

In this version of the master argument we construe Berkeley as seeking a certain *de dicto* conception, reflected in the antecedent of premise 1, and claiming that a necessary condition for attaining this conception is that one achieve or be able to achieve a certain *pure de re* conception, noted in the consequent of premise 2, in which one conceives the sensible object itself. There is, however, another reading of those passages, one in which the apparent *de dicto* conception— conceiving the possibility of a sensible object existing unperceived— just *is*, for Berkeley, the sort of *pure de re* conception here described. The rationale for this reading is straightforward: PR 22, containing the apparent *de dicto* notion, in effect lays down a challenge, to which section 23 is a response. The very thing one is challenged to do in PR 22 is claimed capable of accomplishment in PR 23. This suggests that Berkeley does not have in mind two different sorts of conception but just one, namely, *pure de re* conception. Exactly the same challenge pattern occurs in the *Dialogues*:

> *Philonous:* . . . I am content to put the whole upon this issue. If you can conceive it possible for any mixture or combination of qualities, or any sensible object whatever, to exist without the mind, then I will grant it actually to be so.
>
> *Hylas:* If it comes to that, the point will soon be decided. What more easy than to conceive a tree or house existing by itself, independent of, and unperceived by, any mind whatsoever? I do at this present time conceive them existing after that manner. (D 200)

The master argument suggested by this second reading of the relevant passages is considerably simpler:

Master Argument, Second Version

(1) If one cannot conceive a sensible object existing unperceived, then the *esse est percipi* thesis ($=C$) is true.

(2) One cannot conceive a sensible object existing unperceived.

(3) Thus, the *esse est percipi* thesis, or C, is true.

Of these two readings, and two resulting arguments, I believe the second is the more plausible as an interpretation of what Berkeley wants.

I do not have conclusive evidence militating in favor of this reading, but still there is some. It emerges later, after the second version of the master argument has been investigated more fully.

De Re Conceivability

Why can one not conceive a sensible object existing unperceived, as alleged in premise 2? We know Berkeley's answer: when one tries to accomplish this feat, one is *eo ipso* conceiving that very object. The natural response is that this makes no difference; the object still exists *unperceived* despite the fact that someone *conceives* it. Berkeley is usually represented as responding to this point with the claim that, no, by *conceiving* the object one thereby *perceives* it. Hence, the object does not exist unperceived. And of course the point is general; no matter who tried to engage in this sort of conception, he or she would in that very process conceive, and thus perceive, the object in question.

If this is Berkeley's reasoning, it certainly seems that he has made an elementary blunder, namely, as many commentators have pointed out, that of conflating conceiving and perceiving. These two mental operations are quite distinct, and Berkeley's argument runs them together.

I doubt if Berkeley is guilty of quite such a notorious error. The reasoning used in defense of premise 2 does not require so wide a claim as

(2a) All conception is perception.

At most the reasoning requires the more modest claim that

(2b) all *pure de re* conception is perception.

In fact, it seems that even (2b) is too strong; Berkeley needs only something such as

(2c) All *pure de re* conception of sensible objects is perception.

This claim, though perhaps implausible, is less so than (2a).

Even so, why would Berkeley have accepted (2c)? In PR 23 he claims that when one tries to conceive a sensible object existing unperceived, one ends up conceiving one's own ideas. He makes the same point, through Hylas, in the *Dialogues*: "But now I plainly see that all I can do is frame ideas in my own mind. I may indeed conceive in my thoughts the idea of a tree, or a house, or a mountain, but that is all" (D 200). So, Berkeley is prepared to accept the view that

   (2d) if one has a *pure de re* conception of a sensible object, then one *de re* conceives an idea.

If we assume that the idea attended to is not an abstract idea, as indeed Berkeley would, then it is easy to see why he would infer (2c) from (2d). Berkeley holds that perceiving *just is* the having of the right sorts of ideas, and given this and (2d), (2c) follows directly.

We can be more specific. What (2d) and the claim that perceiving just is the having of the right sorts of ideas show is that

   (2e) if one has a *pure de re* conception of a sensible object, then one perceives an idea.

Nevertheless, what Berkeley seems to require is something different, namely,

   (2f) If one has a *pure de re* conception of a sensible object, then one perceives that object.

What is needed is some way to relate these last two statements to each other.

The reasoning Berkeley seems to be using in the passages quoted from the *Principles* and *Dialogues* is that *de re* conception of a sensible object inexorably involves perceiving an idea, and the perception of that idea is, as well, the perception of that object. Then, consider trying *de re* to conceive a sensible object existing unperceived. By (2d) one thereby *de re* conceives an idea, and thus, by (2e), one perceives that idea. But then, given the points just made, perception of that idea just is perception of the sensible object in question, in which case it does not qualify as unperceived. Thus, premise 2 of the second version of the master argument is established.

With this reasoning, we still have Berkeley making a serious mistake regarding conception and perception, for we have him accepting the claim that

(2g) if one has a *pure de re* conception of a sensible object, then one perceives an idea, and perception of this idea constitutes perception of that sensible object.

Given (2g), Berkeley has no way to distinguish effectively between imagining an object and perceiving it.[7] But we can see why he is driven to such a conclusion, at least in a way that we could not with (2a). The theory of ideas, that is, the theory that perception not only includes but is actually constituted by the having of appropriate ideas, together with the view that *de re* conceiving of objects requires that one have appropriate ideas, leads directly to this result. In this respect, acceptance of (2g) on Berkeley's part is not quite the egregious error that acceptance of (2a) would be.

Impossible Performances

On the account presented thus far, we see that for Berkeley any attempt to have a *pure de re* conception of an unperceived existent sensible object is doomed to fail. The reason is clear: the very attempt to engage in this sort of conception guarantees its own failure. The sense of 'guarantees' here is worth noting. The very event or activity of attempting *de re* to conceive an unperceived existent sensible object *is* the perception of that object. The attempt, then, is self-defeating. We can even to some extent see why Berkeley speaks of contradictions in this context. For suppose one does attempt the relevant conception. Then one would be *de re* conceiving an existent sensible object, and that very object, *ex hypothesi,* would be unperceived. But *de re* conception of that object, given (2g), is perception of that object. Such an object would thus be both perceived and unperceived. Small wonder that Berkeley speaks of impossibility in this context.

But notice where the impossibility lies. The proposition expressed by 'Person S *de re* conceives an existent but unperceived sensible object' does not of itself imply a contradiction. Instead, it is the conjunction of this proposition and (2g) that implies a contradiction; hence, this conjunction is inconsistent. From this, of course, we cannot infer that either conjunct is inconsistent. Indeed, we know the contrary. We have just noted that the first conjunct does not imply a contradiction, and surely (2g) is contingent. Thus, the 'cannot' in premise 2 of the second version of the master argument is not a logical 'cannot.'

What, then, shall we say of that premise? A clue is provided by a passage from the second dialogue: "The things, I say, immediately perceived are ideas, or sensations, call them what you will. But how can any idea or sensation exist in, or be produced by anything but a mind or spirit? This indeed is inconceivable; and to assert that which is inconceivable is to talk nonsense: is it not?" (D 215). Here we find that, as Berkeley sees it, inconceivability implies nonsense or meaningless. So were we to consider premise 2, we would infer that the proposition expressed by 'Some sensible object exists but is unperceived' would count as meaningless.[8] It is this that lies behind premise 2.

However, should we not then say that the proposition expressed by 'No sensible object exists unperceived,' which is equivalent to *C*, is also meaningless on the grounds, mentioned earlier, that if a proposition is meaningless then so is its denial? To help answer as Berkeley might, it is useful to look again at the end of the second dialogue:

> *Phil:* Now in that which you call the obscure indefinite sense of the word *matter*, it is plain, by your own confession, there was included no idea at all, no sense except an unknown sense, which is the same as none. . . . My business was to shew that you meant *nothing*; and this you were brought to own. So that in all your various senses, you have been shewed either to mean nothing at all, or if any thing, an absurdity. And if this be not sufficient to prove the impossibility of a thing, I desire you will let me know what is. (D 225–26)

Here we find that Berkeley infers impossibility from meaninglessness. Hence, he would also infer this same impossibility from *de re* inconceivability, since the latter implies the meaninglessness of the relevant proposition. Thus, it is impossible that matter exists, and it is impossible that some sense object exists unperceived. Both follow, as Berkeley sees it, from respective inconceivabilities.

Yet to say of something that it is impossible that it should exist is to say that the proposition asserting the existence of that thing is logically false. Is Berkeley, then, simply entirely muddled on all this? Yes and no. Yes, because it is a confusion to run together the alethic modalities with meaninglessness. Logical impossibility is quite distinct from, and does not follow from, lack of meaning. If Berkeley has made this error, he is certainly confused. But it is not clear that he has; rather, he does seem to be groping toward some alternate modality and does seem quite aware of this. Consider these remarks from the second dialogue:

> *Hyl:* But I am not so thoroughly satisfied that you have proved the impossibility of matter in the last most obscure abstracted and indefinite sense.
>
> *Phil:* When is a thing shewn to be impossible?
>
> *Hyl:* When a repugnancy is demonstrated between the ideas comprehended in its definition.
>
> *Phil:* But where there are no ideas, there no repugnancy can be demonstrated between ideas.
>
> *Hyl:* I agree with you.

These remarks come from the same passage quoted just above, in which Berkeley goes on to infer impossibility from meaninglessness. He is there speaking of matter, but what he says carries over directly to the case of *esse est percipi.* We cannot have the relevant ideas, because the *de re* conception in which we would have to engage in order to get them is self-defeating.

We are now in a position to see why the second version of the master argument is preferable to the first: the first would have had us searching for some logical necessity attaching to the *esse est percipi* thesis (C). But we have found that Berkeley's actual arguments on the point lead elsewhere, to something weaker than logical necessity. A focus upon the second version of the master argument helps to bring these points out more clearly. In fact, in the end the examination of the second version of the master argument sheds light on the first. For consider again premise 1 of the first version, namely:

> If one can conceive the possibility of a sensible object existing unperceived, the *esse est percipi* thesis is false.

We noted earlier that the antecedent of this conditional is best read in a *de dicto* manner: what cannot be conceived is that it is *possible that* some sensible object exists unperceived. We noted that Berkeley infers impossibility from inconceivability, and so we said that the *esse est percipi* thesis would come out as a necessary truth on the first version of the master argument. But we now see that this is a mistake, if we take the necessity to be logical, as we did earlier. For as we notice in the second premise of the first version of the master argument, *de re* conceivability is reckoned a necessary condition for the appropriate *de dicto* conceivability, and Berkeley takes the former to imply something other than logical impossibility. So even the first version of the master argument does not show that the *esse est percipi* thesis, or *C,* is a necessary truth for Berkeley, not even when one assumes that inconceivability implies impossibility.[9]

What these considerations show or at least support is that the *esse est percipi* thesis, or *C,* is not understood by Berkeley to be a logically or conceptually necessary truth. Instead, its necessity consists merely in the fact that the attempt to conceive its denial requires that one successfully complete an act of *de re* conception, which conception in this particular case is peculiar in that it is always self-defeating.

Notes

Earlier versions of this essay were read at the University of Illinois (Urbana), the meetings of the Australasian Association of Philosophy in Brisbane, and the University of Western Ontario. I acknowledge helpful comments and criticism from David Schwayder, Steven Wagner, Robert McKim, Lloyd Reinhardt, André Gallois, Robert Imlay, Martha Bolton, and David Raynor.

1. Jaakko Hintikka, "Cogito, Ergo Sum: Inference or Performance?" in *Descartes,* ed. Willis Doney (New York: Doubleday, 1967).

2. K. Marc-Wogau, "Berkeley's Sensationalism and the *Esse Est Percipi* Principle," in *Locke and Berkeley,* ed. C. Martin and D. Armstrong (New York: Doubleday, 1968).

3. The contention made here that Berkeley himself held that God is a perceiver is, of course, perfectly consistent with the claim made by some commentators to the effect that Berkeley's God is not really a perceiver.

4. It is true that Berkeley sometimes speaks of the concept of matter as being inconsistent, or as including or involving a direct contradiction. Although I cannot argue for it here, my view of these passages is that in all cases Berkeley is referring to a contradiction between the supposition of matter and the truth of the *esse est percipi* thesis. If I am right, then, Berkeley is hardly in a position to use the alleged inconsistency in the concept of matter in an argument for *C.*

5. See my "Abstract Ideas and the '*Esse* Is *Percipi*' Thesis," *Hermathena* 139 (Winter 1985), pp. 47–62. For related discussion, see Margaret Atherton, "Berkeley's Anti-Abstractionism," and Martha Bolton, "Berkeley's Objection to Abstract Ideas and Unconceived Objects," both in *Essays on the Philosophy of George Berkeley,* ed. Ernest Sosa (Dordrecht: Reidel, 1987).

6. Kenneth P. Winkler says, "One of Berkeley's most deeply held beliefs is that conceivability and possibility coincide: a state of affairs is conceivable, he thinks, if and only if it is possible." See George Berkeley, *A Treatise Concerning the Principles of Human Knowledge,* ed. Winkler (Indianapolis: Hackett

Publishing Co., 1982), p. xvi. If Winkler is right, then Berkeley also accepts that if a state of affairs is inconceivable, then it is impossible, for this is implied by the principle Winkler cites.

7. On this point, see I. C. Tipton, "Berkeley's Imagination," in *Essays on the Philosophy of George Berkeley,* pp. 85–102.

8. In the passage just quoted, Berkeley infers lack of meaning from *de dicto* inconceivability. I am here assuming that he would draw the same inference from *de re* inconceivability.

9. Another reason to prefer the second version of the master argument over the first was given earlier, namely, that the challenge Berkeley issues and then responds to seems to use just one notion of conceivability.

8

Berkeley's Notion of Spirit

Charles J. McCracken

Ideas and spirits are the two great categories of Berkeley's ontology. Part One of the *Principles of Human Knowledge* examined ideas. Part Two was to examine spirits. But Part Two never appeared. "I had made a considerable progress in it; but the manuscript was lost . . . and I never had leisure since to do so disagreeable a thing as writing twice on the same subject," Berkeley explained to his friend Johnson.[1] Nor was he ever to give a detailed account of his concept of mind or spirit in any later work. His notebooks, however, reveal a good deal about his struggle to get clear about the nature of spirit. His notion of spirit there underwent some notable changes. I want here to trace those changes, then suggest a problem in the view of spirit he finally settled on.

Berkeley's initial concept of mind was fairly Cartesian. Descartes held that the mind has two faculties: the understanding, by which I passively perceive (*percipio*) ideas, and the will, by which I actively assent to or deny them. Further, thoughts and ideas, according to Descartes, are but 'modes of thinking' (*façons de penser*), i.e. of that thinking substance that is the mind (*Meditations*, III and IV; *Principles of Philosophy*, I, 17). Early in his first notebook, Berkeley seems to have accepted much in this view. Thus, he took the mind to have active and passive powers, which he described as 'powers to cause thoughts' and 'powers to receive thoughts', or as those "interior operations of the mind, wherein the mind is active, [and] those that obey not the acts of volition, and in which the mind is passive, [which] are more properly called sensations or perceptions" (228, 286).[2] And rather than taking ideas to be distinct from minds, Berkeley at first supposed them, as

145

had Descartes, to be modifications of minds (or of 'persons' as he called minds, until it occurred to him that by so doing he might needlessly embroil himself in controversy about the Trinity). Thus, an early entry declared, "Nothing properly but persons, i.e., conscious things, do exist; all other things are not so much existences as manners of the existence of persons" (24). Berkeley's early ontology, then, countenanced only one kind of thing: minds—things having active and passive powers (which he later regularly called 'will' and 'understanding', as Descartes had done), while the ideas minds perceive he took to be but modifications or 'manners of the existence' of minds. It is thus not surprising that in many early entries he used 'thoughts' and 'ideas' as synonyms (e.g. 164, 228, 280, 299). Even as late as entry 474, he could still write that "according to my doctrine, all things are *entia rationis, i.e. solum habent esse in intellectu*" (a claim he later repudiated on the verso page, at 474a).

Gradually, however, Berkeley began to see in this division of spirit into active and passive components the basis of a new dualism—one that would divide things into two radically unlike species: wholly active beings and wholly passive beings. He first effected this division in a surprising way: He divorced the understanding from the will, and identified the understanding wholly with its ideas, the spirit wholly with its will. He first ventured on this view in this notable set of entries:

> Consult, ransack your understanding: what find you there besides several perceptions or thoughts? What mean you by the word 'mind'? . . . Mind is a congeries of perceptions. Take away perceptions and you take away the mind. Put the perceptions and you put the mind. Say you: the mind is not the perceptions, but that thing which perceives. I answer: you are abused by the words 'that' and 'thing'. These are vague, empty words without a meaning. (579–81)

This passage brings to mind, of course, Hume's view that the self is "nothing but a bundle or collection of perceptions." But Berkeley was here speaking, I think, not of *spirit per se,* but only of that passive aspect of spirit that he called 'the understanding'. When he uses 'mind' in this passage, he seems to use the word as Malebranche sometimes did, *viz.* as a synonym for the understanding and in contrast to the will. That it is only the understanding, not the spirit as a whole, that he is here identifying with its ideas is suggested by the fact that only a few entries later he wrote, "The understanding seemeth not to differ from

its perceptions or ideas. Qu: what must one think of the will and passions?" (587).

Berkeley effected this identification of ideas with the understanding
by denying any distinction between three things Locke had kept separate: the understanding, the understanding's perception of ideas, and
the ideas the understanding perceives. For Locke, our idea of a white
spot is an "idea of sensation"; but our idea of our *perception* of a white
spot is "the first and simplest idea we have from reflection" (*Essay
Concerning Human Understanding*, II, 9, 1). Now Berkeley grew suspicious of this distinction, asking himself "if there be any real difference
betwixt certain ideas of reflexion and others of sensation, e.g. 'twixt
perception and white, black, sweet, etc.? Wherein I pray you does the
perception of white differ from *white*?" (585, emphasis added). The
idea and the *perception* of the idea, it seemed to him, are the same.
And further, "the understanding seemeth not to differ from its perceptions and ideas" (587).

Here, then, we find him suggesting, albeit in a tentative way, the
identity of an idea with our perception of it, and of the understanding
with (the sum of) its ideas or perceptions. A few entries later, tentative-
ness gave way to conviction: "The distinguishing betwixt an idea and
perception of the idea has been one great cause of imagining material
substances. . . . The understanding [is] not distinct from particular perceptions or ideas" (609, 614). Understanding, perception of ideas,
ideas: these are but several expressions for the same thing (cf. 578,
656, 681).

Only two further steps were needed for Berkeley to reach a thor-
ough-going dualism of idea and spirit: namely, to separate the will from
the understanding and to identify the spirit wholly with the will. He
soon took both steps. Entries 614–615 already hint at some notable
distinction between understanding and will: "The understanding not
distinct from particular perceptions or ideas. The will not distinct from
particular volitions." At 643, he more definitely proclaimed the will
"*toto coelo* different from the understanding, i.e., from all our ideas. If
you say the will, or rather a volition, is something, I answer there is an
homonymy in the word 'thing' when applied to ideas and volitions and
understanding and will. All ideas are passive, volitions active" (643). A
bit later he put it more simply: "The will and the understanding may
very well be thought two distinct beings" (708; cf. 362a, 681).

With will and understanding divorced and the understanding identified wholly with its ideas, all that Berkeley had to do to reach his new

dualism was to identify the spirit wholly with the will; and this he now proceeded to do: "The soul is the will properly speaking and, as it, is distinct from ideas" (478a—this was Berkeley's response to his query at 478, "How is the soul distinguished from its ideas?"). "The spirit, the active thing, that which is soul and God, is the will alone" (712). This identification of spirit with the will alone is stated or implied in many other entries, e.g., 706, 788, 814, 828, 829. Thus he arrived at a fundamental dualism of wholly active beings and wholly passive beings.

But this early version of his dualism was untenable. For if the will and the understanding are separated, then the will will perceive nothing and so will be blind. Berkeley at first embraced this odd conclusion. "I say nothing which is perceived or *does perceive* wills" (659, emphasis added). But he soon began to see its untenable consequences. For if the will *is* the spirit, and yet perceives nothing, then the *spirit* perceives nothing—which is contrary to the very doctrine Berkeley wants to prove, *viz.* that the existence of a thing depends on its being perceived by some spirit. A will that perceived nothing would be blind, for it would have no idea of what it was willing; and a passive understanding—separated from the will—would have no power to direct its attention from one idea to another. Berkeley can be seen mulling these problems over in several entries in which he wonders whether there can be perceptions without volitions or volitions without perceptions (cf. 611–13, 624, 645). At length, he concluded that "without perception there is no volition" (674) and that "there can be no perception, no idea, without will" (833). The upshot seemed clear: "It seems to me that will and understanding, volition and ideas, cannot be severed, and that either cannot be possibly without the other" (841).

These reflections led Berkeley to see that the understanding must be distinguished from its ideas and restored to the spirit. But, eager to preserve his doctrine that spirit is "altogether active and not at all passive" (706), he now sought to construe the understanding as itself active: "Understanding in some sort an action" (821). And what is its activity if not thinking and perceiving? "Thought itself, or thinking, is no idea; 'tis an act, i.e., volition, i.e., as contradistinguished to effects, the will" (808; cf. 777). Of perception he now wrote, "There is somewhat active in most perceptions, i.e., such as ensue upon our volitions" (672a). Where he had once written, "The understanding [is] not distinct from particular perceptions or ideas" (614), he now corrected himself on the *verso* page: "The understanding, taken for a faculty, is not really distinct from the will" (614a).

Earlier he had spoken of will and understanding as "two distinct beings." But now he held them to be the *same* thing, differing only in the objects they are directed toward: "Will, understanding, desire, hatred, etc., so far forth as they are acts or active differ not; all their difference consists in their objects, circumstances, etc." (854). At the end of his notebooks, then, Berkeley took spirit to be an essentially active being, with will and understanding distinguished not even as different faculties or kinds of action, but only by differences in the relations that the spirit, in acting, stands in to its effects. " 'Tis one will, one act, distinguished by the effects. This will, this act, is the spirit, operative principle, soul, etc." (788).[3]

This view, however, was implausible for two reasons. First, the difference between willing and perceiving cannot be explained solely by differences in the *things* that I will and that I perceive—for one and the same thing (e.g. the motion of my arm) may on occasion be the object both of my volition (I move it voluntarily) and my perception (I see it move). And second, perceiving something, in an important sense, is not an *action* at all. Berkeley himself stressed this in the *Three Dialogues*. When Hylas sought to distinguish "the *act* of the mind perceiving" from the object perceived, Philonous asked whether there can be any "act of the mind" save an "act of will" and Hylas allowed that there cannot be. But what act of the will, asks Philonous, is involved when I smell a smell or see a colour? I act, to be sure, when I pick the flower, put it to my nose, and inhale: but it is not in these acts that the perception of the flower's smell consists but in what follows upon them. And in that "I do not find my will concerned any farther. Whatever more there is, as that I perceive such a particular smell or any smell at all, this is independent of my will, and therein I am altogether passive." In the same way, opening and focusing your eyes often depends on your will. "But doth it in like manner depend on your will, that in looking on this flower, you perceive white rather than any other colour?" Hylas grants that it does not. "You are then in these respects altogether passive," concludes Philonous.

Note here that it is *you* who are "altogether passive," and not just the *rose* you perceive. To be sure, that too, on Berkeley's view, is altogether passive, for it produces no effects, including your perceptions of it. But you too are not the cause of your perceiving this smell, this colour; you too are passive in perceiving them. "Since therefore you are in the very perception of light and colours altogether passive, what is become of that action you were speaking of, as an ingredient in every sensation?"[4]

There are really, then, on Berkeley's view, *two* things that are passive in sense-perception: the idea and the perceiver of the idea—for neither is the cause of the spirit's perceiving of this colour, this smell. But Berkeley blurs these two distinct passivities—of the idea perceived and of the mind insofar as it is perceiving by sense—by calling them both "passions or sensations in the soul."[5] But, in fact, the 'passion in the soul' is not the same as the passive idea: for though the *idea* is not, for Berkeley, the cause of my perceiving it, *I* am not the cause of my perceiving it, either. Both ideas and I (insofar as I perceive by sense) are passive. Berkeley's final view of spirit, therefore, is not that of the notebooks, where he sometimes called spirit 'pure act' (701, 828; but cf. 870). Instead, it is that a spirit is in some ways active (when willing things), and in some ways passive (when perceiving them by sense).

Berkeley himself later put it thus: "That the soul of man is passive as well as active, I make no doubt."[6] But if so, what kind of thing are we to take spirit to be? It cannot simply be that "the substance of a spirit is that it acts, causes, wills, operates" (829)—for that will not explain how a spirit can passively perceive. Nor can it simply be that a spirit is a thing that perceives (whose existence *is* 'percipere', as Berkeley declared at 429)—for that will not explain its capacity to act and will. Shall we say that a spirit is the *being* or *thing* that *has* the 'faculties' or 'powers' of willing and perceiving? Or, as Berkeley himself put the question when he still believed in abstract ideas, "Qu: whether being might not be the substance of the soul; or whether being, added to the faculties, complete the real essence and adequate definition of the soul?" (44; at 154 he answered this question affirmatively). On that view the spirit itself would be a bare particular—one that would take 'perceives such and such' and 'wills such and such' as predicates. But once Berkeley gave up abstract ideas, any talk of mere 'things' or 'existents' became anathema; to speak of a "positive abstract idea of quiddity, entity, or existence" was now seen as "a downright repugnancy and trifling with words" (*Principles*, 81).

For a while, Berkeley replaced the view that the soul is a bare particular that has the faculties of willing and perceiving—"a complex idea made up of existence, willing, and perception," as he himself put it when he still accepted this notion (154)—with a "bundle" view of the self. Thus, as we've seen, he at one point proclaimed "the will not distinct from particular volitions" (615). "You ask, do these volitions make one will? What you ask is merely about a word, unity being no more [than that]" (714). And he said the same of the understanding. But this view too he abandoned. "I must not say that the understanding differs not from the particular ideas, or the will from particular volitions. The spirit, the mind, is neither a volition nor an idea" (848–9). The unity of an apple, to be sure, is merely nominal, merely a unity imposed by the mind on a bundle of ideas (*Principles*, 1). But the unity of the spirit is a real, not merely a nominal, unity. Berkeley came repeatedly to insist that "a spirit is one simple, undivided, active being," an "indivisible substance" (*Principles*, 27, 89, 141).

But if spirit is not simply a thing that wills, nor again simply a thing that perceives, nor an indeterminate thing or bare particular of which 'volitions' and 'perceptions' can be predicated, nor finally a mere bundle of particular volitions and perceptions, what is it? The one alternative that remains, it seems, is to say that spirit is a thing whose very essence *consists* in willing and perceiving, that willing and perceiving are not faculties or powers of the soul but its very substance—or, as Berkeley himself put it, that the existence of the soul *is percipere* and *velle* (429a). But how much light does this shed on the nature of spirit? Spirit, for Berkeley, is a simple, indivisible thing, yet one that can be in very different states, and the problem is to understand what sort of thing it is that, though perfectly unitary, can be the subject of these different states, or can exercise these different faculties.

Berkeley himself had a nominalist's profound distrust of attempts to distinguish a thing from its states or faculties. It was this that led him, at 614–615, to try to reduce will and understanding to collections of particular volitions and ideas; this that led him to reject talk of 'a being which wills' or 'a thing which perceives' as "vague, empty words without a meaning" (499a, 581; cf. 829); this that made him loath to speak of spirit as "a thinking substance . . . which perceives and supports and ties together the ideas" (637). This same suspicion caused him, late in the notebooks, to resolve not to mention understanding and will as faculties at all but simply to say they are included in 'all that is active' (848), and still later to write, "I must not say will and understanding are all one, but that they are both abstract ideas, i.e., none at all; they not being even *ratione* different from spirit, *qua* faculties, or active" (871). This same distrust of the distinction between a thing and its faculties led him, in the *Principles*, to denounce the attempt to "frame abstract notions of the powers and acts of the mind, and consider them prescinded, as well from mind or spirit itself, as from their respective objects and effects" (*Principles,* 143).

But once he allows, as in the *Dialogues,* that willing is an active state, perceiving a passive state, he can no longer hold that spirit is nothing but "one will, one act" (788). Instead, he needs to show how a thing that is perfectly simple and unitary can be simultaneously in such radically different states as those of actively willing and passively perceiving. To say it can because its nature consists in willing and perceiving amounts to no more than saying that a spirit can will and perceive because it is the kind of thing that wills and perceives. But that bare tautology goes no way towards revealing what, on the one hand, the source of a spirit's unity and indivisibility is, nor, on the other, what it is in spirit that allows it, though one, to be qualified by very different sorts of predicates.

Perhaps, had Berkeley written Part Two of the *Principles,* he would have shown how to solve this puzzle. But it is interesting that, after losing the unfinished manuscript, he never again tried to write that second part. Was it really that he "never had leisure . . . to do so disagreeable a thing as writing twice on the same subject"? He *did* write twice on the same subject (in the *Principles* and the *Three Dialogues*), and he did find leisure to write works on the topics of the other projected parts of the *Principles* (in *De Motu* and *The Analyst*). Of the topics the unwritten parts of the *Principles* were to treat of, the only one he never devoted a detailed study to was the nature of spirit. Maybe his prudent good sense suggested to him that about this topic it was as well to say no more.

Notes

1. *The Works of George Berkeley, Bishop of Cloyne,* ed. A. A. Luce and T. E. Jessop (Nelson, 1949), Vol. II, p. 282.

2. All numbers, unless otherwise indicated, refer to the numbered entries of the *Philosophical Commentaries,* in *Works,* Vol. I. A lowercase 'a' after a number indicates a later addition to or emendation of an entry. I have modernized Berkeley's spelling and punctuation, and have enclosed words he is mentioning, rather than using, in quotation marks.

3. Cf. MS addition to the *Principles,* 138, in *Works,* Vol. II, p. 10.

4. *Works,* Vol. II, pp. 194–7.

5. Ibid., p. 197.

6. Letter to Johnson, 24 March 1730, in *Works,* Vol. II, p. 293.

9

The Representation of Causation and Hume's Two Definitions of "Cause"

Don Garrett

In *A Treatise of Human Nature* I.iii.2 (entitled "Of probability; and of the idea of cause and effect"), Hume sets out to "explain fully" the relation of cause and effect (Hume 1978; henceforth "THN"). Twelve sections and ninety-five pages later, at the climax of THN I.iii.14 ("Of the idea of necessary connexion") he comes to:

> collect all of the different parts of this reasoning, and by joining them together form an exact definition of the relation of cause and effect, which makes the subject of the present enquiry. [THN 169]

He then proceeds, notoriously, to give not one but "two definitions . . . of this relation." The first definition states that:

> We may define a CAUSE to be 'An object precedent and contiguous to another, and where all the objects resembling the former are plac'd in like relations of precedency to those objects, that resemble the latter.' [THN 170]

The second definition states that:

> 'A CAUSE is an object precedent and contiguous to another, and so united with it, that the idea of the one determines the mind to form the idea of the other, and the impression of the one to form a more lively idea of the other.' [THN 170]

Near the end of Section VII of *An Enquiry Concerning Human Understanding* (entitled "Of the Idea of Necessary Connexion"), Hume provides a similar pair of definitions (Hume, 1975; henceforth "EHU"). Although there are several minor differences between the *Treatise* definitions and their more streamlined *Enquiry* counterparts[1] the similarities are sufficiently great that I will treat the *Enquiry*, not as providing two additional definitions, but simply as providing alternative versions of the same two definitions that occur in the *Treatise*. For in both works, the first definition—which I will call "C1"—appeals to what Hume calls *constant conjunction*, while the second definition—which I will call "C2"—appeals instead to a psychological process of *association*.

Why does Hume provide two different definitions for the same crucial concept? And which definition or definitions—if either—does he regard as correct or adequate? We cannot hope to understand his famous discussion of causation fully without the answers to these two fundamental interpretive questions. Yet although these questions have produced considerable discussion, there has been little consensus about the answers to them. My aim in this paper is to answer them definitively. In the first section of this paper, I will describe the various considerations that make it seem so difficult to determine Hume's attitude towards the two definitions. In the second section, I will seek to shed new light on the questions by examining the problem that the definition of causation poses within Hume's own theory of mental representation and the argument that leads him to the definitions he offers. In the third section, I will develop an analogy between Hume's definitions of 'cause' and his definitions of 'virtue', explain why he offers two definitions of 'cause', and argue that he regards both definitions of 'cause' as correct. I will then conclude by commenting briefly on the importance of understanding Hume's treatment of the concept of causation.

1. Four Interpretations and Their Evidence

Which of his two definitions of 'cause' does Hume ultimately regard as correct? There are four possible answers to this question: "both," "only C1,": "only C2," and "neither." Each of the four alternatives has its proponents among commentators.[2] We may distinguish no fewer than eight different kinds of evidence bearing on the choice among these four alternatives: (1) evidence that Hume endorses both C1 and C2; (2) evidence that he does not endorse both C1 and C2; (3) evidence that he endorses at least C1; (4) evidence that he does not endorse C1; (5) evidence that he endorses at least C2; (6) evidence that he does not endorse C2; (7) evidence that he endorses at least one of C1 and C2; and (8) evidence that he does not endorse either C1 or C2. I will present the various pieces of evidence in that order.

1.1　Evidence That Hume Endorses Both C1 and C2

There are at least two reasons to think that Hume regards both definitions as correct. First, there is the manner of their initial presentation. As already noted, he introduces them in the *Treatise* by announcing that he will "collect all the different parts of this reasoning, and by joining them together form an *exact definition* of the relation of cause and effect" [THN 169; emphasis added]. He then goes on to say that because:

> the nature of the relation depends so much on that of the inference, we have been oblig'd to advance in this seemingly preposterous manner, and make use of terms before we were able *exactly to define them or fix their meaning.* We shall now *correct this fault* by giving *a precise definition of cause and effect.* [THN 169; emphasis added]

Although the forthcoming definition is thus characterized as "exact" and "precise," it so far sounds as though there is to be only one such definition. However, he next asserts that:

> there may *two definitions be given of this relation, which are only different by their presenting a different view of the same object,* and making us consider It either as a *philosophical* or as a *natural* relation; either as a comparison of two ideas, or as an association betwixt them. [THN 169–170; emphasis added]

It seems unlikely that Hume would offer only one of these two definitions as "exact" and "precise" without telling us which one it is. Instead, C1 and C2 are apparently both intended to be definitions of the kind promised, and can be treated as one because they differ "only by presenting a different view of the same object." Although Hume's introduction of the definitions in the *Enquiry* is somewhat more apologetic, even there he implies that the two definitions are the only "just" ones that can be given. He then goes on to say that we "may" define 'cause' either by C1 or by C2, and he confirms their parallel definitional status by applying each in turn to an example (namely, what it means to say that "the vibration of this string is the cause of this particular sound") [EHU 77].

Secondly, Hume explicitly cites *both* definitions of 'cause' in order to justify further claims. In the *Treatise*, for example, he draws four "corollaries" from his discussion of causation. The third of these (concerning the alleged necessity of the claim that every beginning of existence has a cause) is justified entirely by appeal to the two definitions, each of which is quoted in full [THN 172]. And in both the *Treatise* and the *Enquiry*, he cites C1 and C2 in order to justify the two definitions of 'necessity' that he employs in his discussions of "liberty and necessity" [THN 409 and EHU 97]. These two definitions of 'necessity', in turn, play an irreplaceable role in Hume's argument that all human actions are just as necessary as the behavior of inanimate objects. Thus, the evidence so far strongly suggests that Hume endorses both C1 and C2 as correct definitions of 'cause'.

1.2 Evidence That Hume Does Not Endorse Both C1 and C2

Yet there is also a serious reason to deny that Hume endorses *both* C1 and C2. For as J. A. Robinson was perhaps the first to insist (Robinson, 1962), not only are the two definitions not logically *equivalent* to each other, it appears that they are not even *coextensive*. Robinson argues that in order to satisfy (either version of) C1, an object must be the temporally prior member of a pair of objects that instantiates a general regularity; but in cases where instances of this general regularity have not been *observed*, it seems that the pair of objects will not be *associated* in the mind, and hence that the prior object will not satisfy (either version of) C2. Conversely, in order to satisfy (either version of) C2, an object must be the prior member of a pair of objects that are psychologically associated; but in cases where this psychological association results from observation of the conjunction of objects in an *unrepresentative sample*, it seems that the pair of objects will not instantiate any truly *general regularity*, and hence that the prior object will not satisfy (either version of) C1. In short, unobserved regularities seem to prevent the set of causes defined by C1 from being even a subset of those defined by C2, while observed but unrepresentative samples seem to prevent the set of causes defined by C2 from being even a subset of those defined by C1.

If, as it thus appears, C1 and C2 are not coextensive, and if Hume is actually endorsing both of them as correct, then he must either be proposing definitions of two different causal relations, or else contradicting himself by strictly implying that the very same things both are and are not causes. On the one hand, he insists that his two definitions provide "different views of the *same* object" [THN 169–170; emphasis added], exhibit "*the* relation of cause and effect in . . . two lights" [EHU 77; emphasis added], and give rise to senses of causal necessity that "are at bottom *the same*" [EHU 97; emphasis added]. Moreover, he actually draws as a corollary of his discussion of causality the conclusion that all causes are of the *same kind . . .* there is but *one kind of cause* [THN 171; emphasis added]. But on the other hand, it is difficult to accept the view that Hume, at the very climax of his most careful and sustained line of argument, in two different works, effectively contradicts himself within a single page by successively endorsing two obviously incompatible definitions of the same central term. The necessary conclusion seems thus to be that he cannot really be endorsing both definitions as correct; he must either be endorsing only one, or be endorsing neither.

1.3   Evidence That Hume Endorses at Least C1

Hume makes a number of additional remarks—both before and after the definitions, in the *Treatise* and in the *Enquiry*—that seem to imply the correctness of C1. Here is one example:

> We have no other notion of cause and effect, but that of certain objects, which have been *always conjoin'd* together, and which in all past instances have been found inseparable. [THN 93; emphasis added; see also THN 173; EHU 96n; and EHU 159]

Such passages strongly suggest that Hume either endorses C1 alone, or else endorses both C1 and C2.

1.4   Evidence That Hume Does Not Endorse C1

Yet there is also a serious reason to deny that Hume really regards C1 as a correct definition of 'cause'. Near the beginning of his investigation of the causal relation in the *Treatise,* he isolates as "essential" to it the relations of (i) contiguity in space, (ii) priority of time in the cause before the effect, and (iii) "a NECESSARY CONNEXION [which]

. . . is of much greater importance, than any of the other two" [THN 76–77]. Similarly, in the *Enquiry*, he implies that it is impossible to "*define* a cause, without comprehending, as a part of the definition, a *necessary connexion* with its effect" [EHU 95]. C1 mentions priority and (in the *Treatise* version) spatial contiguity, but as Norman Kemp Smith observes,[3] it makes no explicit mention of the allegedly more important element of a "necessary connexion." Furthermore, Hume asserts in both works that in order to understand the idea of necessary connection, we should trace it to the impression from which it is derived [THN 157, EHU 62]; and he eventually identifies this impression as an internal impression of "the determination of the mind to pass from any object to its usual attendant" [THN 165; see also EHU 75]. Yet C1 makes no explicit mention of this impression nor of this determination. Thus, it seems that Hume either endorses C2 alone, or else endorses neither C1 nor C2.

1.5 *Evidence That Hume Endorses at Least C2*

Hume makes at least one additional remark that seems to imply the correctness of C2:

> When we say, therefore, that one object is connected with another, *we mean only that* they have acquired a connexion in our thought, and give rise to this inference, by which they become proofs of each other's existence. [EHU 76; emphasis added]

This passage strongly suggests that Hume either endorses C2 alone, or else endorses both C1 and C2.

1.6 *Evidence That Hume Does Not Endorse C2*

Yet there are also three serious reasons to deny that Hume really regards C2 as a correct definition of 'cause'. First, although C2, unlike C1, does refer at least obliquely to the "determination of the mind" whose internal impression Hume claims to be the true origin of the idea of necessary connection, this mention of "determining" itself gives rise to a new difficulty, as several commentators have noted.[4] For when C2 refers to an object whose idea "determines the mind" to form an idea of (or "conveys the thought to," in the *Enquiry* version) a second object, and to an object whose impression likewise "determines" the mind to form a lively idea of the second, it seems that 'determine' (and 'convey to') can only be verbal variations of 'cause'. Yet Hume is quite explicit that it is not just the single word *'cause'*, but *all equivalent causal terms* that stand in need of definition [THN 77; THN 157; EHU 62; EHU 96n]; and if we seek to define *'determine'*, as a synonym for 'cause', by appeal to C2 itself, the result will be circular. This difficulty renders it questionable whether Hume could have intended C2 to stand as a correct definition of 'cause'.

Secondly, it seems questionable whether Hume would or could accept the correctness of C2 in light of other doctrines to which he is committed. For example, as Wade Robison observes (Robison, 1977, p. 160), Hume refers in both the *Treatise* and the *Enquiry* to "a vast variety of springs and principles, which are hid, by reason of their minuteness or remoteness" [THN 132; EHU 87]; yet such unobserved causes do not produce any association in the mind and hence they seem, by C2, not to be causes at all. Similarly, THN I.iii.15—"Rules by which to judge of causes and effects"—makes one's beliefs about the presence or absence of causal relations subject to considerable criticism and correction; yet it seems difficult to be mistaken about the occurrence or non-occurrence of psychological processes of association and inference in the mind, as specified by C2.

And thirdly, C2 seems to have a number of implications that have struck many readers as rendering it simply too implausible for a philosopher as astute as Hume to accept: (i) that an object is a genuine cause even when it becomes psychologically associated with another solely as a result of observing an unrepresentative sample; (ii) that the existence or non-existence of a causal relation is relative to each individual mind (since objects may be associated in one mind without being associated in another); and (iii) that there would be no causation at all unless there were minds. Moreover, Hume seems to recognize the implausibility of these implications when he writes:

> As to what may be said, that the operations of nature are independent of our thought and reasoning, I allow it; and accordingly have observ'd, that objects bear to each other the relations of contiguity and succession; that like objects may be observ'd in several instances to have like relations; and that all of this is independent of, and antecedent to the operations of the understanding. [THN 168]

Thus it seems that Hume either endorses C1 alone, or else endorses neither C1 nor C2.

1.7   Evidence That Hume Endorses at Least One of C1 and C2

There is considerable reason to think that Hume endorses at least *one* of the two definitions. For in both the *Treatise* and the *Enquiry*, he famously insists that we can neither understand nor meaningfully speak of causation as involving any "power," "force," "real connexion" or "ultimate principle" residing in or between the cause and effect themselves [THN 162; THN 168; THN 267; and EHU 77]. This is a stringent limitation that both C1 and C2 satisfy, and one that would be difficult to satisfy otherwise. Hence, the limitation strongly suggests that Hume endorses C1, C2, or both.

1.8   Evidence That Hume Does Not Endorse Either C1 or C2

Yet there are also two serious reasons to deny that Hume regards *either* definition as correct. First, when offering the two definitions, he notes with apparent sympathy the objection that both of them are "defective" or otherwise problematic because "drawn from objects foreign to the cause" [THN 170; and EHU 77]. Robison, among others, takes these remarks to be an "explicit rejection" of the definitions (Robison, 1977, p. 160).

Secondly, the ultimate endorsement of either C1 or C2 as a definition of 'cause' strikes many commentators, including Oswald Hanfling, John P. Wright, Donald Livingston, and Galen Strawson,[5] as incompatible with Hume's remarks—particularly in the *Enquiry*, but also in the *Treatise*—referring to the "secret powers" or "ultimate principles" that "bind causes and effects together," powers and principles of which we must always remain ignorant [for example, THN 159; THN 169; THN 267; EHU 30–31; EHU 39; EHU 63; and EHU 65–66]. These remarks seem to imply that Hume ultimately recognizes and employs a sense of the term 'cause' that presupposes such secret powers and ultimate principles, and hence is stronger than both C1 and C2. Thus, it seems that Hume rejects both C1 and C2 as definitions of 'cause'.

2.   Two "Neighboring Fields": Definitions of Relations and the Necessary Connection Argument

Each of the four possible interpretations of Hume's attitude toward his two definitions is subject to serious objections. Although each interpretation has been adopted by a number of commentators, the defenses offered for each interpretation consist chiefly of references to some of its strengths—many of which, as we have seen, are simply abilities to avoid objections that apply to other interpretations—with little attempt to refute the objections that apply to the interpretation being defended. The attempt to understand Hume seems thus to have reached an impasse.

When Hume's attempt to understand "the nature of that *necessary connexion,* which enters into our idea of cause and effect" reaches an impasse of its own in *Treatise* I.iii.2, he proposes that we:

> proceed like those, who being in search of any thing, that lies conceal'd from them, and not finding it in the place they expected, beat about all the neighboring fields, without any certain view or design, in hopes their good fortune will at last guide them to what they search for. 'Tis necessary for us to . . . endeavor to find some other questions, the examination of which will perhaps afford a hint, that may serve to clear up the present difficulty. [THN 77–78]

He then proposes the investigation of two such questions.[6] Similarly, I propose that *we* beat the neighboring fields with two questions of our own. First, what does Hume think is required to *define* an abstract relational term? And secondly, what *argument* leads him to offer the two definitions of 'cause' that he provides?

2.1 Definitions of Relations

In *An Essay Concerning Human Understanding* III.iv.5 (Locke, 1975), John Locke offers to show "from the Nature of our *Ideas,* and the Signification of our Words . . . *why some Names can, and others cannot be defined,* and which they are." He then continues:

> 6. I think, it is agreed, that *a Definition is* nothing else, but *the shewing the meaning of one Word by several other not synonymous Terms.* The meaning of Words, being only the Ideas they are made to stand for by him that uses them; the meaning of any Term is then shewed, or the Word is defined when by other Words, the *Idea* it is made the Sign of, and annexed to in the Mind of the Speaker, is as it were represented, or set before the view of another; and thus its Signification ascertained: This is the only use and end of Definitions; and therefore the only measure of what is, or is not a good Definition.

7. This being premised, I say, that the *Names of Simple* Ideas, and those only, *are incapable of being defined.* The reason whereof is this, That the several Terms of a Definition, signifying several *Ideas,* they can altogether by no means represent an *Idea,* which has no Composition at all: And therefore a Definition, which is properly nothing but the shewing the meaning of one Word by several others not signifying each the same thing, can in the Names of simple *Ideas* have no Place. (Locke, 1975, p. 422).

In this passage, Locke makes four claims about definitions: (i) that the purpose of a definition, and hence the measure of a good definition, lies in its showing the meaning of a term by conveying the idea that the term "signifies"; (ii) that the definition of a term cannot simply be one or more synonymous terms; (iii) that all terms signifying simple ideas are indefinable; and (iv) that *only* terms signifying simple ideas are indefinable.

Throughout his discussions of definitions of various terms, Hume implies that definition is an attempt to convey the idea that a term signifies, and hence he implies his agreement with the first claim [see, for example THN 50; THN 77; THN 277; EHU 60; see also *An Enquiry Concerning the Principles of Morals* (Hume, 1975; henceforth "EPM") 201–202. His rejection of synonyms as definitions for casual terms, already mentioned previously, is evidence of his acceptance of the second claim. He also accepts the third claim, as his discussions of the indefinability of pride and humility, love and hatred, and the will, all indicate [THN 277; THN 329; THN 399].[7] Hume is considerably less committal, however, about the fourth claim—i.e., the Lockean doctrine that *only* simple ideas are indefinable. Instead, he writes only that "Complex ideas may, *perhaps,* be well known by definition, which is nothing but an enumeration of those parts or simple ideas, that compose them" [EHU 62; emphasis added]. Elsewhere, he asserts that mathematicians must allow that "equality" is indefinable [EHU 156n, original 1748 and 1750 editions only; see also THN 637], even though, as a *relation* between quantities, an idea of equality must be classified as complex, for both Locke and Hume. Similarly, he argues that there can be no entirely satisfactory definitions of 'straight' or 'curve', even though these are both clearly complex ideas on his view [THN 49].

Why should Hume decline to endorse the Lockean thesis that all terms representing complex ideas are definable? One good reason may be found in a respect in which Hume's theory of mental representation differs crucially from Locke's. According to Locke, abstract or general ideas derive their generality from their own representational indeterminacy. This indeterminacy is the result of separating or *abstracting* these ideas from some or all of the other ideas that accompany them in what he calls "real existence" (Locke, 1975, III.xi.)]. Thus, for Locke, the abstract idea of a triangle is simply indeterminate with respect to the proportion of the sides or angles, and the abstract idea of a human being is simply indeterminate with respect to eye-color, presence or absence of hair, and facial details. Hume, on the other hand, rejects Locke's account in favor of the theory that "all general ideas are nothing but particular ones, annexed to a certain term, which gives them a more extensive signification" [THN 17].[8] Upon noticing a resemblance among objects, Hume claims, we apply a single term to them all, notwithstanding their differences. The term is directly associated with the determinate idea of a particular instance. This determinate idea nevertheless achieves a general *signification*—and hence *serves as* an abstract idea   because the term also revives the "custom" or disposition to call up ideas of other particular instances. We are especially disposed to call up ideas of *counterexamples,* if we can find them, to claims employing the term that we encounter in the course of reasoning. Thus, for example, noticing certain resemblances among a number of animals, I call them all "dogs." A particular occurrence of this term brings to mind the idea of a particular dog, say Lassie, and revives a custom of calling up other ideas of dogs as needed. If, for example, the claim is made that all dogs are collies, my idea of Lassie does not itself provide a counterexample, but I will quickly find an idea of, say, Rin Tin Tin coming to mind, and I will therefore be able to reject the claim.

In this example, my idea of Lassie, though entirely particular and determinate, serves as my abstract idea of "dog." Yet to define the term 'dog', it will clearly not be enough to produce the complex idea of Lassie in another person's mind by naming all of that idea's simpler parts. For as Hume would be well aware, the idea of Lassie can equally well represent Lassie herself, or all collies, or all mammals. (And similarly, an idea of some other dog could also serve as the abstract idea of "dog.") Thus, if a Humean definition of an abstract idea is to succeed, it must somehow convey to other persons the ability to call up *any member* of an appropriate set of ideas of particular instances, so that the "custom" of doing so can be "revived" by later occurrences of the term defined. For the sake of convenience, I will call this appropriate set of ideas of particular instances associated with a general term its *"revival set."* This ability to call up any member of the revival set for a term can be conveyed only by characterizing what all of the instances or their ideas have in common. Now, in Hume's view, resemblance is sometimes, but not always, a matter of having the same kind of simpler parts in common [THN 637]. For example, ideas of eagles and ideas of griffins resemble each other by including the same kind of head; but two colors can resemble each other without having any parts in common. When the resemblance among particular instances is a matter of having simpler parts in common, definitions of abstract ideas will still be relatively easy; when it is not, definition may become more difficult or impossible. Hume finds 'straight' and 'curved' difficult to define precisely because the resemblance among all straight lines and the resemblance among all curved lines are not resemblances based on shared common elements, and hence cannot be easily conveyed in simpler terms.

Let us now apply these considerations to Humean definitions of terms for *relations.* Among all the various terms that signify abstract ideas, we may expect that terms for relations will often pose particular problems of definition. Since conceiving a relation always requires a comparison of two ideas, according to Hume [THN 13–14], an abstract idea of a relation must evidently consist of an idea of a particular *pair* of objects standing in the appropriate relation; and the idea of this pair must be associated with a general term that revives the custom of forming ideas of other pairs of objects similarly related. Because the particular idea that *serves* as the abstract idea will always be of at least two objects, the abstract idea *itself* will always be complex. However, an adequate definition must convey not merely this idea, but the ability to call up any member of the revival set of ideas of related pairs. Hence, there is no guarantee that the relation in which the members of these pairs stand to each other can be specified in *any* non-synonymous terms (i.e., by anything other than another term also associated with the same "custom"), and hence there is no guarantee that the relation can be *defined* at all, in Hume's sense.[9]

There is, however, at least one case in which we can be confident that a relation *will* be definable: namely, when the respect in which the related objects are being compared itself consists in two or more other relations. And such appears, at least initially, to be the case with the relation of cause and effect, a relation which—as we have seen— Hume characterizes at the outset as involving the three relations of priority, contiguity, and necessary connection [THN 76–77]. Indeed, this characterization fails to *complete* the definition of cause and effect only because the idea of necessary connection is itself initially obscure, and so itself in need of clarification. Appealing to his principle that obscure ideas may be clarified by finding the impressions from which they are derived, therefore, he sets out an argument concerning the origin of the idea of necessary connection, at the conclusion of which he immediately offers his definitions of 'cause'. The question of how that argument gives rise to those definitions is our *second* neighboring field.

2.2   The Necessary Connection Argument

In both the *Treatise* and the *Enquiry*, Hume presents his two definitions as the outcome of an argument concerning the idea of necessary connection. He elegantly summarizes the *Enquiry* version of that argument immediately after he presents the two definitions [EHU 78–79]. The argument, as summarized there, may be outlined as follows in Hume's own words:

1. Every idea is copied from some preceding impression or sentiment. [Hume's "Copy Principle"]
2. [W]here we cannot find any impression, we may be certain that there is no idea. [from 1]
3. In all single instances of the operation of bodies or minds, there is nothing that produces any impression . . . of power or necessary connexion.
4. In all single instances of the operation of bodies or minds, there is nothing that . . . can suggest any idea . . . of power or necessary connexion. [from 2 and 3]
5. [W]hen many uniform instances appear, and the same object is always followed by the same event; we then begin to entertain the notion of cause and connexion.
6. [W]hen many uniform instances appear, and the same object is always followed by the same event . . . [w]e then *feel* a new sentiment or impression, to wit, a customary connexion in the thought or imagination between one object and its usual attendant. . . .
7. [T]his idea [of necessary connexion] arises from a number of similar instances, and not from any single instance. [from 4 and 5]

8. [This idea of necessary connexion] must arise from that circumstance, in which the number of instances differ from every individual instance. [from 1 and 7]
9. [T]his customary connexion or transition of the imagination is
   the only circumstance in which they differ.
10. [T]his sentiment [i.e., the customary connexion or transition or
    determination of the imagination] is the original of that idea
    which we seek for. [from 6, 8, and 9]

Although the additional support that Hume offers for some of these
points differs between the *Treatise* and *Enquiry* versions, the ten
claims themselves may fairly be said to constitute the framework of the
argument in both works.

It may initially seem strange that Hume should treat this argument
as the justification for his two definitions of 'cause', since the *term*
'cause' appears only once (in premise 5), and then only tangentially. In
the *Treatise,* of course, the transition from the argument to the definitions is mediated partly by the earlier claim that necessary connection
is one of the three relations essential to the relation of cause and effect.
In both works, however, the transition is also mediated by an even
more specific conception of what the relation between necessary connection and "cause and effect" is presumed to be. Hume expresses
this conception in his tentative definitions of two terms that he reports
to be synonyms for 'necessary connexion'. These are 'power', which
he defines as "that very circumstance in the cause, by which it is enabled to produce the effect" [EHU 67–68]; and 'efficacy', which he
defines as "that very quality, which makes [causes] be follow'd by their
effects" [THN 156].[10]

For Hume, this argument shows that, although we have both an impression and an idea of "necessary connexion" as an *internal feeling*
of "transition" or "determination," we have no impression or idea of
any necessary connection that is an additional relation or quality to be
found *in* or *between* the members of individual cause-and-effect pairs.
(We mistake the internal impression for the impression of a relation or
quality intrinsic to individual cause-and-effect pairs, according to
Hume, because we tend to "spread" this impression of necessary connection onto the objects, much as we ascribe spatial locations to sensory qualities, such as sounds and smells, that have no location [THN
167].) Thus, we have no idea of any additional relation or quality *intrinsic to* the members of individual cause-and-effect pairs by means of

which priority and (in the *Treatise*) contiguity can be supplemented to complete the definition of the causal relation; our representations of the casually-related pairs themselves simply turn out to have no such further content. At the same time, however, the argument also explicitly shows what *is* common, beyond the relations of priority and perhaps contiguity, to the entire set of ideas of cause-and-effect pairs—i.e., to the revival set whose members the term 'cause' or 'cause and effect' determines us to call up. Specifically, each cause-and-effect pair whose idea we become disposed to call up is such that all objects *similar to the first* have been followed by objects *similar to the second,* which results in a determination of the mind to pass *from the idea of the one to the idea of the other.* Thus, it seems that we can specify the membership of the revival set of ideas of cause-and-effect pairs in either of two ways, depending on whether we choose (i) to describe the shared (though not intrinsic) feature of the *pairs of objects* whose ideas become included in the revival set, or (ii) to describe the shared feature of the *ideas of pairs* that are included in the revival set themselves. That is, we can define 'cause and effect' either in terms of the *constant conjunction* that in fact produces the determination or transition of psychological *association* and *inference,* without specifying the psychological process to which it gives rise; or we can define 'cause and effect' in terms of the association and inference, without specifying the features of objects that in fact give rise to it. These two approaches provide two different "views of," or two different "lights on," the revival set of ideas signified by 'cause'; and they correspond, of course, to C1 and C2.

3. The Two Definitions Reconsidered

Our consideration of the two "neighboring fields" strongly suggests that Hume would accept *both* C1 and C2 as representing acceptable alternate strategies for specifying the revival set of ideas of cause-and-effect pairs that must be conveyed in order to convey a representation of the causal relation and hence to define the term 'cause'. This suggestion is further strengthened by an analogy with another notable case in which, according to Hume, we mistakenly "spread" an internal impression onto the objects—namely, that of virtue or personal merit. Here, too, Hume offers not one but two definitions, which I will call "V1" and "V2." On the one hand, he writes that:

[V1] Personal Merit consists altogether in the possession of mental qualities, *useful* or *agreeable* to the *person himself* or to *others.* [EPM 268]

And he explicitly characterizes this as a "delineation or definition" of "virtue or merit" [EPM 277]. Yet he also writes just a few pages later that:

[V2] The hypothesis which we embrace is plain. . . . It defines virtue to be *whatever mental action or quality gives to a spectator the pleasing sentiment of approbation* . . . [EPM 289; see also EPM 261n]

Just as in the case of 'cause', we have a class of objects possessing a feature that produces a characteristic psychological effect on observers. However, in this case the objects are mental qualities of persons, rather than pairs of objects or events; their common feature is usefulness or agreeableness to the possessor or others, rather than the constant conjunction of resembling objects; and the psychological effect is the sentiment of moral approbation, rather than association and inference. Just as he does in the case of 'cause', Hume delineates the revival set of ideas signified by the general term 'virtue' in two ways. First, he provides a definition [V1] that specifies the feature of the objects (usefulness-or-agreeableness) that in fact produces the characteristic psychological effect, without specifying *what* that effect is. He then offers a second, alternative, definition [V2] that specifies the class of objects by means of the characteristic psychological effect on observers (the sentiment of approbation), without specifying *what* feature of the objects actually gives rise to this effect. Significantly, Hume seems in this case quite clearly to endorse *both* definitions as correct; and the analogy thus provides at least some further reason to think that he also regards both definitions of 'cause' as correct.

We have already seen that there is considerable textual support for the interpretation of Hume as endorsing both of his two definitions of 'cause'. This support lies in (i) their manner of presentation, (ii) his uses of them to derive further conclusions, (iii) his further remarks seeming to endorse each of them, and (iv) their conformity to his limitations on what can meaningfully be said and thought about causal relations. On the other hand, there were also a number of serious objections left outstanding to the view that Hume endorses both definitions. Let us now determine whether the insights gained from the two "neighboring fields," and from the analogy with his two definitions of 'virtue', can shed new light on those objections.

3.1   The Incompatibility Objection

First, how can C1 and C2 represent acceptable alternate definitions of the same relation when they are not even coextensive? The analogy with Hume's two definitions of 'virtue' should make us reconsider the nearly-universal assumption that the two definitions are *not* coextensive.

V2's reference to "the spectator" might easily be interpreted as a reference to some *individual* human observer. And so interpreted, V2 defines a "subjective," or person-relative, sense of 'virtue', according to which a given mental quality is a virtue for a particular person if and only if it produces approbation *in that person*. Indeed, such a sense is not without its uses for Hume. It is, for example, the only sense for him in which what he calls the "monkish virtues" of celibacy, fasting, penance, mortification, self-denial, humility, silence, and solitude [EPM 270] could actually be called *"virtues"*: that is, they *function psychologically as* virtues for the monkish, even though people of better moral sensibility rightly (he claims) regard them as vices. Nevertheless, the "spectator" mentioned in V2 has been widely construed instead to be a *generalized* or "ideal" spectator—e.g., one who correctly assesses the consequences of mental qualities, has a well-developed human moral sense, and suffers from no interfering biases such as those deriving from religion, special relations with persons under evaluation, or other eccentricities of perspective. So interpreted, V2 defines a more "absolute" sense of 'virtue'; and—if Hume's theory of moral judgment is correct—V2 so interpreted is *coextensive* with V1.

Now, Hume's reference to "the mind" (or, in the *Enquiry* version, "the thought") in C2 is strikingly similar to his reference to "the spectator" in V2. As before, the reference to "the mind" may be interpreted as a reference to some individual human observer. So interpreted, of course, C2 provides a "subjective," person-relative, sense of 'cause', according to which one object is a cause of another object for a particular person if and only if it is prior (and, perhaps, contiguous) to the other object and psychologically associated with it, in the way that C2 specifies, *for that person*. Such a subjective sense is, once again, not without its uses for Hume. For example, when he discusses the effects of resemblance and contiguity in heightening our sympathy, he notes that "relations of blood, being a species of causation, may sometimes contribute to the same effect" [THN 318]. What matters for the operation of this mechanism is not, of course, whether the object of our sympathy is *objectively* related to us by blood, but whether we *take* him or her to be so related. (If people could not sympathize on the basis of mistaken beliefs about blood relationships, the plotlines of most daytime television dramas would have to be radically revised.)[11] C2, so interpreted, provides a sense in which objects *function psychologically as* casually related to other objects for the inexperienced, the hasty, or the credulous, even though the better-informed and wiser may rightly judge them not to be causally related. Nevertheless, there is no reason why the "mind" (or "thought") of C2 cannot *instead* be construed to be a generalized or *"ideal"* mind or spectator—e.g., one who accurately views all and only representative samples; has a well-developed human inferential mechanism; and suffers from no interfering biases such as those deriving from religion or eccentricities of the imagination.[12] And in fact, it is just this "idealized" construal of C2's reference to "the mind" that is demanded by Hume's discussions of "liberty and necessity." For after using C2 to generate a sense of necessity that requires "the inference of the understanding from one object to another" (as described previously), he goes on to argue that *all* human actions are necessary in this sense—not just those human actions that happen to be observed by one or more human observers. Thus interpreted, C2 defines a more "absolute" sense of 'cause'; and—if his general theory of causal judgment is correct—C2 so interpreted is *coextensive* with C1, at least as C1 is usually understood.

I say "at least as C1 is usually understood" because C1 itself proves to be somewhat ambiguous on closer investigation. Hume explicitly characterizes C1 as involving "constant conjunction" [THN 170]—yet he generally treats "constant conjunction" as something that an individual person may or will *already have observed* at a given time.[13] Furthermore, in two of his seeming endorsements of C1, he writes that:

> We have no other notion of cause and effect, but that of certain objects, which *have been always conjoin'd* together, and which *in all past instances have been found* inseparable. [THN 93; emphasis added]

and:

[W]e have no other idea of this relation [of cause and effect] than that of two objects, which *have been frequently conjoined* together. [EHU 159; emphasis added]

Moreover, in his sample application of C1 to the affirmation that "the vibration of this string is the cause of this particular sound," he writes that we mean only "that this vibration is followed by this sound, and that all similar vibrations *have been followed* by similar sounds" [EHU 77; emphasis added]. Thus, it becomes doubtful whether C1 should be understood "absolutely," as taking within its scope *all* times and *all* places, or whether it should be understood more "subjectively," as tacitly restricted to the *past* experience of a *particular* observer. As-suming the correctness of Hume's general theory of causal judgment, C1 on its *absolute,* unrestricted, reading will be coextensive with C2 on its *absolute,* idealized-spectator, reading; and C1 on its *subjective,* restricted, reading will be coextensive with C2 on its *subjective,* person-relative, reading. In short, the two definitions are coextensive on *either* their "absolute" or their "subjective" readings," so long as both are read in the same way.

It must be granted that Hume does not explicitly distinguish the two possible readings of each definition, nor, accordingly, indicate explicitly which he prefers (although I have little doubt that he would ultimately prefer the absolute reading, at least for most purposes, for reasons that will emerge shortly). But an understanding of his theory of abstract ideas helps to explain *why* he does not draw this distinction explicitly, and why he writes sometimes in terms suggestive of the one reading and sometimes in terms suggestive of the other. I argued earlier that when one seeks to provide a Humean definition of a term signifying an abstract idea, one seeks to convey the ability to call up any of the mem-bers of an appropriate set of ideas associated with that term; and I defined the *"revival set"* of a term as the set of ideas that it is appro-priate to convey for a successful Humean definition. But what exactly is the membership of that set? Is it the set of ideas that I, as the definer, am actually accustomed to revive when I hear the term in question—a set which thus constitutes my own present representation of the causal relation—even though there are members in that set that I would de-lete, and other ideas that I would add, upon greater experience and reflection? Or is it rather the set of ideas that I would revive if I actually had greater or unlimited experience and reflection?

Given the Lockean tradition that my words mean, for me, whatever ideas I actually use them to signify, there is a sense in which conveying the former set does convey the actual signification of the term in my *present idiolect,* even though the latter set better characterizes the ideas that I should use the term to signify, and on which we will ultimately tend, with more experience and reflection, to converge. Moreover, the very distinction between the two readings will often be hidden from me under normal circumstances; it can be disclosed only by second-order reflection on my own fallibility. For if I first try to list the members of the set of ideas that I take to fall under a general term, and then try to list the members of the set of ideas that really *should* fall under a general term, I will of course specify the same set both times—this is just a particular consequence of the tautological general fact that I do presently believe all of my present classificatory beliefs. Only when I reflect more *generally* on my fallibility in classifying will I conclude that the two sets probably differ, and even then I cannot actually *specify* the individual differences in membership. Further exacerbating this difficulty is the fact that Hume's theory of abstract ideas—like Berkeley's—is developed primarily with examples of simple geometrical shapes whose features of resemblance are readily-observable spatial qualities. As a result, *problems* or *mistakes* about what to include in a revival set are, in these cases, either rare or non-existent.[14] For all of these reasons, Hume's theory of abstract ideas prevents him from *focusing* on the difference between the absolute and subjective interpretations of his two definitions, and hence he is not careful to eliminate the ambiguity between them in his writing. As it happens, the phrasing of C1 more immediately suggests the absolute reading, while the phrasing of C2 more immediately suggests the subjective reading. An understanding of Hume's theory of mental representation, as it applies to relations, shows not only how his two definitions can be reconciled, but also why they initially appear to be incompatible.

It may also be objected that, even if the two definitions are *coextensive* (on each reading), they are still not logically *equivalent,* and that this is a reason why Hume would not endorse them both. As we have seen, however, Hume's primary concern is to convey a mental representation of causation by delineating the membership of the revival set, not with doing so in *logically equivalent ways.* To be sure, unless the two definitions are not just coextensive but *necessarily* coextensive, they will yield different results in application to counterfactual suppositions and other possible worlds. Once again, however, the analogy with Hume's two definitions of 'virtue' is helpful. Given human nature *as it is,* the class of mental qualities that are useful or agreeable to their possessors or others has (Hume holds) the same membership as the class of mental qualities that produce approbation in an ideal human spectator. If we treat 'idealized human spectator' *as designating a particular psychological make-up rigidly,* in Kripke's sense (Kripke, 1980), then the two definitions (on their absolute readings) will also be *necessarily* coextensive (i.e., coextensive in every possible world). If we treat 'ideal human spectator' non-rigidly, on the other hand, then there will be possible worlds in which "idealized spectators" have different psychologies, and so they will not feel approbation in response to all and only those mental qualities that are useful or agreeable to their possessors or others. But this is still no problem for Hume. In application to such worlds, he may say, the concept of 'virtue' would then simply come apart, and it would become an arbitrary question whether to say that useful and agreeable qualities would no longer be *virtues* in those worlds, or to say that virtues would no longer produce moral *approbation.* The case of 'cause' is completely parallel: whether the two definitions are *necessarily* coextensive or not (on their absolute readings) depends on whether we treat 'the idealized mind' as designating a certain psychological make-up rigidly or not. If we do, then C1 and C2 will be necessarily coextensive. If we do not, then there will be possible worlds in which idealized minds have different psychologies, and so will no longer associate objects that are constantly conjoined. But again, this is no problem for Hume. In application to such worlds, he may say, the concept of 'cause' would then simply come apart, and it would become an arbitrary question whether to say that constantly conjoined objects would no longer be *causes and effects* in those worlds, or to say that causes and effects would no longer be *psychologically associated.*

3.2   The Objection from C1

Another objection to the interpretation of Hume as endorsing both definitions was derived from the fact that C1 makes no explicit mention of necessary connection or its impression, even though Hume characterizes necessary connection as "of much greater importance" than priority or contiguity [THN 77], and claims that it must be "comprehended" as a part of the definition of cause [EHU 95–96]. We can now see from our analysis of his argument concerning necessary connection, however, that both definitions "comprehend" the necessary connection, in the sense that both specify the set of pairs that are taken to be related by a necessary connection—even though the idea of necessary connection itself turns out to be something other than what was expected. C2 characterizes the set of *ideas* that give rise to the internal impression of necessary connection directly, while C1 characterizes the same set indirectly, by characterizing the *objects* whose ideas give rise to this impression. That both definitions do sufficiently "comprehend" the necessary connection, for Hume, is shown both by the fact that he uses both definitions to generate definitions of 'necessity' for use in his discussions of "liberty and necessity," and by his claim that "this constancy [i.e., constant conjunction] forms the very essence of necessity" [EHU 96n].[15] Thus, I conclude that the present interpretation can also overcome this objection.

3.3   Objections from C2

Further objections to the interpretation of Hume as endorsing both definitions were derived from (i) the apparent circularity of C2, (ii) its apparent incompatibility with other Humean doctrines, and (iii) the appearance that it gives rise to implausible consequences. As we have seen, Hume's general strategy is to convey our representation of causation by delineating the revival set of ideas of cause-and-effect pairs in two different ways—first by appealing to a feature of the objects (i.e., constant conjunction), and secondly by appealing to a feature of the ideas (i.e., association). This general strategy is itself potentially sound, as we can see in his application of it to the closely-related case of the two definitions of 'virtue'. The complication in the case of 'cause' derives from the fact that the relevant feature of the *ideas* happens to be an associative relation which is itself also a causal relation; hence, the *ideas* of cause-and-effect pairs are *themselves* cause-and-effect pairs whose own (second-order) *ideas also* belong to the revival set. It is perhaps because the threatened circularity derives from the specific case of defining 'cause', rather than from the more general definitional strategy, that Hume does not seem to notice it more explicitly. In any case, however, he can identify cases of the mind being "determined" (or the thought being "conveyed") without a circular appeal to C2 in either of two ways. First, he can identify cases of "determination" by the occurrence of the characteristic *impression* of determination that Hume cites as the source of our idea of necessary connection, a remedy suggested by Robison and others (Robison, 1977, p. 160; and Botwinick, 1980, p. 98). Alternatively, he can identify cases of mental "determination" by the *constant conjunction* of the associated ideas. To adopt the second alternative is, of course, to make the application of C2 partly dependent on the feature of constant conjunction mentioned in C1. But it will still be the case that C1 and C2 specify the revival set of ideas of cause-and-effect pairs in two different ways—i.e., by appeal to a feature of the cause-and-effect pairs and to a feature of their ideas, respectively. *Both* definitions will thus still be correct and valuable, and both will serve their intended purposes.[16]

It should now be evident that the two remaining objections derived from C2 depend entirely on its subjective reading. When read *absolutely*—i.e., as referring to an idealized mind—C2 is perfectly compatible with the existence of "a vast variety of springs and principles, which are hid, by reason of their minuteness and remoteness" [THN 132; EHU 67]; and it is also compatible with the existence of, and need for, the "Rules by which to judge of causes and effects" set out in *Treatise* I.iii 15. Indeed, these rules become, in part, rules for making oneself more like an idealized mind. Furthermore, on the absolute reading, C2 implies neither (i) that objects to be conjoined in unrepresentative samples are always real causes; nor (ii) that the existence or non-existence of a causal relation is relative to individual minds; nor (iii) that there would be no causation at all unless there were minds. On the other hand, these are all implications of the *subjective* reading of *C1*, just as much as they are implications of the subjective reading of C2. Thus, what originally appeared as objections to the view that Hume endorses C2 now become, instead, reasons to think that he would ultimately prefer the absolute readings of *both* definitions over their subjective counterparts—at least as conveying the *objective* or *ideal* use of the term 'cause'—if he were to focus on the ambiguity between the two readings. Hence, I conclude that the present interpretation can also overcome the objections specifically from C2 as well.

3.4   Objects Foreign to the Cause and Secret Powers

It now remains only to consider the two objections suggesting that Hume rejects both C1 *and* C2 as defective and/or too weak. The first of these objections appeals to his remarks concerning the fact that his definitions are "drawn from objects foreign to the cause." The definitions are "drawn from objects foreign to the cause," of course, because C1 refers not only to the cause-and-effect pair itself, but also to *"objects resembling"* the cause and effect; while C2 refers not only to the cause-and-effect pair itself, but also to both the "mind" (or "thought") and to the *ideas* of the cause-and-effect pair.

However, Hume does not say in the *Treatise* that either of his definitions is "defective" for this reason; rather, he addresses himself to those who would *"esteem"* them to be "defective" because "drawn from objects foreign to the cause." He challenges those who "express this delicacy" to "substitute a juster definition in its place." Such a definition would, of course, restrict itself to some relation or quality of each individual cause-and-effect pair that did not involve reference to any other objects (such objects as classes of *resembling* objects, on the one hand, or the mind and the *ideas* of the objects on the other). But he has already argued, as we have seen, that no such relation or quality can be represented; hence, any attempt to convey a revival set by reference to such a relation or quality must fail. Thus, after briefly reviewing his argument concerning necessary connection, he reports that he will "repose" himself on his present "sentiments" about these matters "as on establish'd maxims" [THN 170]. Nor does he say in the *Enquiry* that his definitions' reliance on "objects foreign to the cause" renders them defective. Instead, he says that it constitutes an "inconvenience" [EHU 77]—as surely it does, since we can neither determine whether two objects are related as cause and effect without considering other objects as well, nor convey a representation of causation without appeal to such further objects. He does also imply that our *ideas* of "cause and effect" are "imperfect" because we cannot represent any necessary connection as a quality or relation intrinsic to cause-and-effect pairs themselves, as we should like to do, and that a definition that *could* convey such a representation would be "more perfect." But this does not entail that his two definitions, which capture and convey the representation of causation that we actually *have,* are themselves defective or mistaken. On the contrary, they do convey "justly" the ideas that our terms actually "signify," as Hume immediately goes on to affirm.

The last remaining objection concerns Hume's frequent use, especially in the *Enquiry,* of such phrases as 'secret power' and 'ultimate principle'. Whenever he uses these terms, it is in the course of arguing that we do not have any impression of, and cannot form an idea of, any secret power or ultimate principle in the cause itself that *makes* the cause give rise to its effect. Still, his constant reference to our *ignorance* of such powers and principles suggests to many readers that he does nevertheless believe that there is something unrepresentable in causes themselves that somehow accounts for their causal efficacy. It is, of course, un-Humean to say that Hume believes in unrepresentable powers and principles. That is because belief is, for him, a lively idea; and hence a specific belief requires a specific representation of *that which is to be believed.* It is also true, however, that for Hume there is no *contradiction* in the general supposition that there are things or qualities (nature unspecifiable) that we cannot represent. And he never denies, needs to deny, or seeks to deny, that there may be such things or qualities in causes [THN 168]. His repeated and pointed failure to deny the existence of such things is part of the generally more conciliatory tone of the *Enquiry.* But none of these facts count, for him, against the acceptability of his two definitions. For his definitions are not intended to be reductive in the sense of claiming that there are no relations between causes and effects other than constant conjunction or psychological association. Instead, they are intended to capture the revival set of ideas of cause-and-effect pairs that the term 'cause' and its related abstract idea signify; and in doing so, they successfully convey the representation of 'cause' that we actually use, which is the abstract idea for which the term stands. This they do "exactly," "precisely," and "justly," in his view; whereas any phrase to which no definite representation corresponds cannot capture this set. Thus, his remarks about "secret powers" and "ultimate principles," important though they are,[17] do not refute the claim that Hume endorses both definitions of 'cause' as correct.

4. Conclusion

I have argued in this paper that Hume regarded *both* of his two definitions of 'cause' as correct, and that the difficulties which have led most of Hume's commentators to reject this interpretation can be overcome. In arriving at this conclusion, I have appealed (i) to the details of his theory of mental representation (more specifically, to his theory of abstract ideas as applied to ideas of relations); (ii) to the content of his argument concerning necessary connection; and also (iii) to the analogy between his two definitions of 'cause' and his two definitions of 'virtue'.

I believe that an accurate understanding of Hume's attempt to define 'cause' is of particular philosophical interest for many reasons. First,

Hume's two definitions constitute a crucial episode in the history of thought about the causal relation, so that to understand them more clearly enables us to understand more clearly our own place as inheritors of that history. Secondly, Hume's approach to understanding the causal relation remains one of a very small number of live general approaches to explicating that relation. It is therefore important to understand that approach as clearly as possible; and a grasp of the subtlety and consistency of Hume's own development of it makes a significant contribution to that understanding. Thirdly, Hume's attempt to define 'cause' exhibits the close relation between his theory of causal judgment and his theory of moral judgment, and it points the way to a consistent interpretation of the latter as well. This is characteristic: much of the philosophical value in studying Hume is to be found not simply in what he says about particular philosophical topics, but in what he says or implies about the relations between philosophical topics. Finally, the specific resolution I have offered to the puzzle about Hume's two definitions of 'cause' illustrates a more general fact: that the solutions to puzzles in the interpretation of Hume's philosophy are often to be found in a better understanding and application of his views about the nature of understanding itself—that is, in what might nowadays be called his views in "cognitive science." There is an important reason why this should be so. It is because Hume himself operates on the premise that an understanding of both the principles and the details of our cognitive processes will enable us to arrive at better answers to philosophical questions—including, but not limited to, questions about the nature of the most fundamental concepts that we use. He seeks to understand the underlying mechanisms of those cognitive processes unblinkingly, as contingent products of nature, yet in a way that will ultimately refine rather than undermine our deep human commitment to the theoretical and practical outcomes of those contingent mechanisms. His account of our thought about and representation of the causal relation is just one instance of that project, but it is an instance that he believed had important consequences for our moral and religious, as well as our scientific, commitments. Although some of the details of his cognitive science may be outdated, that project itself most certainly is not.

Notes

Earlier versions of this paper were read at Princeton University, the University of Cincinnati, and the University of Utah. I am grateful to the participants for their helpful comments.

1. The *Enquiry* version of the first definition omits the *Treatise* version's reference to spatial contiguity, a reference which the *Treatise* itself treats as problematic (since some causes and effects are not spatially located at all) [THN 75 and 75n]. The *Enquiry* version of the second definition omits the *Treatise* version's reference to the inference from an impression to a lively idea; and it also lacks the *Treatise* version's implication that the psychological determination must operate in both directions, i.e., from idea of effect to idea of cause, as well as from idea of cause to idea of effect.

2. Among those who more or less explicitly endorse the answer "both" are Richards, 1966; MacRae, 1969; Beauchamp and Rosenberg, 1981, Chapter 1; and Pears, 1990. Among those who more or less explicitly endorse the answer "only C1" are Robinson, 1962; Ducasse, 1966; p. 142; and Capaldi, 1975; see also Basson, 1958, pp. 74–76. Among those who more or less explicitly endorse the answer "only C2" are Church, 1968, pp. 81–86; and Botwinick, 1980, pp. 92–98. Among those who more or less explicitly endorse the answer "neither" are Anderson, 1966, Chapter 15; Robison, 1977; Stroud, 1977 and 1978; Hanfling, 1979; Wright, 1983, Chapter 4; Livingston, 1984, p. 158; Flew, 1986, p. 74, and also 1961, p. 124; Craig, 1987, Chapter 2; and Strawson, 1989.

3. Smith, 1941, pp. 91–92. See also Flew, 1961, p. 123.

4. See Smith, 1941, p. 401, and Ducasse, 1966. Another version of the circularity objection, involving "necessary connexion," may be found in Whitehead, 1969, p. 163.

5. Oswald Hanfling, 1979; Wright, 1983; Livingston, 1984; and Strawson, 1989; see also Craig, 1987, Chapter 2.

6. These questions are: "For what reason we pronounce it *necessary*, that every thing whose existence has a beginning, shou'd also have a cause?" and "Why we conclude, that such particular causes must *necessarily* have such particular effects?"

7. Although, as I have argued elsewhere, Hume does not draw his simple/complex distinction in the same *way* that Locke draws his. For example, the idea of extension is simple for Locke but complex for Hume. See Garrett, 1985.

8. In doing so, he is of course elaborating on Berkeley's theory of abstract or general ideas, which he praises as "one of the greatest and most valuable discoveries that has been made of late years in the republic of letters" [THN 17]. For another, rather different, attempt to apply Hume's theory of abstract ideas to the topic of his analysis of causation, see Robison, 1982.

9. In fact, he writes concerning the relational terms 'inheritance' and 'contract' that:

> these terms . . . stand for ideas infinitely complicated; and to define them exactly, a hundred volumes of laws, and a thousand volumes of commentators have not been found sufficient [EPM 201–202].

The "infinite complexity" is, presumably, not with the *particular* abstract ideas associated with the two terms, for Hume insists elsewhere that the mind cannot have ideas with an infinite number of parts; rather, the infinite complexity is in the membership of the terms' revival sets.

10. This seeming indifference to whether necessary connection is a *relation between* causes and effects or a relational quality of causes, incidentally, reflects

a Lockean indifference to any distinction between ideas of relations and ideas of relational qualities. It is also manifest in Hume's willingness to say both that C1 and C2 define "a cause" and that they define "the relation of cause and effect."

11. Similarly, when Hume discusses the belief-enhancing capacity of "cause and effect" in the case of religious relics [EHU 43], what matters for belief-enhancement is not whether the object was actually used by a saint, but whether we take it to have been used by a saint.

12. For a tentative step in the direction of such an interpretation, see Robinson, 1966.

13. This point was first suggested in Robison, 1977, p. 160–161, and made again in greater detail in Robison, 1982. See also Jacobson, 1984.

14. Indeed, even actually unobserved shapes are easily classified, simply by imagining them.

15. See also Fogelin, 1985, Chapter IV, for an indication of this point.

16. In fact, a similar dependence occurs in the opposite direction, as well. C1 refers to classes of "resembling" objects. But what amount of resemblance is sufficient? Clearly, we cannot specify any particular kind or amount of resemblance, except to say that it must be resemblance *sufficient to lead to inference and association in the mind.* Thus, C1 can only be further explicated by reference to the feature of ideas that is prominently mentioned in C2. This does not render C1 circular, however, any more than the further explication of C2 by means of the feature prominently mentioned in C1 renders C2 circular.

17. And much more could be said about them than I have said here.

References

Anderson, Robert
1966 *Hume's First Principles,* Lincoln: University of Nebraska Press.

Basson, A. H.
1958 *David Hume,* London: Pelican.

Beauchamp, Tom L., and Rosenberg, Alexander
1981 *Hume and the Problem of Causation,* New York: Oxford University Press.

Botwinick, Aryeh
1980 *Ethics, Politics and Epistemology: A Study in the Unity of Hume's Thought,* Lanham, Md.: University Press of America.

Capaldi, Nicholas
1975 *David Hume: The Newtonian Philosopher,* Boston: Twayne.

Chappell, V. C. (ed.)
1966 *Hume: A Collection of Critical Essays,* Garden City, N.Y.: Doubleday Anchor.

Church, Ralph

1968   *Hume's Theory of the Understanding*, London: Allen and Unwin.

Craig, E. J.

1987   *The Mind of God and the Works of Man*, Oxford: Clarendon Press.

Ducasse, C. J.

1966   "Critique of Hume's Conception of Causality," *Journal of Philosophy*, vol. 63.

Fogelin, Robert

1985   *Hume's Skepticism in the Treatise of Human Nature*, London: Routledge and Kegan Paul.

Flew, Anthony

1961   *Hume's Philosophy of Belief*, London: Routledge and Kegan Paul.

1986   *David Hume: Philosopher of Moral Science*, Oxford: Basil Blackwell.

Garrett, Don

1985   "Simplicity and Separability in Hume's Empiricism," *Archiv für Geschichte der Philosophie*, vol. 67, no. 3.

Hanfling, Oswald

1979   "Hume's Idea of Necessary Connection," *Philosophy*, vol. 54.

Hume, David

1975   *Enquiries Concerning Human Understanding and Concerning the Principles of Morals*, edited by L. A. Selby-Bigge, third edition revised by P. H. Nidditch, Oxford: Clarendon Press.

Hume, David

1978   *A Treatise of Human Nature*, edited by L. A. Selby-Bigge, second edition revised by P. H. Nidditch, Oxford: Clarendon Press.

Jacobsen, Anne Jaap

1984   "Does Hume Hold a Regularity Theory?" *History of Philosophy Quarterly*, vol. 1.

Kripke, Saul

1980   *Naming and Necessity*, Cambridge, Mass.: Harvard University Press.

Livingston, Donald

1984   *Hume's Philosophy of Common Life*, Chicago: University of Chicago Press.

Locke, John

1975   *An Essay Concerning Human Understanding*, edited by P. H. Nidditch, Oxford: Clarendon Press.

MacRae, Robert

1969   "Hume on Meaning," *Dialogue* (Canada), vol. VIII.

Morice, G. P. (ed.)

1977   *David Hume: Bicentennary Papers*, Austin: University of Texas Press.

Pears, David

1990   *Hume's System: An Examination of the First Book of His Treatise*, Oxford: Oxford University Press.

Richards, Thomas J.
1966   "Hume's Two Definitions of Cause," in Chappell (ed.), 1966.

Robinson, J. A.
1962   "Hume's Two Definitions of Cause," *The Philosophical Quarterly*, Vol. XII; reprinted in Chappell (ed.), 1966.
1966   "Hume's Two Definitions of 'Cause' Reconsidered," in Chappell (ed.), 1966.

Robison, Wade
1977   "Hume's Causal Scepticism," in Morice (ed.), 1977.
1982   "One Consequence of Hume's Nominalism," *Hume Studies*, vol. VIII, no. 2.

Smith, Norman Kemp
1941   *The Philosophy of David Hume*, London: MacMillan.

Strawson, Galen
1989   *The Secret Connexion: Causation, Realism, and David Hume*, Oxford: Clarendon Press.

Stroud, Barry
1977   *Hume*, London: Routledge and Kegan Paul.
1978   "Hume and the Idea of Causal Necessity," *Philosophical Studies*, vol. 33, no. 1.

Whitehead, Alfred North
1969   *Process and Reality*, New York: The Free Press.

Wright, John P.
1983   *The Sceptical Realism of David Hume*, Minneapolis: University of Minnesota Press.

10

Hume's Inductive Skepticism

Kenneth Winkler

This essay is an attempt to understand—and to appreciate—the following extraordinary paragraph:

> In a word, human life is more governed by fortune than by reason; is to be regarded more as a dull pastime than as a serious occupation; and is more influenced by particular humour, than by general principles. Shall we engage ourselves in it with passion and anxiety? It is not worthy of so much concern. Shall we be indifferent about what happens? We lose all the pleasure of the game by our phlegm and carelessness. While we are reasoning concerning life, life is gone; and death, though *perhaps* they receive him differently, yet treats alike the fool and the philosopher. To reduce life to exact rule and method, is commonly a painful, oft a fruitless occupation: And is it not also a proof, that we overvalue the prize for which we contend? Even to reason so carefully concerning it, and to fix with accuracy its just idea, would be overvaluing it, were it not that, to some tempers, this occupation is one of the most amusing, in which life could possibly be employed.[1]

This is the final paragraph of Hume's essay on "The Sceptic," one of a series of four essays on philosophical "characters."[2] I have heard philosophers question whether these sentences (or any others in the series) can be taken to express Hume's own opinions. This is a good question, but philosophers tend to ask it in the wrong spirit, making the cozy assumption that any sentence in the *Treatise of Human Nature* or the *Enquiry Concerning Human Understanding*, "serious" works of philosophy, *can* be taken to express Hume's own opinion. I object to this *as an assumption* (though not as a working hypothesis,

to be confirmed by its interpretive success): discovering intentions in
a work of "serious" philosophy is, I think, no easier than finding them
in what we now call works of "literature."³ In this essay I will, at least
for the most part, put methodological questions to one side. I will try
to persuade the reader of four things: that Hume is a skeptic; that his
skepticism presents him with a difficult problem; that his response to
the problem is interesting and profound; and that his skepticism, together with his response to the problem it raises, is something that
deserves our admiration, even if we cannot give it our agreement.

On my view, Hume is a skeptic about many things, but I propose to
concentrate here on his *inductive* skepticism—his skepticism regarding expectations about the unobserved. It will be useful to have a brief
summary of the skeptical argument I find in him, but my aim here is
not to defend this interpretation of his argument. It is to defend the
attribution (to Hume) of its conclusion.

i.   Our inductive expectations suppose, as their foundation, that
     the future will resemble the past.
ii. It implies no contradiction that the course of nature may
     change.
iii. Hence there is no *a priori* argument for the proposition on
     which our expectations rest. (Here Hume assumes that if a
     proposition can be known *a priori*, its negation implies a con-
     tradiction.)
iv. All arguments are either *a priori* or inductive.
v.   So (from [iii] and [iv]) any argument for the proposition must
     be inductive.
vi. But in view of (i), any such argument would suppose, as its foun-
     dation, the proposition it aspires to establish.
vii. Hence there is no non-circular argument for the proposition.
viii. And thus there is, in view of (i), no reason for any of our induc-
     tive expectations.⁴

According to Hume we needn't worry about losing our expectations as
a result of this argument. "Nature will always maintain her rights, and
prevail in the end over any abstract reasoning whatsoever" (*Enquiry* 5,
p. 41). The skeptic finds himself or herself "absolutely and necessarily
determin'd to live, and talk, and act like other people in the common
affairs of life" (*Treatise*, p. 269).

1. Hume's Skepticism

It is surprisingly difficult to say what a skeptic is, and it isn't often noticed that section 12 of Hume's first *Enquiry* begins with this very question. It is, in fact, the question that moves the section forward. After observing that there are no *complete* skeptics—men or women bereft of "opinion or principle concerning any subject, either of action or speculation"—Hume writes:

> This begets a very natural question; What is meant by a sceptic? And how far it is possible to push these philosophical principles of doubt and uncertainty. (*Enquiry* 12, p. 149)

In many cases, as this passage perhaps suggests, Hume's uses of "skepticism" can be replaced by "doubt," and his uses of "skeptic" by "doubter." "Skeptical" is trickier. At times it means "doubt-provoking" or "doubt-insinuating," as in the phrase "skeptical arguments." At other times it means "doubt-complying," as in the phrase "skeptical solution" (from the title of *Enquiry* 5). But Hume's "skepticism," as the passage also suggests, is *philosophical* doubt, doubt sustained by philosophical considerations. This means that fully defining "skepticism" will be as difficult as defining "philosophy." I propose to work with the following definition, which will be adequate, I hope, for the purposes at hand: A skeptic with regard to a particular belief is someone who thinks, on philosophical grounds, that there is no reason for the belief. The absence of a reason has, the skeptic thinks, normative bearing, but it isn't easy to say what that bearing comes to. The skeptic needn't think that the belief should be abandoned, all things considered. The skeptic may, for example, hold the belief on faith, much as the narrator of *Enquiry* 11 claims to believe in providence and a future state. Yet from a certain point of view—the point of view of "reason"— the belief (according to the skeptic) should not be held. Whether it should not be held, period, depends on the relative authority of the point of view.

I have referred to the point of view as the point of view of "reason," and a fully adequate definition of skepticism would tell us what that point of view is. (From the fact that it is so hard to refute a skeptic, people sometimes infer that it must be easy to be one. Perhaps it is. But it isn't easy to be a self-conscious skeptic—one who is aware of himself or herself as a skeptic, and therefore has articulate beliefs about the nature of philosophy, and about the point of view from which the skeptic's attitudes are formed.) It is the point of view of that faculty "which judges of truth and falsehood" (*Treatise*, p. 417), and supports such judgments with good arguments.[5] It is, therefore, the point of view of *true* reason, reason as it should be understood. And this means that it is *not* the point of view of reason as the rationalists construe it. Here I depart from those who think that Hume is, in the end, not a skeptic at all. They take him to believe that there is no *rationalist* reason for believing in the uniformity of nature. And since Hume disputes the rationalist construal of reason, they see him not as a skeptic, but merely as an enemy of rationalism.

This is the view of Thomas Beauchamp and Alexander Rosenberg.[6] They admit that Hume sometimes *seems* to be saying that we have no reason to accept the conclusions we arrive at by induction, but they insist this is no more than an appearance. "The whole point of [Hume's] 'critique' of induction," they say, is to combat rationalism, the belief that *a priori* reason is "capable of deriving sweeping factual conclusions." "Far from being a sceptical challenge to induction," they write, "Hume's 'critique' is little more than a prolonged argument for the general position that Newton's inductive method must replace the rationalistic model of science" (p. 43). They think Hume *does not even raise* the general question of justification to which inductive skepticism is a response. More recently, Annette C. Baier has argued against "any sceptical reading except the one that attributes 'true' meta-scepticism" (p. 55).[7] Meta-scepticism, she explains, is "scepticism turned on itself, diffidence about the sceptic's conclusions" (p. 302). And these conclusions say only that " 'reason' as the rationalists construe it" cannot do what earlier philosophers asked of it; they say nothing, directly, about the enlarged conception of reason Hume himself embraces at the end of Book III (p. 66; see also pp. 96–7). The *Enquiry*'s "sceptical doubts" about induction, for example,

> concern the ability of demonstrative "argument" or "ratiocination" to establish a conclusion such as "this bread will nourish me." It is the rationalist's "reason" whose limits are shown, or perhaps more generally, it is our ability to give any algorithm to spell out how we perform causal inferences that Hume has real doubts about—"we cannot give a satisfactory reason, why we believe, after a thousand experiments, that a stone will fall, or fire burn" (E. 162). . . . His sceptical doubts have their "sceptical solution," and it is the true meta-sceptic who provides that solution. For

just what have we shown once we have shown the limits of "ratiocination" and algorithmic thinking? The mind has other resources, other abilities. "If the mind be not engaged by argument to make this step, it must be induced by some other principle of equal weight and authority" (E. 41). . . . The true meta-sceptic, whose diffidence about his doubts mitigates those doubts, sees how little is shown once the limits of our algorithm-addicted reason are shown. (p. 301)

I want to suggest that these commentators are mistaken, and that something closer to the traditional view of Hume as a skeptic—as a philosopher struck by the limits of *reason,* rather than by the limits of rationalism—is correct.[8]

Before turning to those reasons I want to say a word or two about the context of Hume's account of inductive inference. Beauchamp and Rosenberg write that "the single most important rationalistic view under scrutiny in [Hume's] work is the Cartesian (and even Lockean) belief that there can be synthetic *a priori* knowledge about the world derived from self-evident principles" (pp. 42–3). As it stands this claim is unconvincing, partly because the unifying theme of Locke's *Essay* is that reason *cannot* derive sweeping factual conclusions, and partly because the Cartesian belief *as they state it* (even making allowance for the anachronistic introduction of "synthetic *a priori*") was not a live presence at the time Hume wrote. As Mary Shaw Kuypers explains, "by Hume's time . . . it was the common opinion that the a priori method of Descartes had reversed the proper order of investigation and that Newton had shown the only true way to validate scientific results."[9]

Yet there is something in what Beauchamp and Rosenberg are saying; our task is to isolate and clarify it. We can do so, I think, if we turn our attention to the notion of *intelligibility.* Much of Hume's philosophy is an attack on a certain employment of this notion, an employment illustrated by such claims as, "the only intelligible way in which bodies can operate is by impulse." (This claim is borrowed, with some modification, from Locke's *Essay.*) To say that something is an intelligible view of a subject matter is to say that its truth is *comprehensible.* This (according to the early modern philosophers who made such claims) gives us an *a priori* reason for preferring it to rival hypotheses that are unintelligible.[10] Such affirmations of intelligibility are fairly common not only among so-called rationalists such as Descartes, Malebranche, and Leibniz, but among so-called empiricists such as Boyle, Locke, and Berkeley. Locke for example wholeheartedly agrees that we cannot arrive *a priori* at sweeping factual conclusions, and he would agree with the Hume of Beauchamp and Rosenberg that the inductive method (as exemplified by Newton) is the only proper method in natural philosophy. But Locke accepts corpuscularian mechanism (and the distinction between primary and secondary qualities on which it rests) at least partly because he finds it more intelligible than its rivals. That Hume is suspicious of such arguments is suggested by some remarks he makes at the end of the final volume of his *History*. He writes there that Boyle "was a great partisan of the mechanical philosophy; a theory which, by discovering some of the secrets of nature, and allowing us to imagine the rest, is so agreeable to the natural vanity and curiosity of men."[11] Newton, on the other hand, while he seemed "to draw off the veil from some of the mysteries of nature, . . . showed at the same time the imperfections of the mechanical philosophy; and thereby restored her ultimate secrets to that obscurity in which they ever did and ever will remain" (volume 6, p. 329). Newton tried but failed to account for gravitational attraction by mechanical means. (Hume takes note of the attempt in a footnote to *Enquiry* 7). The proper response to Newton's failure (and the similar failures of others) is not, Hume thinks, to insist that some such account must succeed, but to recognize that gravity, like elasticity, cohesion of parts, and communication of motion by impulse, may be a brute fact—one we can accept, but never comprehend. "The most perfect philosophy of the natural kind only staves off our ignorance a little longer" (*Enquiry* 4).

As far as Hume is concerned, the only legitimate employment of intelligibility equates it with consistency. If we abstract from experience, anything can be the cause of anything; all consistent views of a subject matter are equally intelligible, and all are equally arbitrary. Hence there is no such thing as (non-zero or non-unary) probability antecedent to experience. Hume's target, then, is not exactly *Cartesian* rationalism, but any view making the appeal to intelligibility that Hume renounces. This might be described as rationalism "in the broad sense"—a rationalism to which Boyle and Locke, in their defense of mechanism, both subscribe.

Nothing I have said so far threatens Beauchamp and Rosenberg's main thesis. But if we turn to Hume's works and ask ourselves whether rationalism, *even in the broad sense I have identified,* is the primary object of Hume's concern, I think the answer will be no. Hume is actuated in part by what can only be described as a purely theoretical interest in the justification of conclusions from experience. His theoretical concern should be viewed not only against the background of rationalism, but against the background of similar expressions of concern. Joseph Butler's *Analogy of Religion, Natural and Revealed,* was published in 1736, two or three years before Book I of the *Treatise.* In the Introduction to the *Analogy,* Butler complains, as Leibniz had done, about the poor state of the science of probability:

> It is not my design to inquire further into the nature, the foundation, and measure of probability; or whence it proceeds, that *likeness* should beget that presumption, opinion, and full conviction, which the human mind is formed to receive from it, and which it does necessarily produce in every one; nor to guard against the errors to which reasoning from analogy is liable. This belongs to the subject of logic, and is a part of that subject which has not yet been thoroughly considered.[12]

The *Analogy* is not a contribution to logic, and Butler raises the problem of the nature and foundation of probable reasoning only to put it aside. But according to Hume himself, Book I of the *Treatise is* a contribution to logic, a study whose sole end, as he states in the Introduction, "is to explain the principles and operations of our reasoning faculty, and the nature of our ideas." In Book I of the *Treatise* Hume sets out to remedy the situation of which Butler had complained, and his discussion of induction is addressed not only to rationalists, but to empiricists who share Butler's theoretical concern with the nature and foundation of probability. Thus in the *Abstract* of the *Treatise* Hume acknowledges Leibniz's complaint that the usual logics are "too concise when they treat of probabilities" (p. 647). "The author of the *treatise of human nature* seems to have been sensible of this defect," he writes, "and has endeavoured, as much as he can, to supply it" (p. 647). Butler's use of "reason" is therefore relevant to an understanding of Hume's. In the *Analogy* Butler observes there is a probability that "all things will continue as we experience they are." He adds,

> This is that *kind* of presumption, or probability, from analogy, expressed in the very word *continuance,* which seems our only natural *reason* for believing the course of the world will continue to-morrow, as it has done as far as our experience or knowledge of history can carry us back. Nay it seems our only *reason* for believing, that any one substance, now existing, will continue to exist a moment longer; the self-existent substance only excepted. (*Works,* volume 1, p. 17; the emphasis on the two occurrences of "reason" is my own.)

Butler uses the word "reason" in (to borrow from Beauchamp and
Rosenberg) "a looser sense approximating our ordinary usage in these
contexts today" (p. 43). If we assume that Hume, in his discussion of
induction, uses "reason" as Butler does here, we will arrive at a very
natural reading of Book I of the *Treatise*. But it will be a reading that
makes Hume an inductive skeptic, because the restriction on the scope
of "reason" that is central to the reading proposed by Beauchamp and
Rosenberg will have been dropped. In the passage quoted, Butler himself is only a step away from raising the problem of induction. Seen
against this background, the passages in the *Treatise* and the first *Enquiry* that have always *seemed* to raise the problem clearly *do*.

My use of Butler to understand Hume does not depend on a claim
of influence. But it is worth recalling that Butler is among the philosophers identified in the introduction to the *Treatise* as putting the science of man "on a new footing" (p. xvii). Hume presented Butler with
a copy of the book, and he excluded a section disparaging belief in
miracles in order to avoid offending him. It is perhaps also worth observing that Butler's use of the word "presumption" both recalls
Locke's definition of probable judgment as the joining or separating of
ideas when "their Agreement or Disagreement is not perceived"—as it
is in (certain) knowledge—"but *presumed* to be so" (*Essay Concerning Human Understanding* IV.xiv.4, Locke's emphasis), and anticipates Hume's observation, on p. 90 of the *Treatise*, that "probability is
founded on the *presumption* of a resemblance betwixt those objects,
of which we have had experience, and those, of which we have had
none" (my emphasis).[13]

Beauchamp and Rosenberg are not the only commentators whose
interpretation of Hume on reason precludes the kind of skeptical interpretation I want to defend here. Don Garrett, for example, is highly
critical of Beauchamp and Rosenberg (Hume, he argues, does not restrict himself to "an arbitrarily narrowed sense of 'reason' "), but in the
end he agrees that in, for example, *Treatise* I.iii.6 (the book's most
thorough discussion of inductive inference), Hume never expresses
"an *evaluation* of the epistemic worth of inductive inferences."[14] Reason, for Hume, is "neither a normative epistemic term (as proponents
of the skeptical interpretation have assumed) nor a term for some narrow aspect or conception of reasoning that Hume intends to denigrate
or abuse" (p. 92). Reason, he argues, is simply Hume's name "for the
general faculty of making inferences or producing arguments—just as
it was for Locke" (p. 92). For Garrett, "reason" belongs to the vocabu-

lary of cognitive psychology, and Humean claims that others take to be expressions of skeptical doubt are either non-normative conclusions within cognitive psychology or scientific reports of feelings. I want to argue, against both these interpretations, that Hume raises the kind of normative question whose presence is denied by Beauchamp and Rosenberg and minimized (if not altogether denied) by Garrett. Because of the differences between the two views, it will be useful to discuss them one by one. I will begin with Beauchamp and Rosenberg.[15] My case against them has two parts: one taking issue with their claim that in the *Treatise*, "reason" means *reason as the rationalists construe it;* the other showing that in the final section of the *Enquiry*, Hume is manifestly concerned with the evaluation of our inductive practices.

At *Treatise* I.iii.6, Hume tells us that even after experience has disclosed the constant conjunction of causes and effects, " 'tis impossible for us to satisfy ourselves by our reason, why we shou'd extend that experience beyond those particular instances, which have fallen under our observation" (p. 91). It is *imagination* that induces us to extend our experience beyond the testimony of our senses and our memory (p. 225, pp. 265–6), and Hume deliberately contrasts imagination with reason in an important footnote on pp. 118–19. "When I oppose it to reason," he writes, "I mean the [faculty, by which we form our fainter ideas], excluding our demonstrative and probable reasonings." Reason is spoken of here as the faculty responsible for *all* our reasonings, probable as well as demonstrative. It is not the reason of the rationalists. The point is important enough to bear repeating in a second footnote, this time in Book II, where the faculty earlier described as "reason" is called "the understanding":

> To prevent all ambiguity, I must observe, that where I oppose the imagination to the memory, I mean in general the faculty that presents our fainter ideas. In all other places, and particularly when it is oppos'd to the understanding, I understand the same faculty, excluding only our demonstrative and probable reasonings. (p. 361)

Reason or understanding, Hume argues in the *Treatise*, is not the ultimate source of our inductive expectations, and to assign those expectations to the imagination, as Hume does, is to cancel any prospect of their justification, as Hume makes clear in another passage in I.iii.6:

> I ask, why in other instances you presume that the same power still exists, merely upon the appearance of these qualities? Your appeal to past expe-

rience decides nothing in the present case; and at the utmost can only prove, that that very object, which produc'd any other, was at that very instant endow'd with such a power; but can never prove, that the same power must continue in the same objection or collection of sensible qualities; much less, that a like power is always conjoin'd with like sensible qualities. Shou'd it be said, that we have experience, that the same power continues united with the same object, and that like objects are endow'd with like powers, I wou'd renew my question, *why from this experience we form any conclusion beyond those past instances, of which we have had experience.* If you answer this question in the same manner as the preceding, your answer still gives occasion to a new question of the same kind, even *in infinitum;* which clearly proves, that the foregoing reasoning had no just foundation. (p. 91)[16]

Hume's own *Abstract* of the *Treatise* provides further evidence that he is raising a question of justification, and arguing that the answer to the question is negative.[17] There Hume reaches the conclusion that Adam—a man "created in the full vigour of understanding" but "without experience" (p. 650)—would not be able to *demonstrate* that the course of nature must remain the same (p. 651). The reason Hume gives is familiar: "What is possible can never be demonstrated to be false; and 'tis possible the course of nature may change, since we can conceive such a change" (p. 651). But "I will go farther," he continues, and assert

that he could not so much as prove by any *probable* arguments, that the future must be conformable to the past. All probable arguments are built on the supposition, that there is this conformity betwixt the future and the past, and therefore can never prove it. This conformity is a *matter of fact,* and if it must be proved, will admit of no proof but from experience. But our experience in the past can be a proof of nothing for the future, but upon a supposition, that there is a resemblance betwixt them. This therefore is a point, which can admit of no proof at all, and which we take for granted without any proof. (pp. 651–2)

Proof, here, does not mean demonstration; in the eighteenth century the two were often distinguished. Here it means "non-demonstrative argument."[18]

In the next paragraph we are told

we are determined by CUSTOM alone to suppose the future conformable to the past. . . . There is nothing in . . . objects, abstractly considered, and independent of experience, which leads me to form any such conclusion: and even after I have had experience of many repeated effects of this kind, there is no argument, which determines me to suppose, that the effect will be conformable to past experience. The powers, by which bodies operate, are entirely unknown. We perceive only their sensible qualities: and what *reason* have we to think, that the same powers will always be conjoined with the same sensible qualities? . . . 'Tis not, therefore, reason which is the guide of life, but custom. That alone determines the mind, in all instances, to suppose the future conformable to the past. However easy this step may seem, reason would never, to all eternity, be able to make it. (p. 652)

Surely "reason" here is not confined to *a priori* reason. The word is clearly intended to pick up the earlier occurrence of *proof* as well as that of *demonstration.* There is no *argument* or *reason* (in *our* sense of "reason") for the connecting proposition; and since "our experience in the past can be a proof of nothing for the future, but upon a supposition, that there is a resemblance betwixt them," past experience does not give us a *reason* (in our sense of "reason") for any particular inductive expectation.

A skeptical reading of Hume on induction is strongly supported by *Enquiry* 12, by its overall structure as well as its details. The most significant divisions in *Enquiry* 12 are *not* the ones corresponding to Hume's three labeled parts, and a reader who pays too much attention to those labels is likely to lose a proper sense of the whole. The largest division of thematic significance is a division between *antecedent* skepticism, a topic confined to the first two pages of the part Hume labels "I," and *consequent* skepticism, a topic that spans all three parts. Antecedent skepticism is skepticism *"antecedent* to all study and philosophy" (p. 149); the most prominent example is the methodological skepticism of Descartes, which Hume dismisses as unattainable and in any event incurable (p. 150). A more moderate version of antecedent skepticism, which recommends clarity and self-evidence in principles, caution in the derivation of conclusions, and accuracy in the examination of consequences, is praised by Hume as "a necessary preparative to the study of philosophy" (p. 150).

Consequent skepticism is skepticism *"consequent* to science and enquiry, when men are supposed to have discovered, either the absolute fallacious of their mental faculties, or their unfitness to reach any fixed determination in all these curious subjects of speculation, about which they are commonly employed" (p. 150). "Science and enquiry" is understood by Hume to be quite broad; it covers not only inductive inquiry but the philosophical inquiry undertaken by Berkeley in his discussion of the senses, and by Berkeley and Bayle in their discussions of space. Consequent skepticism regarding the evidence of sense is discussed in Part I. The discussion of consequent skepticism regarding reasonings begins with Part II. The distinction between abstract reasoning and moral reasoning (i.e., reasoning concerning matters of fact) creates a further division in the text, marked by italics: skepticism regarding *abstract* reasoning is discussed in Part II (beginning on p. 156), and skepticism regarding *moral* reasoning is discussed in Parts II and III (beginning on p. 158). Hume classifies consequent skepticism regarding moral reasoning as either *Pyrrhonian* (and *"excessive"*) or *academical* (or *"mitigated"*). He argues in Parts II and III that Pyrrhonian skepticism is neither durable nor useful, but he defends mitigated skepticism as a species of doubt that rightly encourages us to be modest, and to confine our inquiries to matters of common life and experience.

The architectonic of *Enquiry* 12 clearly indicates that Hume wanted the section to be seen as divided, but, I think, as a divided *whole.* A certain general topic is covered in all three labeled parts, and the treatment of skepticism regarding the senses (in Part I) and of skepticism regarding abstract reasoning (in Part II) should therefore condition the interpretation of the passages on moral reasoning in Parts II and III. All three discussions come under the heading of consequent skepticism. Now questions of justification are, I submit, clearly raised in Parts I and II, and if the discussions in those parts are as closely related to the discussion of moral reasoning as Hume's arrangement suggests, his discussion of moral reasoning should also be seen as raising the question of justification, the *external* question which Beauchamp and Rosenberg take to be foreign to Hume's concerns.

My claim that questions of justification are clearly raised in Parts I and II is easy to document. We are told on p. 150 of Part I that philosophers bring our sense "into dispute." The supposition that the images presented by the senses exist in an external universe is "destroyed by the slightest philosophy, which teaches us, that nothing can ever be present to the mind but an image or perception" (p. 152). "No man, who reflects, ever doubted, that the existences, which we consider, when we say, *this house* and *that tree,* are nothing but perceptions in the mind, and fleeting copies or representations of other existences, which remain uniform and independent" (p. 152). Yet philosophy "finds herself extremely embarrassed, when she would *justify* this new system, and obviate the cavils and *objections* of the sceptics. . . . To justify this pretended philosophical system, by a chain of clear and convincing argument, or even any appearance of argument, exceeds the power of human capacity" (p. 152, emphasis mine). "This is a topic," Hume concludes, "in which the profounder and more philosophical sceptics will always triumph, when they endeavour to introduce an universal doubt into all subjects of human knowledge and enquiry" (p. 153).

The last two pages of Part I are devoted to another skeptical topic, "derived from the *most* profound philosophy," which is even more disturbing. It is universally allowed that such qualities as color, hardness, and heat are merely "perceptions of the mind, without any external archetype or model, which they represent." But the same must then be said of extension, because an extension "that is neither tangible nor visible, cannot possibly be conceived" (p. 154). This "objection," Hume says, goes farther than the last, because it represents the opinion of external existence as "contrary to reason," not merely as indefensible by reason. Hume explains in a footnote that this objection is drawn from Berkeley, whose arguments "*admit of no answer*" (p. 155).

The language of Part I is consistently one of justification: Hume is speaking of skeptics who dispute our beliefs and of philosophers who respond by trying to justify them. The discussion of abstract reasoning in Part II is couched in the same terms. The skeptics, Hume says, endeavor to find "objections" (p. 156). And the objections they find turn out to be very powerful: they throw reason into "a kind of amazement and suspense"—the same attitude of "amazement and irresolution and confusion" Hume had earlier declared to be the effect of Berkeley (p. 155). This gives reason "a diffidence of herself, and of the ground on which she treads" (p. 157). She becomes "so dazzled and confounded, that she scarcely can pronounce with certainty and assurance concerning any one object" (p. 157). The skeptics have raised a question of justification, and reason is dazzled and confounded because it is beyond her power to answer it.

The language of justification is carried over into the discussion of moral reasoning, which opens on p. 158 with another mention of objections: "The skeptical objections to *moral* evidence, or to the reasonings concerning matter of fact, are either *popular* or *philosophical*."

The popular objections turn out to be weak, but "those philosophical objections, which arise from more profound researches," afford the skeptic "ample matter of triumph" (p. 159):

> [The skeptic] justly insists, that all our evidence for any matter of fact, which lies beyond the testimony of sense or memory, is derived entirely from the relation of cause and effect; that we have no other idea of this relation than that of two objects, which have been frequently *conjoined* together; that we have no argument to convince us, that objects, which have, in our experience, been frequently conjoined, will likewise, in other instances, be conjoined in the same manner; and that nothing leads us to this inference but custom or a certain instinct of our nature; which it is indeed difficult to resist, but which, like other instincts, may be fallacious and deceitful. While the skeptic insists upon these topics, he shows his force, or rather, indeed, his own and our weakness; and seems, for the time at least, to destroy all assurance and conviction. (p. 159)

The threat of fallaciousness or deceitfulness would loom only if justification were under discussion. And the argument displays our weakness, and works to destroy all assurance or conviction (however temporary the destruction), only because it leads to the conclusion that our inductive expectations cannot be justified. Hume does go on to say that "no durable good" can ever result from such "*excessive* scepticism"—note that the argument Hume describes as leading to excessive skepticism is an accurate summary of his own argument in *Enquiry* 4—but he does not quarrel with the truth of the argument's conclusion.[19] In fact Part II closes with an endorsement of it: mankind are not able, Hume writes on p. 160, "to satisfy themselves concerning the foundation of these operations, or to remove the objections, which may be raised against them."

When Hume turns to mitigated skepticism in Part III, the excessive skepticism of the earlier section is not left behind. Excessive skepticism is, in fact, the best route to mitigated skepticism. To convince us that our inquiries should deal only with common life, Hume writes, "nothing can be more serviceable, than to be once thoroughly convinced of the Pyrrhonian doubt" (p. 162). Once convinced of the "imperfection," "narrow reach," and "inaccurate operations" of our faculties, we will never be "tempted to go beyond common life":

> While we cannot give a satisfactory reason, why we believe, after a thousand experiments, that a stone will fall, or a fire burn, can we ever satisfy

ourselves concerning any determination, which we may form, with regard to the origin of worlds, and the situation of nature, from, and to eternity? (p. 162)

The inquiry into the origin and destiny of worlds that Hume condemns here is not (or not necessarily) an *a priori* inquiry. Butler's *Analogy*, which is aggressively inductivist, is an example of it. Butler's announced methodology is to

> join abstract reasonings with the observation of facts, and argue from such facts as are known, to others that are like them; from that part of the Divine government over intelligent creatures, which comes under our view, to that larger and more general government over them, which is beyond it; and, from what is present, to collect what is likely, credible, or not incredible, will be hereafter. (*Works*, volume 1, p. 7)

This is the methodology Hume attacks in section 11 of the *Enquiry* Our inability to give a satisfactory reason why we believe that stone will fall or a fire burn would not be of use in curtailing our pretensions if the reason we are unable to give were not a reason in "a looser sense approximating our ordinary usage in these contexts today" (Beauchamp and Rosenberg, p. 43).

Although my observations about *Enquiry* 12 have been directed against Beauchamp and Rosenberg, I believe they also weigh heavily against Garrett's interpretation, which gives the *Enquiry* less attention than I think it deserves. But to be entirely fair to Garrett I need to look more closely at the *Treatise*, particularly the concluding section of Book I, which Garrett discusses in great detail.

Although there is some evidence on the other side, in chapter 4 of his book Garrett makes a very powerful case against a skeptical reading of *Treatise* I.iii.6, taken in isolation from *Treatise* I.iv (and in particular from I.iv.7).[20] I therefore want to concentrate on Garrett's interpretation of I.iv.7, the concluding section of Book I. In chapter 10 of his book Garrett surveys all five of the skeptical arguments that Hume considers in this section. The first of the five arguments—the one that bears most directly on inductive skepticism—is that belief depends on "seemingly trivial idea-enlivening mechanisms that are not 'founded on reason'" (Garrett, p. 208). Garrett argues that the only form of skepticism Hume derives from this argument is that "human reason is . . . subject to many infirmities," and we should therefore use more-than-ordinary caution in regulating our assent (p. 215). "At no point," Garrett writes, does Hume endorse a prescription to the effect that beliefs based (for example) on such seemingly trivial mechanisms "should be *rejected* or *suspended*" (p. 215). In particular, in his response to the influence of seemingly trivial belief-enlivening mechanisms, although Hume expresses "a temporary feeling of diminished confidence," he does not "offer or defend any epistemic evaluation of that feeling nor any recommendation concerning the future treatment of the beliefs that result from those mechanisms. On the contrary, his strictly reportorial language concerning his own sentiments quite carefully refrains from making any such evaluations or recommendations" (p. 215). Garrett reaches similar conclusions about the remaining skeptical considerations surveyed in *Treatise* I.iv.7. Even Hume's readiness "to reject all belief and reasoning" and to "look upon no opinion even as more probable or likely than another" (*Treatise*, pp. 268–9)—the result, according to Garrett, of all five of his skeptical arguments—is no "*recommendation* to reject belief and reasoning," but merely "a cognitive psychologist's report of strong but temporary skeptical sentiments" (p. 232), sentiments that are soon replaced by commitment to an epistemic norm that Garrett calls "the Title Principle": "Where reason is lively, and mixes itself with some propensity, it ought to be assented to. Where it does not, it can never have any title to operate on us" (*Treatise*, p. 270).

Although I share Garrett's view that Hume does not, all things considered, recommend a rejection or suspension of (say) our inductive expectations, I think he asks for more than caution. He asks us to recognize that from the point of view of reason, these expectations do not merit our allegiance. The sentiments that Hume reports in *Treatise* I.iv.7 are expressions of this point of view, one whose authority we continue to feel even if we cannot help but form the beliefs it calls into question, as the final section of the *Enquiry* emphatically affirms.

I would like to offer an alternative to Garrett's reading of I.iv.7, though here I can do no more than sketch it. Hume writes on p. 265 of the section that "after the most accurate and exact of my reasonings, I can give no reason why I shou'd assent to it; and feel nothing but a *strong* propensity to consider objects *strongly* in that view, under which they appear to me." I take it that "it" refers back to the most accurate and exact of his reasonings. He goes on to survey several examples of such reasoning; they show that his beliefs depend on seemingly trivial idea-enlivening mechanisms that are (as he claims in the next paragraph) "inconstant and fallacious." Hume's point in the sentence quoted from p. 265 is that he has no good reason to assent to anything—not even to the very philosophical arguments that portray his belief-forming mechanism as trivial, inconstant, and fallacious. In a similar spirit he says, on p. 270, that he cannot satisfy himself "concerning the reasonableness" of applying his reason at all.

The sentiments that Hume reports here are certainly temporary, but I see no evidence that Hume is enforcing a rigid boundary between sentiments or feelings on the one hand and epistemic evaluations on the other. The feelings Hume reports are, after all, responses to epistemic data (that a propensity is apparently trivial, or inconstant, or fallacious, or contradictory in its deliverances), and they lead us to consider general epistemic strategies (*adhere only to the established principles of imagination,* for example, or *condemn all refined reasonings*). At several points in *Treatise* I.iv.7, Hume moves the discussion forward by enlarging a sentiment or instinctive propensity into a deliberate policy. For example, a "seemingly trivial property of the fancy, by which we enter with difficulty into remote views of things" leads Hume to consider the general maxim "that no refin'd or elaborate reasoning is ever to be receiv'd" (p. 268). The sentiments reported in I.iv.7 are not *mere* sentiments; they are often the engine of epistemic policy.[21] Garrett's non-skeptical reading seems to rest on a non-Humean dismissal of their evaluative significance.

In Garrett's view, Hume's skepticism is sublimated in his Title Principle. Like many of the other epistemic policies discussed in I.iv.7, the Title Principle arises out of a sentiment—the return of good humor. As Hume says just before he introduces the Principle, philosophy itself "has nothing to oppose" to the splenetic and indolent sentiments that urge its abandonment. Philosophy "expects a victory more from the returns of a serious good-humour'd disposition, than from the force of reason and conviction" (p. 270). When good humor returns, the Title Principle is endorsed. But is Garrett right to say that it is the end of Hume's journey?

It does not seem to be so even in the *Treatise,* where after observing that philosophy mixes with the curiosity of strong minds, Hume says that superstition mixes with the novelty-seeking propensities of weak ones.[22] This suggests that mixing with a propensity is not enough to give philosophy the edge. Hume's final defense of philosophy in Book I of the *Treatise* is not, as the Title Principle would have it, simply that philosophy mixes with some propensity, but that it is, in general though not without exception, a safer and more agreeable guide than its rivals (p. 271).[23] We should prefer, Hume writes on p. 271, the "safest and most agreeable" guide, and it is on this ground, rather than on the basis of the Title Principle, that he then "make[s] bold to recommend philosophy," and to "give it the preference to superstition of every kind of denomination." The last word of Book I in defense of philosophy, then, is not merely that it is in accord with some of our inclinations (a privilege it shares with superstition), but that it gives us a surer promise of safety and pleasure.

This is, to my mind, a rather lame defense, not only because of its vagueness and failure to specify standards of safety or pleasure, but because it is not directly responsive to Hume's own skeptical arguments. The curiosity that had once driven him to skepticism returns to Hume just as Book I comes to a close (p. 271), but we are not *then* told what we should make of the earlier arguments. In my view, the *Enquiry* develops Hume's *mature* defense of philosophy, and it is more compelling than the defense that closes Book I of the *Treatise* precisely because it makes use of Hume's skeptical arguments. According to the concluding section of the *Enquiry,* those arguments show "the whimsical condition of mankind, who must act and reason and believe; though they are not able, by their most diligent enquiry, to satisfy themselves concerning the foundation of those operations, or to remove the objections, which may be raised against them" (*Enquiry* 12, p. 160).[24] In view of the "imperfection" of our faculties, their "narrow reach, and their inaccurate operations" (p. 162), philosophy is more "reasonable" (p. 163) than superstitious hypothesizing. Here Hume's earlier skeptical arguments are *recollected;* their skepticism is in an important way preserved, giving us an enduring reason to confine ourselves to common life, and to be modest in our conclusions, even though the more immediate effects of skepticism—amazement, irresolution, confusion—are affirmed to be temporary. Because his final defense of philosophy *incorporates* skepticism (as I earlier defined it), I conclude that Hume is a skeptic.

2. The Problem

Now for the problem. If I am right, Hume is an inductive skeptic. But it is also clear that Hume wants to rank instances of inductive reasoning. He wants to be able to say that some inductive arguments are better than others, and in both the *Treatise* and the *Enquiry* he formulates rules—rules for judging of cause and effect—by which inductive reasoning should be conducted. The problem is this: shouldn't an inductive skeptic take all inductive arguments to be equally bad? If they all rest on an assumption it is beyond our power to justify, by what right can we call one better, or another worse? Inductive skepticism seems to be inconsistent with inductive *discrimination,* and one argument that can be made against my skeptical interpretation is that it renders the *Treatise* and the *Enquiry* inconsistent. It renders them inconsistent, it might even be said, with the very science of human nature they seek to promote, because the basic principles of that science—*every simple idea is a copy of a precedent impression; there are three and only three principles of association among ideas*—are inductively defended.[25]

The problem can be sharply drawn in a particular case. In section 10 of the *Enquiry,* Hume argues that it is unreasonable to believe in miracles. He begins by defining a miracle as a violation of the laws of nature, a fair definition because the theologians he is attacking presuppose it. If an event violates the laws of nature, they reason, it must be caused directly by God, and if he has taken the trouble to intervene on a given occasion, the person apparently responsible for the event (Moses in the court of the Pharaoh, for example) must be acting on God's authority. But there is, Hume observes, uniform experience in favor of every (known) law of nature. There must therefore be uniform experience against any miraculous event. This yields a "full proof" against the miracle, and even if there is also a proof in favor of it (one based on the trustworthiness of the witnesses who report it), "in that case, there is proof against proof, of which the strongest must prevail, but still with a diminution of its force, in proportion to that of its antagonist" (p. 114). No testimony is sufficient to establish a miracle, then, "unless the testimony be of such a kind, that is falsehood would be more miraculous, than the fact, which it endeavours to establish; and even in that case there is a mutual destruction of arguments, and the superior only gives us an assurance suitable to that degree of force, which remains, after deducting the former" (p. 116). Hume then argues that the testimony in favor of religious miracles is always shaky. He concludes that it is unreasonable to believe in them. "Upon the whole, we may conclude," he writes, "that the *Christian Religion* not only was at first attended with miracles, but even at this day cannot be believed by any reasonable person without one. Mere reason is insufficient to convince us of its veracity: And whoever is moved by *Faith* to assent to it, is conscious of a continued miracle in his own person, which subverts all the principles of his understanding, and gives him a determination to believe what is most contrary to custom and experience" (p. 131).

The apparent contradiction between Hume's inductive skepticism and his conclusions about belief in miracles is brought out very clearly by C. S. Lewis.[26] He first summarizes Hume's argument in *Enquiry* 10:

> Ever since Hume's famous *Essay* [on Miracles] it has been believed that historical statements about miracles are the most intrinsically improbable of all historical statements. According to Hume, probability rests on what may be called the majority vote of our past experiences. The more often a thing has been known to happen, the more probable it is that it should happen again; and the less often the less probable. Now the regularity of Nature's course, says Hume, is supported by something better than the majority vote of past experiences: it is supported by their unanimous vote, or, as Hume says, by "firm and unalterable experience." There is, in fact, "uniform experience" against Miracle; otherwise, says Hume, it would not be Miracle. A Miracle is therefore the most improbable of all events. It is always more probable that the witnesses were lying or mistaken than that a Miracle occurred. (pp. 122–3)

But this argument, Lewis contends, rests on a belief in nature's uniformity that no one can possibly justify:

> The whole idea of Probability (as Hume understands it) depends on the principle of the Uniformity of Nature. Unless Nature always goes in the same way, the fact that a thing had happened ten million times would not make it a whit more probable that it would happen again. And how do we know the Uniformity of Nature? A moment's thought shows that we do not know it by experience. We observe many regularities in Nature. But of course all the observations that men have made or will make while the race lasts cover only a minute fraction of the events that actually go on. Our observations would therefore be no use unless we felt sure that Nature when we are not watching her behaves in the same way as when we are: in other words, unless we believed in the Uniformity of Nature. Experience therefore cannot prove uniformity, because uniformity has to be assumed before experience proves anything.

"The odd thing," Lewis then writes, "is that no man knew this better than Hume. His *Essay on Miracles* is quite inconsistent with the more radical, and honourable, skepticism of his main work." If Hume is genuinely skeptical about induction, Lewis contends, he cannot fairly condemn belief in miracles.

Hume sometimes speaks in ways that make the problem very clear. In section 12 of the *Enquiry*, for example, he speaks of the "undistinguished" or indiscriminate doubts of what he describes as "Pyrrhonism, or *excessive* skepticism." He recommends a *"mitigated"* skepticism in which the indiscriminate doubts of the Pyrrhonian are, "in some measure, corrected by common sense and reflection" (p. 161). But what sort of correction can take place if the reasoning in question is inductive? It seems that any condemnation of inductive reasoning should be "undistinguished" or across-the-board.

3. Hume's Response

To solve Hume's problem would be to *insulate* the evaluations he wants to make from the skepticism I think he embraces. And there are passages suggesting that this might be accomplished by the sheer force of nature. In *Enquiry* 5, for example, Hume assures us that we needn't fear that skepticism,

> while it endeavours to limit our enquiries to common life, should ever undermine the reasonings of common life, and carry its doubts so far as to destroy all action, as well as speculation. Nature will always maintain her rights, and prevail in the end over any abstract reasoning whatsoever. Though we should conclude, for instance, as in the foregoing section, that, in all reasonings from experience, there is a step taken by the mind which is not supported by any argument or process of the understanding; there is no danger that these reasonings, on which almost all knowledge depends, will ever be affected by such a discovery. If the mind be not engaged by argument to make this step, it must be induced by some other principle of equal weight and authority; and that principle will preserve its influence as long as human nature remains the same. What that principle is may well be worth the pains of enquiry. (pp. 41–2)

That principle is custom or habit, "a species of natural instincts, which no reasoning or process of the thought and understanding is able either to produce or to prevent" (pp. 46–7). "Nature," Hume writes in section 12, "is always too strong for principle. And though a Pyrrhonian may throw himself or others into a momentary amazement and confusion by his profound reasonings; the first and most trivial event in life will put to flight all his doubts and scruples, and leave him the same, in every point of action and speculation, with the philosophers of every other sect, or with those who never concerned themselves in any philosophical researches" (p. 160). "I may, nay I must yield to the current of nature, in submitting to my senses and understanding," Hume writes in the closing section of Book I of the *Treatise*, "and in this blind submission I shew most perfectly my skeptical disposition and principles" (p. 269).[27]

These passages, especially the last, favor what I will call *natural* insulation: nature protects everyday life from skeptical interference by making us believe that the future will resemble the past. To suppose that a skeptical argument could rid us of the belief is to overestimate the power of reason. If reason is too weak to establish nature's uniformity, it is also too weak to extinguish the belief once we discover it to be without foundation. Hume's argument against the reasonableness of belief in miracles simply takes place after nature has done its work. It makes an assumption that is itself unreasonable, but since it is also inevitable, nothing in the argument for inductive skepticism will disturb those who make the other argument.

This is not entirely satisfying. We do not merely *believe* in the uniformity of nature. We think we are *right* to do so. And so a suspicion of inconsistency lingers: if we continue to say that the uniformity assumption is unreasonable, we shouldn't single out any particular belief for criticism. Our peculiar hostility toward belief in miracles seems to be inconsistent with the skeptical assessment of our belief in uniformity.[28] It seems that we need a more powerful kind of insulation, insulation that might be called *normative*. And something deserving of this name seems to be what Hume has in mind, even in the passages I've quoted.

Our submission to the uniformity of nature is not in fact blind. Nature gives us more than a brute belief in nature's uniformity; it cooperates with human nature to make that belief a norm—one we can identify, reflect on, and to some extent even improve. Here is an outline of the process—the *normalizing of the natural*—as Hume understands it:[29]

Step 1: The commitment to uniformity is established, just as it is in an animal. At this point it might be described as something brute. "It is there—like our life."[30]

Step 2: We become aware of the commitment. (This could take place by introspection, but it needn't. We might infer it by observing ourselves and others, as Butler perhaps did. Or we might become aware of it by noticing that our beliefs about matters of fact depend on it, as Hume does in *Enquiry* 4.)

Step 3: We observe that the commitment is conjoined (not constantly, but reliably) with practical success. (This step in the process could be further analyzed. We observe that the commitment is conjoined with the formation of beliefs we deem "good," in view of their consequences.)

Step 4: We come to see the commitment as a cause of practical success. We therefore approve of it. We come to see it as a virtue, or something like a virtue.[31]

Step 5: We see that people vary in the skill with which they make use of the past. This allows us to arrive at rules, inductively grounded, for judging of cause and effect. It becomes natural to speak of habits conforming to these rules as virtues, because good inductive habits are not possessed by everyone, or by everyone to the same degree. And we may make deliberate use of the rules as we form inductive expectations. Our expectations will then be *oblique* (rule-mediated) rather than *direct* responses to observed regularities.

Note that the process as described is wholly natural.[32] We can now condemn belief in miracles as unreasonable, because it goes against a norm validated by the process. But do we still have insulation? And—a prior question—do we still have skepticism? Don't the five steps show that induction is reasonable after all?

I want to say that skepticism persists because there is another norm, one that our inductive commitment fails to meet. This norm is harder to specify than the one that emerges from the five steps, and its origin in human nature is obscure.[33] I will call it "the love of truth," borrowing from Hume's observation that "every passion is mortified by [skepticism], except the love of truth; and that passion never is, nor can be, carried to too high a degree" (*Enquiry* 5, p. 41). Hume does not explain, here or elsewhere, what the passion involves.[34] There is evidence, though, that it is a passion for finding foundations known to be neither fallacious nor deceitful.[35] Although its origin is obscure, Hume recognizes its tenacity, at least for some. "This skeptical doubt," he writes in the *Treatise,* "is a malady, which can never be radically cur'd, but must return upon us every moment, however we may chace it away, and sometimes may seem entirely free from it" (p. 218). "I cannot forbear," he writes later in the same book, "having a curiosity to be acquainted with the principles of moral good and evil, the nature and foundation of government, and the cause of those several passions and inclinations, which actuate and govern me. I am uneasy to think I approve of one object, and disapprove of another; call one thing beautiful, and another deform'd; decide concerning truth and falsehood, reason and folly, without knowing upon what principles I proceed" (p. 271). The obscurity of its origin is (from the viewpoint of the passion itself) no objection to it, because our account of our empirically-conditioned commitment to induction rests on assumptions which (from the viewpoint of the passion) have no justification.

It now looks as if we are admitting two sets of norms, and with them two standards of reasonableness. Reasonableness$_c$—the standard of "common life"—is reasonableness relative to the norms that emerge from the five steps. Reasonableness$_p$—the more demanding standard of foundational philosophy—is reasonableness relative to the desire for foundations known to be free of fallacy.[36] So perhaps we do have insulation—the insulation of one set of norms (and the judgments it warrants) from another. Our belief in uniformity is unreasonable$_p$, but we can still condemn belief in miracles for running counter to that belief—for being unreasonable$_c$.

Our recognition of two sets of norms can also be described as a recognition of two species of philosophy. One is foundational philosophy, animated by the passion for foundations known to be neither fallacious nor deceitful. The other is a philosophy whose conclusions are, as Hume says "nothing but the reflections of common life, methodized and corrected" (*Enquiry* xii, p. 162). There are important similarities between these two species of philosophy.[37] But in the end they are not faithful to the very same set of standards.

Yet it is hard to believe that these two sets of standards have nothing to do with one another, and Hume admits as much when he writes that one of the best ways of achieving mitigated skepticism is "to be once thoroughly convinced of the force of the Pyrrhonian doubt, and of the impossibility, that anything, but the strong power of natural instinct, could free us from it" (*Enquiry* xii, p. 162). "While we cannot give a satisfactory reason"—a reason$_p$—"why we believe, after a thousand experiments, that a stone will fall, or a fire burn; can we ever satisfy ourselves concerning any determination, which we may form, with regard to the origin of worlds, and the situation of nature, from, and to eternity" (p. 162). As we saw in our discussion of Garrett's non-skeptical interpretation, the failures of reason$_p$ give us what we must now regard as a reason$_c$ for limiting our inquiries to common life and experience.[38]

It may help to ask from what viewpoint the two standards can be acknowledged. It cannot be the viewpoint of foundational philosophy, which will tolerate only one. So it must be the viewpoint of common life. And Hume seems to be telling us that when we occupy this viewpoint (after passing through the fires of Pyrrhonism), *the authority of the other is not entirely forgotten.* As Philo explains in the opening part of the *Dialogues Concerning Natural Religion,* "if a man has accustomed himself to sceptical considerations on the uncertainty and narrow limits of reason, he will not entirely forget them when he turns his reflection on other subjects; but in all his philosophical principles and reasoning, I dare not say, in his common conduct, he will be found different from those who either never formed any opinions in the case, or have entertained sentiments more favourable to human reason."[39] This is why the viewpoint provides insight into our whimsical (or as we would now say, absurd) condition. We are whimsical or absurd because: (a) we cannot help but believe things we cannot justify; and (b) we realize this; yet (c) the realization cannot free us of the beliefs, or of the painful suspicion that justification is required. The paragraph with which I began portrays another aspect of the same malady. Our passions and interests, as Malebranche observed, justify themselves. They take themselves with utmost seriousness, and they are sometimes able to make us see things their way. But we are also able to see that they don't deserve to be taken seriously, although (at the moment we see this, or a second later) we continue to take them seriously. Either we shuttle back and forth between passionate absorption and skeptical detachment, or (an alternative that seems to me more faithful to Hume's intentions) we invent a state of mind in which our commitments seem monumentally important and at the same time absolutely arbitrary. If Hume is a great philosopher it is partly because of his many clever and deeply disturbing arguments, and partly because he challenges us to form and sustain states of mind in which two or more conflicting tendencies are somehow given their due.

I have argued in this essay that we *can* give each its due, at least up to a point. We can insulate the norms at work in section x of the *Enquiry* against the corrosive force of the norms at work in section iv. We therefore answer Lewis, but we do not answer the reader who wonders, with Terence Penelhum, why our failure to satisfy the norms at work in section iv gives us a reason—a positive reason—to confine our enquiries to common life.[40] Hume is persuaded that it gives us such a reason (and my skeptical interpretation rests in part on his belief in it), but I have so far been unable to discover what it is, or even what it could be.

I would like to conclude by returning to the love of truth. It is true that Hume says almost nothing about its content or origin. But *Enquiry* 12 can be read as a comment on its limitations. If the love of truth is the passion that animates the skeptic, an enquiry into the proper limits of doubt and uncertainty (the professed topic of the section, as we have seen) is at the same time an enquiry into the proper limits of the passion. Perhaps we are meant to be suspicious of it. (If it were subjected, after all, to empirical criticism—if we were to ask what rewards it brings in common life—it would not fare too well.) This suspicion might engender the "true" skepticism Hume describes in the conclusion of Book I of the *Treatise*. "A true sceptic," Hume writes there, "will be diffident of his philosophical doubts, as well as of his philosophical conviction" (p. 273). But we can remain skeptics even if our identification with the passion is not wholehearted. Hume's search for the principles behind his judgments and tastes can be read as an attempt to achieve a kind of inner harmony or constancy. As he writes in a passage already quoted, "I am uneasy to think I approve of one object, and disapprove of another; call one thing beautiful, and another deform'd; decide concerning truth and falsehood, reason and folly, without knowing upon what principles I proceed" (p. 271). Earlier Shaftesbury (another of Hume's acknowledged predecessors in the science of human nature) had written in a similar vein of observing, "with diligence, what passes" in his mind, "what Connexion and Consistency, what Agreement or Disagreement I find *within*."[41] Shaftesbury asks

> Whether, according to my present *Ideas,* that which I approve this Hour, I am like to approve as well the next: And in case it be otherwise with me; how or after what manner, I shall relieve my-self; how *ascertain* my *Ideas,* and keep my Opinion, Liking, and Esteem of things, *the same.* If this remains unsolv'd; if I am still the same Mystery to my-self as ever; to what purpose is all this Reasoning and Acuteness? Wherefore do I admire my Philosopher, or study to become such a one, my-self?

Shaftesbury does not want to be alienated from any of his ideas or passions; he wants all of them integrated into a self of which he can wholeheartedly and perpetually approve. Hume settles for less—his own search for constancy or harmony ends, I have been arguing, in failure—and in doing so he makes the tensions of the *Treatise* and the *Enquiry* seem not merely inevitable (for some dispositions) but, to my mind at least, worth cultivating.

Notes

Earlier versions of this essay were delivered at Vassar College (in October 1992), Brandeis University (in March 1993), Duke University (in March 1994), and Brown University (in March 1998). I am grateful to my audiences on those occasions for their many helpful comments and questions.

1. "The Sceptic," in Eugene F. Miller (ed.), *David Hume: Essays Moral, Political, and Literary* (Indianapolis: Liberty Classics, 1985), p. 180.

2. The others are "The Epicurean," "The Stoic," and "The Platonist." "The Sceptic" is longer than the three others put together.

3. For Hume, philosophical works were part of "literature."

4. The summary is based on *Treatise* I.iii.6, "Of the inference from the impression to the idea," and *Enquiry Concerning Human Understanding* iv, "Sceptical doubts concerning the operations of the understanding." All page references to the *Treatise* and the *Enquiry* are to the editions prepared by L. A. Selby-Bigge and P. H. Nidditch, *A Treatise of Human Nature*, second edition (Oxford: Clarendon Press, 1976), and *Enquiries Concerning Human Understanding and Concerning the Principles of Morals*, third edition (Oxford: Clarendon Press, 1975).

5. In my emphasis on reason as a faculty that produces good arguments (as in much else) I am in agreement with P. J. R. Millican, "Hume's Argument Concerning Induction: Structure and Interpretation," in Stanley Tweyman (ed.), *David Hume: Critical Assessments*, volume 2 (London: Routledge, 1995), pp. 91–144.

6. In their book *Hume and the Problem of Causation* (New York: Oxford University Press, 1981). Page references are provided in the text.

7. *A Progress of Sentiments: Reflections on Hume's* Treatise (Cambridge, Mass.: Harvard University Press, 1991). Page references are in the text.

8. Baier's views differ in important ways from those of Beauchamp and Rosenberg. She takes Hume to be attacking a somewhat broader notion of reason (an "intellectualist" notion), and she argues that as the *Treatise* moves beyond Book I, Hume renders reason both passionate and social. I have trouble seeing what *controls* this development. (From Baier's viewpoint my mention of control may be a sign of intellectualism run wild.) Can *anything* claim the protection of "reason," so long as it is sustained by passionate engagement and social practice? I discuss Baier's interpretation in a review that appeared in *The Philosophical Review* 103 (1994), pp. 755–62. In interpreting Hume as a skeptic I am, on many points, in accord with Barry Stroud, *Hume* (London: Routledge Kegan Paul, 1977), and "Hume's Skepticism: Natural Instincts and

210   *Kenneth Winkler*

Philosophical Reflection," *Philosophical Topics* 19 (1991), pp. 271–91; Robert J. Fogelin, "The Tendency of Hume's Skepticism," pp. 114–31 in his *Philosophical Interpretations* (New York: Oxford University Press, 1992), and "Hume's Scepticism," pp. 90–116 in David Fate Norton (ed.), *The Cambridge Companion to Hume* (Cambridge: Cambridge University Press, 1993); and Millican, "Hume's Argument Concerning Induction: Structure and Interpretation."

9. *Studies in the Eighteenth-Century Background of Hume's Empiricism* (Minneapolis, 1930), p. 7. There are similar remarks in Barbara J. Shapiro, *Probability and Certainty in Seventeenth-Century England* (Princeton: Princeton University Press, 1982). On Locke's eighteenth-century reputation as an empiricist see Gerd Buchdahl, *The Image of Newton and Locke in the Age of Reason* (London: Sheed and Ward, 1961).

10. The existence of an *a priori* reason for preferring the proposition does not make it an *a priori* truth. There may be *a priori* reasons for preferring others, and even if there are none, the list of rivals may not be specifiable *a priori*. In Locke's case the alternatives to mechanism (scholasticism, spagyrism) were certainly not specifiable *a priori*: their availability was an accident of history.

11. *The History of England from the Invasion of Julius Caesar to the Revolution in 1688,* new edition (London: Longman, Brown, Green, and Longmans, 1848), volume 6, chapter 71, p. 328.

12. *The Works of Joseph Butler* (Edinburgh: William Whyte, 1813), volume 1, p. 4.

13. I quote from P. H. Nidditch's edition of Locke's *Essay* (Oxford: Clarendon Press, 1975). Hume goes on to ask (*Treatise,* p. 91) why we "presume" the same powers are always joined to the same qualities, in a passage I quote at length below.

14. *Cognition and Commitment in Hume's Philosophy* (New York: Oxford University Press, 1997), p. 94.

15. Some of my criticisms of Beauchamp and Rosenberg are also made by Garrett, *Cognition and Commitment,* pp. 84–85, 87–88, and Millican, "Hume's Argument Concerning Induction," pp. 135–6.

16. Millican also lays emphasis on this passage, both in "Hume's Argument Concerning Induction" (for example on p. 116), and in his comments on Don Garrett's book at the 1997 Hume Conference. In an unpublished paper, "Hume and the Irrelevance of Warrant," David Owen argues that when it is read in context, the passage does not have the force that readers such as Millican and myself suppose it does.

17. The *Abstract* appears on pp. 641–62 in the Selby-Bigge/Nidditch edition of the *Treatise.*

18. Hume distinguishes between demonstrations and proofs in several places, though he never makes quite the distinction I do here.

19. And in Part III, the claim that no durable good results from excessive skepticism is actually qualified. In fact it seems to be repudiated. It is also repudiated by Philo in a passage from the *Dialogues Concerning Natural Religion* that I discuss below.

20. Some of the evidence on the other side is discussed by Millican, both in

"Hume's Argument Concerning Induction" and in his unpublished comments on Garrett's book. In "Hume and the Irrelevance of Warrant," Owen argues for an interpretation of I.iii.6 that is close to Garrett's. Like Garrett in his chapter 4, Owen deliberately confines his attention (at least for the most part) to I.iii.6.

21. Feelings are reported, but the feelings are responses to philosophical failure—to the frustrated hopes of reason. Reason's involvement is signaled by its urge to take the feelings up—to formulate general principles that respond to them.

22. Here it may be worth observing that superstition, as Hume understands it in the *Treatise,* involves "reason" or inference. (Butler's *Analogy* is a clear example of superstition as the *Treatise* understands it. It is not an attempt to account for the known or visible world, but to infer other worlds from the one we know. It is, however, full of inference.) When the Title Principle tells us, then, that reason should be assented to when it is lively and mixed with some propensity, it is not ruling out superstition, which is why, I think, Hume goes on to discuss it. I suppose it could also be said that "reason" (in the Title Principle) is a synonym for philosophy, but the Title Principle would then be resting *everything* on propensity-mixing, which would still leave us without a reason for preferring philosophy to superstition.

23. What Hume means by calling it "more agreeable" is far from clear. On p. 272 he warns against accepting hypotheses merely because they are "specious and agreeable," but perhaps he is thinking of *superstitious* hypotheses— hypotheses which, instead of accounting for visible phenomena, present us "with scenes, and beings, and objects, which are altogether new" (p. 271)—since he speaks of them as the products of a "warm imagination."

24. David Norton emphasizes both the value of the *Enquiry* and the lasting effects of skepticism in his essay "How a Sceptic May Live Scepticism," in J. J. MacIntosh and H. A. Meynell (eds.), *Faith, Scepticism and Personal Identity* (Calgary: University of Calgary Press, 1994), pp. 119–39.

25. I agree with Garrett that this is the most important problem in recent Hume scholarship. I've profited from Garrett's discussion of it in chapter 10 of his book, as well as from David Owen, "Philosophy and the Good Life: Hume's Defence of Probable Reasoning," *Dialogue* 35 (1996), pp. 485–503, and Lorne Falkenstein, "Naturalism, Normativity, and Scepticism in Hume's Account of Belief," *Hume Studies* 23 (1997), pp. 29–72.

26. In his *Miracles: A Preliminary Study* (New York: Macmillan, 1947).

27. Natural insulation may be what Barry Stroud has in mind when he writes that "our natural instincts do not successfully meet or resolve the sceptical doubts; they simply submerge them" (*Hume* p. 115).

28. At least on the assumption that if *p* is unreasonable in view of *q*, and we have no reason for *q*, we have no reason for condemning *p*.

29. In my interpretation of the process I have been influenced by the writings of both Páll Árdal ("Some Implications of the Virtue of Reasonableness in Hume's *Treatise,*" in Donald Livingston and James King [eds.], *Hume: A Reevaluation* [New York: Fordham University Press, 1976], and *Passion and Value in Hume's Treatise,* second edition [Edinburgh: Edinburgh University Press, 1989]) and Annette C. Baier (*A Progress of Sentiments,* especially pp. 97–100).

30. Ludwig Wittgenstein, *On Certainty* (Oxford: Blackwell, 1969), entry 559.

31. On this see Páll Árdal, *Passion and Value in Hume's Treatise.*

32. It therefore invites comparison with Allan Gibbard's efforts in *Wise Choices, Apt Feelings* (Cambridge, Mass.: Harvard University Press, 1990).

33. As Barry Stroud notes, "Hume does not have as elaborate a 'pathology' of philosophy as Kant was to develop" (*Hume,* p. 97).

34. Is it really a love of truth, or a love of justification? And is it a love as opposed to an aversion—perhaps to falsehood, perhaps to unjustification? The section in the *Treatise* devoted to the love of truth—II.iii.10, "Of curiosity, or the love of truth," pp. 448–54 in the Selby–Bigge/Nidditch edition—is of little help in answering these questions.

35. See the *Enquiry,* p. 159, where Hume writes that the instinct upon which induction rests "may be fallacious and deceitful." This recalls Hume's description of Cartesian antecedent doubt on pp. 149–50 in the same section. This doubt is part of an attempt to assure ourselves of the veracity of our faculties "by a chain of reasoning, deduced from some original principle, which cannot possibly be fallacious or deceitful." I want to say, of course, that there is nothing distinctively *rationalist* about the desire here expressed, even if its starkest manifestation is a rationalist one.

36. I am grateful to Justin Broackes for suggesting the label "foundational philosophy."

37. It seems, for example, that each includes the "theory of ideas"—Hume's belief that every genuine idea is derived from a resembling impression.

38. Fogelin ("The Tendency of Hume's Skepticism") denies that these failures give us a reason (in any sense) to mitigate our skepticism. Mitigation is simply the causal upshot of recognizing them. As I suggest below, Part I of the *Dialogues* strongly suggests that it is more than this.

39. Quoted from p. 36 in David Hume, *Principal Writings on Religion* (Oxford: Oxford University Press, 1993), edited by J. C. A. Gaskin.

40. Penelhum presses this question both in *God and Scepticism* (Dordrecht: D. Reidel, 1983) and his reply to the essay by David Norton cited in footnote 25 (p. 270 in MacIntosh and Meynell, *Faith, Scepticism and Personal Identity*). It is a question that Fogelin, in insisting that mitigation is merely the causal upshot of skepticism, neatly sidesteps.

41. *Soliloquy, or Advice to an Author,* volume 1, pp. 299–300 in *Characteristicks of Men, Manners, Opinions, Times* (London, 1711; reprinted Hildesheim: Georg Olms Verlag, 1978). The following quotation appears on p. 300.

11

The Soul and the Self

Robert Fogelin

Section VI of Part IV contains Hume's famous discussion of personal identity. This section has attracted attention because Hume himself expressed his dissatisfaction with it, saying, in an Appendix to the *Treatise*, "I neither know how to correct my former opinions, nor how to render them consistent" (p. 633). He presents his difficulties in these words:

> In short there are two principles, which I cannot render consistent; nor is it in my power to renounce either of them, viz. *that all our distinct perceptions are distinct existences*, and *that the mind never perceives any real connexion among distinct existences*. (p. 636)

At the very least, this passage demands a charitable reading, for the principles cited are not inconsistent with one another. Presumably, these two principles taken together are inconsistent with some third principle that Hume also finds himself incapable of abandoning and that principle must somehow concern personal identity. Yet Hume never says explicitly what is bothering him, and no consensus has emerged among commentators concerning what it might be.[1] Now Hume's discussion of personal identity is preceded by a section concerning the immateriality of the soul. This earlier discussion provides much of the framework for this latter more famous part of the *Treatise*, and, indeed, it may, as I shall argue, be the source of Hume's concerns about the consistency of his system. The section is interesting in another way as well: in declaring that "the question concerning the substance of the soul is absolutely unintelligible" (p. 250), Hume seems to

213

embrace a conceptual skepticism which, as I have argued, is uncharacteristic of the *Treatise*.

Though the discussion will take a number of surprising twists and turns, the section entitled "Of the Immateriality of the Soul" opens straightforwardly by attacking the idea that the soul is an immaterial substance, where it is the soul's substantiality, not its immateriality, that is at issue. Hume asks those philosophers who debate whether the soul is a material or immaterial substance to tell us first, *"What they mean by substance and inhesion?* And after they have answer'd this question, 'twill then be reasonable, and not till then, to enter seriously into the dispute" (p. 232). Hume remarks that this question proved impossible to answer for matter and body, and then suggests, in an obscure passage, that an account of mental substance is burdened with special difficulties of its own:

> As every idea is deriv'd from a precedent impression, had we any idea of the substance of our minds, we must also have an impression of it; which is very difficult, if not impossible, to be conceiv'd. For how can an impression represent a substance, otherwise than by resembling it? And how can an impression resemble a substance, since, according to this philosophy, it is not a substance, and has none of the peculiar qualities or characteristics of a substance? (pp. 232–3)

Hume has in mind a philosopher who maintains that substance itself must be utterly different from any of its qualities, modes, or acts. If impressions are then taken to be qualities, modes, or acts of substance, then they cannot resemble substance and, given Hume's theory of the origin of ideas, we could have no idea (not even a fictitious idea) of substance.

After this dialectical flourish, Hume returns to his normal ways by asking what impression gives rise to the idea of the substance of our minds. His claim is that no such impression or idea can be found—a point he makes by asking a series of questions:

> Is it an impression of sensation or of reflection? Is it pleasant, or painful, or indifferent? Does it attend us at all times, or does it only return at intervals? If at intervals, at what times principally does it return, and by what causes is it produc'd? (p. 233)

Hume completes his critique of the idea of a mental substance by rejecting a definitional trick. If substance is defined as "something which may exist by itself," then every impression or idea will itself be a substance, for every impression and idea is itself a distinct existence. In that case, it will make no sense to say that impressions actually *inhere* in the substance of the mind, since one substance cannot inhere in another. "Thus neither by considering the first origin of ideas, nor by means of a definition are we able to arrive at any satisfactory notion of substance" (p. 234).

With the main argument in hand, Hume turns to the supposed *simplicity* of the soul. He considers a proposed refutation of materialist conceptions of the soul that runs as follows. If the soul is an extended thing, then it will have parts, a top and a bottom, a left side and a right side, etc. From this it follows that any ideas that inhere in such a substance must themselves have a definite spatial location. Yet, according to Hume, "an object may exist, and yet be no where" (p. 235). For example:

> A moral reflection cannot be plac'd on the right or on the left hand of a passion, nor can a smell or sound be either of a circular or a square figure. These objects and perceptions, so far from requiring any particular place, are absolutely incompatible with it, and even the imagination cannot attribute it to them. (p. 236)

From this it follows that there are perceptions which are "incapable of any conjunction in place with matter or body" (p. 236).[2]

Having condemned the materialists, "who conjoin all thought with extension" (p. 239), Hume is quick to point out that a like argument will embarrass their opponents, "who conjoin all thought with a simple and indivisible substance" (p. 239). The reason for this is that some of our ideas are extended:

> to cut short all disputes, the very idea of extension is copy'd from nothing but an impression, and consequently must perfectly agree to it. To say the idea of extension agrees to any thing, is to say it is extended. (pp. 239–40)

Now the immaterialist must labor under the same difficulties that confounded the materialist: he must explain how something extensionless can be locally conjoined with something extended:

> Is the indivisible subject, or immaterial substance, if you will, on the left or on the right hand of the perception? Is it in this particular part, or in that other? Is it in every part without being extended? (p. 240)

So we arrive at a perfect symmetry in the difficulties with both the theory that the subject is a material substance and the theory that the subject is an immaterial substance. Neither theory can explain the local conjunction of the extended with the unextended. Yet it seems that the soul, if it is a substance, must be either a material substance or an immaterial substance. Since both views lead to the same absurdities, we seem forced to abandon the substantial theory of the soul altogether.

> To pronounce, then, the final decision upon the whole; the question concerning the substance of the soul is *absolutely unintelligible:* All our *perceptions* are not susceptible of a local union, either with what is extended or unextended; there being some of them of the one kind, and some of the other. (p. 250) (The italics are mine. I shall return to this passage later.)

The section of the immateriality of the soul contains a third, and very important, argument: Hume clears materialism of the charge that it is absurd in suggesting that matter in motion can give rise to thought. On Hume's account of causality, causal relationships between material and immaterial objects are no more (or less) mysterious than causal relationships between material objects or causal relationships between immaterial objects.

> Now as all objects, which are not contrary, are susceptible of a constant conjunction, and as no real objects are contrary; it follows, that for ought we can determine by the mere ideas, any thing may be the cause or effect of any thing. (pp. 249–50)[3]

This is Hume's solution to one of the central problems of modern philosophy: the so-called mind-body interaction problem. If Hume's theory of causation is correct, this solution is, of course, perfectly adequate.

There are then three central theses in this section of the *Treatise:* (i) both the materialist and the immaterialist face insuperable problems explaining the local union of objects that are extended with those that are not extended; (ii) "the question concerning the substance of the soul is absolutely unintelligible"; and (iii) if causality can be correctly defined in terms of constant conjunction, then "matter and motion may often be regarded as the causes of thought." But even if this correctly summarizes the content of this section, it does not capture its main rhetorical force. As the title indicates, Hume is primarily interested in the doctrine of the immateriality of the soul and, more specifically, with the notion of *simplicity* that is associated with it. This emphasis comes out in a variety of ways. Most interestingly, after completing a largely even-handed critique of both the materialist and immaterialist doctrines of a substantial self, Hume interpolates an additional six pages of criticism aimed specifically at the "doctrine of the immateriality, simplicity, and indivisibility of a thinking substance" (p. 240). Hume, in one of his few lapses into an assertion of guilt by association, claims that anyone who holds that the mind is simple and indivisible must also accept Spinoza's "atheist" doctrine of "the simplicity of the universe, and the unity of that substance, in which he supposes both thought and matter to inhere" (p. 240). He doesn't say why.[4]

Finally, in the closing paragraph of Section V, Hume offers an "apology" that reveals the source of his interest in the simplicity of the mind. He assures the reader that his arguments are in no way dangerous to religion. Such assurances are needed because his denial of the simplicity of the mind seems to deprive religion of one of its standard proofs of the immortality of the soul. Hume's ingenious reply is that his arguments have no such tendency since proofs of the immortality of the soul based upon its supposed simplicity are no good anyway.

> Any object may be imagin'd to become entirely inactive, or to be annihilated in a moment; and 'tis an evident principle, *that whatever we can imagine, is possible*. Now this is no more true of matter, than of spirit; of an extended compounded substance, than of a simple and unextended. In both cases the metaphysical arguments for the immortality of the soul are equally inconclusive. (p. 250)

Hume then gives the discussion a wonderful turn by continuing in these words: "and in both cases the moral arguments and those deriv'd from the analogy of nature are equally strong and convincing" (p. 250). That, of course, does not mean there *are* strong moral and analogical proofs for the immortality of an immaterial soul, and, in fact, the plain implication is just the reverse. Defenders of religion would reject proofs for the immortality of a material soul and thus will not be happy to learn that their proofs for the immortality of an immaterial soul are exactly on a par with them. Hume caps this discussion with a sentence that could have been written by Montaigne:

If my philosophy, therefore, makes no addition to the arguments for religion, I have at least the satisfaction to think it takes nothing from them, but that every thing remains precisely as before (pp. 250–1)

I think we can now understand why Hume spends so much time discussing the simplicity of the soul: it provides an occasion for some mischievous fun at the expense of doctrines of divinity and school metaphysics.

But Hume's discussion of the *simplicity* does not end with Section V of Part IV; it continues into Section VI where the supposed simplicity of the *self* at a time is examined in tandem with its supposed identity over time. In a famous passage he tells us:

> The mind is a kind of theatre, where several perceptions successively make their appearance; pass, re-pass, glide away, and mingle in an infinite variety of postures and situations. There is properly no *simplicity* in it at one time, nor *identity* in different; whatever natural propension we may have to imagine that simplicity and identity. (p. 253)

Hume then goes on at length to explain the origins of "so great a propension to ascribe an identity of these successive perceptions, and to suppose ourselves possest of an invariable and uninterrupted existence thro' the whole course of our lives" (p. 253). This, of course, concerns the *identity* of the self over time and it is only at the end of his discussion that Hume again considers the *simplicity* of the self, remarking that the account he has given of *identity* "may be extended with little or no variation to that of *simplicity*" (p. 263)

In general, the discussion proceeds along the same lines that we found earlier in the section on ancient philosophy, where Hume invoked the associationist principles of resemblance and causality to explain the plain man's (false) belief in the identity of material objects or bodies over time. There is, however, one feature of this discussion that merits digression. At one point Hume makes the following, somewhat obscure, remark:

> Thus the controversy concerning identity is not merely a dispute of words. For when we attribute identity, in an improper sense, to variable or interrupted objects, our mistake is not confin'd to the expression, but is commonly attended with a fiction, either of something invariable and uninterrupted, or of something mysterious and inexplicable, or at least with a propensity to such fictions. (p. 255)

We might think that Hume would argue that debates over personal identity *are* merely verbal just because personal identity is a fiction, but, in fact, he says just the opposite. Later he makes essentially the same point with more clarity:

> as the relations, and the easiness of the transition may diminish by insen-
> sible degrees, we have no just standard, by which we can decide any
> dispute concerning the time, when they acquire or lose a title to the name
> of identity. All the disputes concerning the identity of connected objects
> are merely verbal, except so far as the relation of parts gives rise to some
> fiction or imaginary principle of union, as we have already observ'd.
> (p. 262)

The first sentence makes clear which disputes concerning identity *are* merely verbal: disputes that concern where to draw the line between the preservation and loss of identity through a series of changes. As he says, we have no *just standard* to answer this question. This same no-tion appears in an exchange that occurs in Part XII of the *Dialogues Concerning Natural Religion*. Philo is speaking:

> there is a species of controversy, which, from the very nature of language
> and of human ideas, is involved in perpetual ambiguity, and can never, by
> any precaution or any definitions, be able to reach a reasonable certainty
> or precision. These are the controversies concerning the degrees of any
> quality or circumstance.[5]

So if a dispute broke out among the vulgar as to whether a given per-son was still the same person after some considerable change, then that dispute would be both verbal and incurable. The situation is quite different for the philosophical dispute concerning the existence of a substantial self that endures through changes. Such a substantial self does not exist. It is a fiction. It is a fiction invented—though presum-ably not self-consciously—by philosophers to lend respectability to the belief they share with the vulgar concerning personal identity. The phil-osophical dispute is not verbal and incurable, for we can say that the doctrine that the mind is simple at one time and identical over time is just false.

Returning to the main line of reasoning in the text, Hume seems to be writing with perfect self-confidence. The discussion of the simplicity and identity of the self parallels the earlier discussion of the simplicity and identity of material objects. There may be differences in emphasis between the earlier discussion of material substance and the present discussion of the self. The earlier discussion dwells rather longer on the concept of identity, whereas this latter discussion gives more emphasis to the associative mechanisms that bring about a belief in identity. On the whole, however, the two discussions are very similar and show Hume developing characteristic features of his philosophy with perfect confidence. Why then, in the Appendix to the *Treatise,* does Hume declare himself unable to render his system consistent? Precisely what inconsistency does he have in mind; and why does he find it intractable?

I do not think that I can give a fully satisfactory answer to these questions, for the text, as far as I can see, is underdetermined on these matters. Furthermore, it is all too easy to mix up our opinions about what Hume *ought* to have been worried about with what, in fact, he was worried about. For example, throughout the *Treatise,* Hume adopts two different images of the mind or self. The first, and official, view is that the mind is a bundle (heap, collection) of perceptions. The second view adopts the metaphor of a theatre where the mind appears as a spectator to the scenes presented to it. "The mind is a kind of theatre, where several perceptions successively make their appearance" (p. 253). In this context Hume immediately appends a warning: "The comparison of the theatre must not mislead us. They are the successive perceptions only, that constitute the mind" (p. 253). Well and good, but spectatorial imagery occurs throughout the *Treatise* and often seems essential for the intelligibility of Hume's argument. So it might seem, especially to one who looks back at the *Treatise* from a Kantian perspective, that Hume finally recognized the need for a unified conscious self and then despaired of supplying it, given his own principles. I think that it may be right that Hume ought to have recognized the need for a *transcendental* judging self and it is surely right that his own principles could not have supplied this need, yet I see no evidence in the text that his worries took this form. Indeed, there is one place in the text, the passage just cited, where he specifically warns against taking his spectatorial images literally.

Another more plausible suggestion is that Hume needs a genuinely enduring *empirical* self to underlay the associative mechanisms that form the core of his theory. Jane L. McIntyre formulates this interpretation of Hume's problem in these words: "the concept of a self that is *affected by experience* and therefore must *persist through experience* is precisely the concept of the self that *cannot* be accounted for in the

context of the theory of ideas presented in the *Treatise.*"⁶ With variations in detail, this is the view of Hume's problem that has been presented by MacNabb, Passmore, Robison, and others.⁷ Hume has no
qualms about treating fundamental ideas as fictions, but it seems that
his own theories demand a self that genuinely, and not just seemingly,
endures over time. If Hume saw this point and conceded it, then we
could understand the despair he expresses about the consistency of
his system in the Appendix we are considering. But again I have yet to
see any plausible citation of text indicating that Hume's worries actually
took this form.⁸

Thus far we have examined two suggestions concerning the source
of Hume's anxieties about the consistency of his system: one concerns
the need for a unified *judging* self, something like a Kantian transcendental ego; the other concerns the need for an enduring *empirical* self
as the seat for associationist mechanisms. There is explicit text that
goes against the first interpretation and no text, as far as I can see, that
supports the second. Both interpretations have this in common: they
suppose that the system of the *Treatise* demands a genuine self—not
merely a fictitious self—and is inconsistent without it. Other interpret-
ers of Hume locate his worries in a different place: Hume's problem is
that his position demands a real self as opposed to a fictitious self;
instead he finds his account of the production of this fiction itself inconsistent.

The chief thing to be said on behalf of characterizing Hume's problem in this second way is that it squares quite well with some of Hume's
own language:

> Most philosophers seem inclin'd to think, that personal identity *arises*
> from consciousness; and consciousness is nothing but a reflected thought
> or perception. The present philosophy, therefore, has so far a promising
> aspect. But all my hopes vanish, when I come to explain the principles,
> that unite our successive perceptions in our thought or consciousness.
> I cannot discover any theory, which gives me satisfaction on this head.
> (pp. 635–6)

Notice that this passage does not point to any particular difficulty with
the associationist accounts of the simplicity and identity of the self
given in the main body of the text. There must, it seems, be some
general reason why any such account will face profound difficulties, yet
Hume, for all his self-critical candor, has not said exactly why these

distinct ideas cannot have fictitious connections *via* the principles of association.

As already noted, Hume's account of the identity and simplicity of the self mimics his earlier account of the (fictitious) identity and simplicity of material objects. We can profitably ask why Hume is worried about the one and not the other, for, as David Pears shrewdly remarks, "He does not say anything that is not true of ordinary material objects, and his argument could equally well be applied to the identity of cabbages."[9] In both places he argues that a fiction is generated by the associative mechanisms founded on the relations of resemblance and of cause and effect. Is there anything special about the constituents of the mind that precludes such an associationist account of their membership in a mind that is unified both at a time and over time?

Various writers have noticed that it is not a *necessary* condition for membership in the bundle that a perception stand in a relationship of either resemblance or cause and effect to at least one other member of the bundle. Impressions of sensation illustrate this: an impression of sensation seems not to be *caused* by another perception and, since its content can be novel, it need not resemble any other perceptions either. Yet, for Hume, impressions of sensation are resident in the mind, indeed paradigmatically so. Stroud makes the point this way:

> What Hume needs is a causal chain that runs 'horizontally,' as it were, along the whole series of incoming perceptions that we get from moment to moment. That is what I am arguing does not exist. When I am having an impression of a tree I might turn my head and get an impression of a building, but the first impression is not a cause of the second.[10]

Although Stroud notes this difficulty, he does not argue that this is the source of Hume's anxieties expressed in the Appendix to the *Treatise*. Indeed, it would be very hard to make this case since there does not seem to be a shred of textual evidence indicating that Hume ever considered this particular difficulty.[11]

A second line of argument attacks the *sufficiency* of resemblance and causation to yield the idea of *my* self or of one particular self rather than another. In its simplest form, it can be maintained, as David Pears has maintained, that Hume's position is incapable of explaining the peculiarities of ownership of mental objects.[12] But this is not Hume's worry, nor does Pears suggest it is, for Hume explicitly says that there is nothing about a particular perception in itself that marks it as belonging to one bundle (e.g., the bundle that I am) rather than any other. Starting from this last point Stroud presents his interpretation of Hume's self-doubts:

> There is nothing in any perception, considered in itself, which implies the existence of any other perception, or of anything else whatsoever, and so there is nothing intrinsic to any perception that connects it with some particular series rather than another. So why do perceptions present themselves, so to speak, in discrete, separate bundles?[13]

The individuation of bundles is surely a problem for Hume, but where is the inconsistency Hume complains of? Perhaps discrete bundlehood is inexplicable as so many things are in Hume's philosophy. To this Stroud replies: "To say it is 'inexplicable' for Hume is to say that it is inconsistent with the theory of ideas which he takes to be the only way to make sense of psychological phenomena."[14] I don't find this persuasive, for Hume often admits that psychological phenomena are inexplicable (e.g., the operations of the imagination) without seeming to worry about the consistency of his position.

Garrett provides another ingenious variation on this theme by arguing as follows. Suppose there are two spatially non-locatable perceptions in the minds of A and B respectively. They might, for example, be passions. Furthermore, let us suppose that they occur simultaneously. However, on Hume's theory, are we to assign these two perceptions to different minds? Not by resemblance, for we have assumed that they are qualitatively identical. This leaves causality as the only possibility, but it doesn't seem to work either. Distinct causes can be separated only on the basis of spatial relations, which these perceptions lack, or temporal relations, which these two perceptions lack, or temporal relations, which these two perceptions share. In sum, if A and B both simultaneously feel, say, the same deep sense of foreboding, there would be nothing in Hume's theory that would make sense of the fact that one of these feelings is A's, the other B's.[15]

I think this is a trenchant criticism and it is not immediately clear how Hume would answer it, but again we must ask where Garrett locates the inconsistency that Hume complains of. According to Garrett, Hume surely accepts the following proposition: "It is possible that two qualitatively identical perceptions of any kind, including those that are 'no where,' would occur in different minds at the same time."[16] I have no doubt that, if put to him, Hume would accept this possibility, then, given the argument that Garrett has presented, he would be forced to admit that "either both of [these perceptions] will belong to a given bundle of perceptions or neither of them will."[17]

Again no text is cited to show that Hume was even remotely worried about the ingenious problem that Garrett has posed; more to the point, it does not seem to be something that Hume was likely to be worried about. Hume was uncritically wedded to the way of ideas. He thought that he had immediate access to his own ideas and he simply took it for granted that these ideas were *his*. He saw quite clearly that this position had skeptical consequences concerning what can be *known* beyond the realm of immediate perceptions and it was an important part of his program to develop these skeptical consequences. As far as I can see, however, there is no reason to suppose that Hume entertained the conceptual worries attributed to him by Stroud and Garrett. More strongly, I think that such conceptual problems were quite alien to the standpoint that Hume, along with most philosophers of the seventeenth and eighteenth centuries, uncritically adopted.[18]

Turning now to suggestions I find more persuasive, I think that any suitable account of Hume's worries about personal identity should meet two minimum standards: (i) there should be textual support showing that Hume was at least aware of the issues under consideration; (ii) the inconsistency or difficulty pointed to should concern principles of some importance to Hume himself. I shall consider three proposals that go at least some distance toward meeting these demands.

The first is taken from Terence Penelhum. He claims that

> Hume is forced by his mistaken analysis of our concept of identity to interpret all ascription of identity to changing things as a mistaken ascription, and to regard the relationships that occasion it as distractions which make us overlook the diversity of their successive stages. He accordingly considers our belief in the unity of the self to be a commitment to a fiction.[19]

According to Penelhum, "Hume's fundamental error is his assertion that the idea of identity is the idea of an object that persists without changing."[20]

To see how this conception of identity could lead Hume into immediate trouble, consider the case of a person ascribing identity over time to himself. He might say of himself "I am the person who won the

Grand Prix." If Hume's account of identity is correct, then this person would be saying of himself that he had in no way changed since winning the Grand Prix. That, however, is just false, and he cannot but know that it is false. Of course, Hume is fond of attributing false beliefs to the mass of mankind and then proposing *fictions* behind which they can be hidden. In the present case, however, the falsehood of unchangingness is so palpable that it seems inconceivable that it could be concealed by a fiction. Thus, starting from his curious conception of identity, Hume is led to the paradoxical result that human beings universally accept a belief that should strike them all as false. This, in turn, would lead him to feel uneasy about his account of our *belief* in personal identity. If Penelhum is right, he should have looked more deeply into the concept of identity that was the genuine source of his difficulties.

My second suggestion assumes, along with Stroud and Garrett, that Hume was worried about the *fiction* of self-identity, and, in particular, he finds inconsistent his account of how such a fiction could come into existence. If we return to the discussion of the simplicity of the soul, we can find one good reason why Hume might have worried about the coherence of his position in this regard. Hume there argued that both the materialists and the immaterialists will be embarrassed when asked to explain how extended perceptions and extensionless perceptions can be locally conjoined. Because of the inconceivability of this local conjunction, he drew the conclusion that "the question concerning the substance of the soul is absolutely unintelligible" (p. 250). Later Hume may have realized that the very same considerations cut against the intelligibility of the *wholeness* (including both the *simplicity* and *identity*) of the self. Invoking causal relations between the extended and the extensionless ideas will not relieve this difficulty, for it is the *intelligibility* of conjoining the extended with the extensionless that is at issue, and this is prior to any inquiry concerning the supposed source of this conjunction. If Hume saw that his arguments intended to show the unintelligibility of a *unified* substantial self would apply equally well against *any* notion of a unified self, then we can understand his despair at giving an adequate account of this fiction.

My third proposal is more like those of MacNabb, Passmore, Robison and others in suggesting that Hume's position demands a *genuine* self rather than a merely fictitious self and is inconsistent without one. My reasons for saying this are, however, wholly different from theirs. Perhaps it has been pointed out before, but very little has been made of

the fact that the *initial* appearance of the doctrine that the mind is a
heap or collection of perceptions is in the section on *scepticism with
regard to the senses*. There, as we saw, it was invoked to help Hume
out of a desperate situation. It seems that it is not only false (as Hume
maintains) but actually self-contradictory (as Berkeley held) to assert
that a perception can exist unperceived. We can look again at Hume's
efforts to avoid this difficulty:

> we may observe, that what we call a *mind*, is nothing but a heap or collec-
> tion of different perceptions, united together by certain relations, and
> suppos'd, tho' falsely, to be endowed with a perfect simplicity and iden-
> tity. Now as every perception is distinguishable from another, and may
> be consider'd as separately existent; it evidently follows, that there is no
> absurdity in separating any particular perception from the mind, that is,
> in breaking off all its relations, with that connected mass of perceptions,
> which constitute a thinking being. (p. 207)

In the light of our recent discussions, this passage must appear curious indeed. It starts out by denying the "perfect simplicity and identity" of that "heap or collection of perceptions" which is the mind in
order to make sense of the idea of a perception existing outside of the
mind—i.e., outside of such a heap. The passage concludes by speaking
about the *"connected mass* of perceptions, which constitute a thinking
being." Now in the Appendix it is just this connectedness that Hume
finds himself unable to explain, and this does lead Hume into profound
difficulties. Hume's argument against Berkeley depends upon the notion of an *individual* mind from which a perception may be separated,
but Hume provides no principle for individuating heaps of perceptions
into minds. Strictly speaking, each perception is itself an individual substance and, again strictly speaking, a collection or heap of individual
substances is not an individual substance. More remarkably, on Hume's
principles, each perception is an individual *mind,* and a collection of
minds is not itself a mind. Less strictly, for Hume, perceptions must be
connected together loosely enough to allow separation, while at the
same time they must be connected together closely enough to constitute a mind from which things can be separated. Hume's radical atomism guarantees the first result, but precludes the second. Without both
features (separable perceptions and a unified mind), Hume's theory of
perception no longer contains a response to Berkeley's claim that it is
self-contradictory to suppose that a perception can exist unperceived.[21]

Of the three proposals concerning the source of Hume's worries about personal identity, I prefer the third, both for textual and systematic reasons. Textually, I think it significant that Hume's heap theory of the mind makes its first explicit appearance in the discussion of our belief in the distinct existence of what we perceive. The discussion is systematically important because, as he sees, his whole position is threatened with collapse. There is, however, a challenge that remains embarrassing: if Hume's worries took any of these forms, *why didn't he say so?* I don't know the answer to this and I can only say that this challenge embarrasses everyone who puts forward suggestions on this matter. After all, Hume's explicit statement of his problem is that he cannot render the principle *that all our distinct perceptions are distinct existences* consistent with the further principle *that the mind never perceives any real connexion among distinct existences.* This, taken at face value, is the least plausible interpretation of all.

Notes

1. For a useful summary of the various interpretations of Hume's worries about personal identity, see Don Garrett's "Hume's Self Doubts about Personal Identity," *The Philosophical Review* 90, no. 3, pp. 337–58.

2. At this point Hume pauses to comment on the fact that the plain man, as well as the metaphysician, often falls into the error of assigning a place to things which, properly speaking, can have no place. To illustrate this error, he cites the common belief that the taste of a fig is actually located within the fig. This, Hume thinks, leads to the absurdity of assigning a definite shape to the flavor. Hume seems not to realize that the same absurdity (if it be one) arises when we assign a shape to a hue. By a parity of reasoning, Hume should argue that it is the region with a hue, not the hue itself, that has shape.

3. Hume goes on to remark that this "evidently gives the advantage to the materialist, above their antagonists" (p. 250). Here he seems to forget that the immaterialist also has a problem in explaining causal relationships between material and immaterial objects, e.g., he must explain how an immaterial event (a decision) can bring about a material event (the movement of a limb). Hume's theory thus disembarrasses the immaterialist as well.

4. Hume's understanding of Spinoza plainly relies on Bayle's *Dictionary.*

5. Hume, *Dialogues Concerning Natural Religion*, p. 111. Hume was taken with the idea that disputes concerning where to draw a line on a continuum are merely *verbal.* The notion occurs again in an appendix to *An Enquiry Concerning the Principles of Morals* entitled "Of Verbal Disputes."

6. McIntyre, "Is Hume's Self Consistent?" *McGill Hume Studies* (San Diego, Calif.: Austin Hill Press, 1979), p. 82. McIntyre goes on to suggest that a relatively stable system of overlapping perceptions may provide sufficient

continuity for Hume's purposes. This, however, would make perceptions less *fleeting* than Hume seems to treat them in his discussion of the skepticism with regard to the senses.

7. John A. Passmore, *Hume's Intentions* (Cambridge: Cambridge University Press, 1952), pp. 82ff.; D. G. C. MacNabb, *David Hume: His Theory of Knowledge and Morality* (Oxford: Blackwell, 1966), pp. 151–2; Wade L. Robison, "Hume on Personal Identity," *Journal of the History of Philosophy* 12 (1974), pp. 181–93.

8. Nelson Pike has responded to interpretations of this kind in his "Hume's Bundle Theory of the Self: A Limited Defense," *American Philosophical Quarterly* 20 (1967), pp. 159–65. At the very least, Pike has shown that a response is available which, whether adequate or not, is of a kind that Hume typically accepted. Terence Penelhum ("Hume on Personal Identity," in *Hume*, ed. V. Chappell [New York: Doubleday, 1966], pp. 83ff) and Don Garrett ("Hume's Self Doubts about Personal Identity," *Philosophical Review* 90, no. 3, pp. 343ff) adopt a similar response to this interpretation of Hume's worries.

9. David Pears, "Hume on Personal Identity," in *David Hume: A Symposium*, ed. David Pears (London: Macmillan, 1963), p. 215.

10. Barry Stroud, *Hume* (London: Routledge, 1977), p. 126.

11. S. C. Patten presents a similar view in his "Hume's Bundles, Self-Consciousness, and Kant," *Hume Studies*, vol. 2 (1976), pp. 59–64.

12. Pears, p. 216.

13. Stroud, pp. 138–9.

14. *Ibid.*, p. 140.

15. For an exact statement of this argument, see Garrett, pp. 350–4. A similar line has been adopted by A. H. Basson in his *David Hume* (Baltimore: Penguin, 1958), p. 132.

16. Garrett, p. 350.

17. *Ibid.*, p. 352.

18. Hume's uncritical commitment to the way of ideas did not change in his later writings and, for whatever reason, he did not seem disturbed when it was explicitly challenged by Thomas Reid.

19. Penelhum, *Hume* (New York: St. Martin's Press, 1975), p. 88. This view was first presented by him in his essay "Hume on Personal Identity," in Chappell, *Hume*.

20. *Ibid.*, p. 80. In a brief discussion, MacNabb makes essentially the same point. See MacNabb, pp. 147–8.

21. The consequence that, on Hume's theory, a single perception will constitute a minimum bundle, hence a mind, was pointed out to me by Gareth B. Matthews, citing the following passage from the Appendix to the *Treatise* to support this:

> We can conceive a thinking being to have either many or few perceptions. Suppose the mind to be reduc'd even below the life of an oyster. Suppose it to have only one perception, as of thirst or hunger. Consider it in that situation. Do you conceive any thing but merely that perception? Have you any notion of *self* or *substance*? If not, the addition of other perceptions can never give you that notion. (p. 634)

12

Hume's Scepticism: Natural Instincts and Philosophical Reflection

Barry Stroud

Philosophy for the Greeks was not confined to abstract theory but also was meant as a guide to the living of a good human life. Hume was steeped in the literature of antiquity. I think there is a close kinship between his conception of philosophy and that ancient conception. It is something we tend to miss when we look back at Hume for our own purposes from here and now. I want to try to bring out the connection by identifying what Hume thought philosophical reflection could reveal about human nature, and what he therefore thought the point, or the human good, of philosophical reflection can be. His own direction in philosophy took him closest to that way of life said to have been achieved by certain ancient sceptics.

Some of the most personal, and the most moving, passages in all of Hume's philosophical writings appear in that puzzling, confessional last section of Book One of the *Treatise* prosaically entitled "Conclusion of this Book." Earlier in the Book he has presented his accounts of the origins of some of the most fundamental modes of human thought—causality, identity, enduring objects, the self—and he here steps back to ponder what he calls the "leaky, weather-beaten vessel" in which he is about to launch into the "immense depths of philosophy"[1] still before him in Books Two and Three. Given the discouraging conclusions he has reached earlier about the human understanding, he "despairs" at the "wretched condition, weakness, and disorder of the faculties"[2] which he and all other humans have to rely on. He is stricken with "melancholy," he fancies himself "some strange, uncouth, monster," he finds nothing but "doubt and ignorance" in his mind:[3] "Every step

I take is with hesitation, and every new reflection makes me dread an error and absurdity in my reasoning."[4] Even after "the most accurate and exact" inquiry, he can give no reason why he should assent to any particular conclusion; he simply feels a strong "propensity" to consider objects "*strongly* in that view, under which they appear" to him at the moment.[5]

> When we trace up the human understanding to its first principles, we find it to lead us into such sentiments, as seem to turn into ridicule all our past pains and industry, and to discourage us from further enquiries.[6]

But by the end of that same section, less than ten pages later, he nevertheless finds his spirits raised. His renewed hope of bringing the neglected science of man "a little more into fashion" has somehow served to "compose" his "temper from that spleen, and invigorate it from that indolence, which sometimes prevail"[7] upon him in intense philosophical reflection. He is once again in an "easy disposition," and feels it proper after all to indulge his "inclination in the most elaborate philosophical researches."[8] He continues to philosophize.

What is responsible for such a quick and complete reversal? And why does Hume even mention the matter in what otherwise looks like a purely theoretical treatise on philosophy? I think trying to answer these questions is no mere biographical exercise. I suggest that the interlude is not to be understood as simply an embarrassing personal confession of the youthful author's loss of nerve in the face of his negative conclusions. I think it should be taken seriously as an expression of Hume's philosophy, not just a description of his odd state of mind while writing it. And although the personal, confessional voice is absent from the more polished pages of the later *Enquiry Concerning Human Understanding*, I think the same theme is taken up there and developed more thoroughly and more systematically. If we can understand what goes on in that section of the *Treatise* and in the corresponding parts of the first *Enquiry* we will understand a great deal about what Hume thought philosophy could be, and do.

We must start, as Hume does, with the plight he finds himself in at the end of Book One of the *Treatise*. His examination of the nature of belief and of the role of reason in the genesis of beliefs has shown that even when he is most careful and cautious he will have no more reason to believe any particular conclusion than to disbelieve it; he will simply feel a strong propensity to view things in one way rather than another.

His experience presents him with certain regularities, and habit leads him to expect them to continue in the future. That alone is the source of all his beliefs about matters of fact. If certain ideas did not get "enlivened" by the imagination, and thereby transformed into beliefs, he would never give his assent to anything and never be able to extend his view beyond what is immediately present to his consciousness at the moment. His ability to do so is "founded on" nothing more than the operations of the imagination which serve to make some ideas more "lively" or "vivacious" than some others.

This is in part the discovery that certain operations of the mind must be present if we are able to think and believe and act in the ways we do. In itself that is not something which should throw us into despair. Surely we must acknowledge that *some* features or operations of the mind must be at work if our minds are functioning at all. What specifically troubles Hume is that it is "the imagination" that is at work, and that the quality of the imagination by which "the mind enlivens some ideas beyond others" is "seemingly . . . so trivial, and so little founded on reason."[9]

In calling them "trivial" Hume does not mean that the properties of the imagination are trivial in their effects. Without the operations of the imagination which he is interested in, we could not think at all. Some of those principles are "changeable, weak, and irregular," but there are others which are "permanent, irresistible, and universal," and which serve as "the foundation of all our thoughts and actions, so that upon their removal human nature must immediately perish and go to ruin."[10] So the principles of the imagination are not trivial for human nature; they make it what it is.

In saying that the quality of the imagination by which "the mind enlivens some ideas beyond others" is "so trivial, and so little founded on reason" Hume does not mean that it leaves us uncertain or might lead us astray. He does worry in the *Enquiry* that "custom . . . like other instincts, *may be* fallacious and deceitful,"[11] but that would be cause for vigilance, not despair. Nor does he find himself uncertain whether there are causal connections, enduring objects, and persons. He is not doubt-ridden; he cannot help believing in them. Even his philosophical accounts of belief, reason, causality, and the existence of objects remain convincing to him. That is itself part of his difficulty.

Hume thinks he has discovered that the imagination is a principle "so inconstant and fallacious" that it will inevitably "lead us into errors, when implicitly followed (as it must be) in all its variations."[12] For

example, the power of the imagination is what makes us reason causally, and also what makes us believe in external objects that are not
perceived. But those two operations can sometimes conflict. He thinks
it is not "possible for us to reason justly and regularly from causes and
effects, and at the same time believe the continu'd existence of matter."[13] That is not all. It is the discovery that "the memory, senses, and
understanding are . . . all of them founded on the imagination"[14] that
would "seem to turn into ridicule all our past pains and industry."[15] In
our attempts to understand the world we push on to discover what
really makes things happen as they do. We seek "that energy in the
cause, by which it operates on its effect; that tie, which connects them
together."[16] But Hume's theory of man has shown that "this connexion, tie, or energy lies merely in ourselves" and is only a determination
of the mind acquired by custom.[17] It is "an illusion of the imagination"
to think that we have any insight into the connection even in the most
familiar, everyday cases, let alone in more esoteric matters at the fron-
tiers of science.[18] Causality and most of our other important ideas have
been exposed as mere "fictions" or illusions." That is one source of
Hume's despair.

The predicament causes him despair because it presents him with
the problem, as he puts it, of "how far we ought to yield to these
illusions";[19] and he sees no way to answer the question. To assent to
"every trivial suggestion of the fancy" would lead to so many "errors,
absurdities, and obscurities" that we would be "asham'd of our credulity"; but to try to reject the imagination and "adhere to the understanding" alone would lead nowhere, since "the understanding, when
it acts alone, and according to its most general principles, entirely subverts itself, and leaves not the lowest degree of evidence in any proposition."[20] Hume thinks he has already shown that if we believed only
what we have good reason to believe we would believe nothing. So we
have "no choice left but betwixt a false reason and none at all."[21]

I think what Hume has in mind in speaking of the seemingly "trivial"
qualities or operations of the imagination is that those operations are
found to be only trivially or accidentally connected with the truth of
the beliefs which are their effects. Neither the word 'trivial' nor the
word 'accidental' is quite right, but his point is expressed most clearly
at the end of that section of the *Treatise* called "Of scepticism with
regard to the senses" (I,iv,2). Having explained how various operations
of the imagination lead us from our sense-impressions to a belief in the
continued and distinct existence of objects, Hume confesses that he is

at the moment inclined to place little or no faith in his senses or imagination. He says he "cannot conceive how such trivial qualities of the fancy, conducted by such false suppositions, can ever lead to any solid and rational system."[22] That is because those properties of perceptions which combine to "produce the opinion" of continued existence—namely, constancy and coherence—"have no perceivable connexion with such an existence."[23] What produces our beliefs has no "perceivable connexion" with their truth. I think that is the best description of the unsatisfactory position Hume finds himself in.

It means that, given the ways our minds work, and given what our experience presents us with, we will inevitably come to believe what we do whether that belief is true or not. There is no connection between our believing in the things we believe in—causal connections, enduring objects, and so on—on the one hand, and the existence of such things, on the other. All our beliefs in such things could be false or "illusory" even though it remains perfectly intelligible how we come to acquire them. That is the disturbing feature of Hume's explanations of the origins of our beliefs in terms of the operations of the imagination. He finds that our most important beliefs have a "trivial" or "accidental" origin in the sense that our having those beliefs bears no relation to their being true or to our having any reason to believe them. Their truth or reasonableness does not figure in the explanation of their origin. To say that their origin is "accidental" is of course not to say that the beliefs have no causes at all. It is to say that, given that we have the beliefs in question, it is at best an accident if the beliefs happen to be true; their being true, or their being false, makes no difference one way or the other to our having the beliefs. We would have had them in either case. And that is a disturbing position to find oneself in when reflecting on one's beliefs.

Probably no one is in a position to say with full confidence that none of his beliefs is "accidentally" produced in that way. Perhaps each of us could go so far as to say that we know it must be true of some of our beliefs. But Hume actually specifies a number of very important beliefs and shows of each of them that they have only an "accidental" origin in the sense in question. He shows that that is so for all our beliefs in causal connections, the independent existence of objects, and the enduring self. His theory of their origins explains how we get those beliefs without implying that they are true, or even reasonable.

In fact it is worse than that. Hume does not just fail to assert or to imply the truth of those fundamental beliefs in explaining their origins;

he explicitly denies it. Causal necessity, he says, does not exist in objects.[24] It is a "false opinion" or a "gross illusion" to suppose that objects remain numerically the same after an interruption in our perceptions.[25] And "there is properly no *simplicity* in [a mind] at one time, nor *identity* in different."[26] If we became convinced of these negative conclusions, as Hume's philosophy is meant to convince us, independent objects, and the self, we might well become, with Hume, "asham'd of our credibility," and we might resolve to bring our beliefs more into line with reason and with what we have come to see is the way things really are.

But Hume's "despairing" predicament is that no such resolution could have any effect. We will remain "asham'd of our credulity" if we submit to every "trivial suggestion" of the imagination, but it would be literally fatal if we could somehow avoid the imagination and perform the impossible feat of believing only what is based on reason or solid evidence. Given Hume's negative conclusions about reason, that would mean that we would have no beliefs at all, except perhaps about what is immediately present in our experience at the moment. And that would mean that life would be impossible. Without beliefs:

> All discourse, all action would immediately cease; and men remain in a total lethargy, till the necessities of nature, unsatisfied, put an end to their miserable existence.[27]

There seems to be nothing that can be done. Neither side is tolerable; and yet there seems to be no escape. Despair arises not just from discovering the "illusory" or "fictional" character of our most important beliefs, but from the recognition that we simply cannot avoid indulging in such "fictions" if we are to have any beliefs at all. Hume's theory taken all together shows that most of our beliefs *must* be wrong or unreasonable; given the way we are, we could not have those beliefs unless that were true.

But still, the recognition of this depressing state of affairs is only part of what is needed to understand what Hume is most concerned to show in his philosophical works. The plight or dilemma alone is not enough. What is even more important is the way the dilemma is resolved. He confesses that he simply does not know "what ought to be done" in choosing between "a false reason and none at all." But he does tell us "what *is* commonly done."[28] As a matter of fact, he says, "this difficulty is seldom or never thought of; and even where it has once been present to the mind is quickly forgot, and leaves but a small impression behind it."[29]

What kind of solution is that? How does it help to resolve the predicament for us to be told that most people never recognize the plight they are in, or if they do, that they soon forget about it? This might look like a comment on the idleness or irrelevance of philosophy, of its lack of impact on what human beings actually do. Hume sometimes says things which give that impression: for example, his wry observation that "errors in religion are dangerous; those in philosophy only ridiculous."[30] But I think Hume's point here is no passing jibe at philosophy. It is a very important observation; and, for Hume, a philosophical observation.

For Hume it is essential to one's understanding of human nature, and to one's life—and therefore philosophically important—to recognize the force of natural instinct over the deliverances of reason. It is important to see what actually happens to someone who is rightly convinced of Hume's negative conclusions and is thereby thrown into the plight he describes. What always in fact happens is that "nature" quickly dispels the clouds that "reason" is incapable of dispelling.[31] We find ourselves "absolutely and necessarily determin'd to live, and talk, and act like other people in the common affairs of life,"[32] whatever our philosophical conclusions might have been and whatever doubts or despair we might have arrived at in our philosophical studies. Hume is right to emphasize that philosophers too eat and drink and converse and sometimes even play backgammon as other mortals do. A thoughtful person can perhaps be brought by philosophical reflection temporarily to "renounce all belief and opinion,"[33] but his resolution, however strong, cannot last very long.

External objects press in upon him: Passions solicit him: His philosophical melancholy dissipates; . . .[34]

The bent of his mind relaxes, and cannot be recalled at pleasure: Avocations lead him astray: Misfortunes attack him unawares: And the *philosopher* sinks by degrees into the *plebeian*.[35]

Section IV of *An Enquiry Concerning Human Understanding* is called "Sceptical Doubts Concerning the Operations of the Understanding." That is where Hume establishes the negative conclusions parallel to those reached in Book One of the *Treatise:* in particular, "that it is not reasoning which engages us to suppose the past resembling the future, and to expect similar effects from causes which are, to appearance, similar."[36] The next section is surprisingly called "Sceptical Solution of These Doubts." What is the solution Hume offers? Why does he call it a "sceptical" solution? I will return to this second question after we see what the "solution" is.

The "solution" is the one I have already mentioned from the *Treatise*—that the negative philosophical conclusion about our beliefs and our reasoning will never in fact undermine the beliefs and reasonings of everyday life. The inferences we actually make from our experience will not be affected one way or the other by the true discovery that in all such so-called reasonings there is always a step which is not supported by argument or by any process of the understanding. What that discovery shows is that, since the mind is not engaged by reason, it "must be induced by some other principle of equal weight and authority; and that principle will preserve its influence as long as human nature remains the same."[37] That principle is "Custom or Habit";[38] it is a fundamental principle of human nature which we cannot pretend to explain further.

Hume therefore sums up the first part of the section called "Sceptical Solution of These Doubts" by declaring that "the conclusion of the whole matter" is quite simple. It is that "all belief of matter of fact or real existence" is simply the "necessary result" of a receptive mind's being placed in certain circumstances; coming to believe something after having observed a constant conjunction of objects of two kinds is "an operation of the soul, when we are so situated, as unavoidable as to feel the passion of love, when we receive benefits; or hatred, when we meet with injuries."[39]

> All these operations are a species of natural instincts, which no reasoning or process of the thought and understanding is able either to produce or to prevent.[40]

And that is really the end of the matter. That is the "solution." "At this point," Hume says, "it would be very allowable for us to stop our philosophical researches."[41] The most important general point about human nature has been made.

The point is that "nature breaks the force of all sceptical arguments in time,"[42] or that "nature is always too strong for principle."[43] No philosophy committed only to Hume's negative conclusions could possibly be put into practice as it stands. But this does not imply that we should therefore pay no attention to those negative conclusions or to the philosophical arguments which lead to them. It does not follow that any consideration of such reasonings must be completely idle and without effect.

For Hume we must see and appreciate both the doubts and negative conclusions and the so-called "solution" if we are to discover the important truth about human nature. We must first find the negative "philosophical" or "sceptical" view completely convincing—indeed, unanswerable—in order to perceive and acknowledge the sheer force of custom, habit, or instinct which can submerge it with hardly a trace. If we never philosophized and reached the "sceptical" conclusion, that discovery would be lost to us. We might find out somehow that there are certain things which we cannot help believing, but we would never understand why, or how. And if Hume is right about the overwhelming force of instinct, if we tried to accept the negative "philosophical" view by itself, we would find it intolerable. Even in our purely philosophical moments, we will at best find ourselves in Hume's desperate plight; and even then those moments and that plight cannot last very long. Any doubts we arrive at will be unstable and will produce only "momentary amazement and confusion."[44] But if we never arrived at any of those doubts in the first place, the "solution" would be no solution at all. We must be "once thoroughly convinced of the Pyrrhonian doubt, and of the impossibility, that anything, but the strong power of natural instinct, could free us from it."[45] We must get both. So it is essential for Hume to present both sides: both the "doubts" and the "sceptical solution" of those doubts. That is what he does explicitly in Sections IV and V of *An Enquiry Concerning Human Understanding*. And that is what I think he does less explicitly but more personally and more dramatically in the "Conclusion" of Book One of the *Treatise*.

I turn now to the point, or the payoff, of "resolving" the conflict in Hume's way. It reveals something important about his conception of his philosophical task, and so brings him closer to the ancient sceptics.

Hume adopts and recommends what he calls "the sceptical philosophy," but he uses the words 'sceptical' and 'scepticism' in a variety of ways. He speaks of the "sceptical reasonings"[46] or "sceptical arguments"[47] which lead him to what he calls "total scepticism"[48] or "sceptical"[49] or "Pyrrhonian doubt."[50] I think there is no doubt that Hume as a philosopher believes that those negative conclusions are correct; they represent a significant part of his contribution to philosophy. But his recommendation of what he calls "scepticism" is not simply a recommendation of the acceptance of those sceptical conclusions. He knows that those conclusions are not believable in everyday life. Nature will always submerge them in time. So he does not recommend them as a set of principles to be adopted and used to guide our thought and conduct.

When he acknowledges in the "Conclusion" of Book One of the *Treatise* that he must inevitably "yield to the current of nature" he goes on to remark that "in this blind submission I shew most perfectly my sceptical disposition and principles."[51] And in *An Enquiry Concerning Human Understanding* the "solution" provided by our natural instincts to the philosophical doubts or denials is described as a "sceptical solution." This brings me to the second of the two questions I raised earlier: why does Hume call the "solution" which consists in yielding to the inevitable force of nature a "sceptical solution"?

I believe it is because submission to the forces of nature under certain conditions can be a form of "scepticism" in the sense of the ancient sceptics who reputedly found a trouble-free way of life in following their natural inclinations. Some of them appear to have thought that they could achieve that blessed state only if they had no convictions or beliefs as to how things are. Hume thought no one could live without convictions or beliefs, but he saw himself in the old sceptical tradition at least in his recommendation of acquiescence in the face of what is most fully "natural." Richard Popkin has for this reason called Hume a "Pyrrhonist."[52] Even if human belief and reasoning cannot be avoided, if they are as natural and predictable as any other events in the world, Popkin thinks there is no need to try to avoid them on sceptical principles. Accepting the inevitability of beliefs and convictions would be "merely a legitimate extension of the Pyrrhonian principle of living according to nature."[53]

But it is equally important in Hume's view to acknowledge the naturalness and virtual inevitability of reflecting philosophically on the human condition. At the end of Book One of the *Treatise* he confesses that he finds himself "naturally inclin'd" towards philosophical reflection; he "cannot forbear" indulging in it; he is "uneasy" to find he does not understand certain things.[54] Even if he could manage to ignore it, he says, "I *feel* I shou'd be a loser in point of pleasure; and this is the origin of my philosophy."[55] Human beings are easily led to philosophize.

It is true that "profound philosophical researchers" will always leave us dissatisfied. We will inevitably be led to the "temporary melancholy and delirium"[56] of what Hume calls "Pyrrhonism, or *excessive* scepticism."[57] But arriving even for a moment at such unstable and incredible results can nevertheless be a good thing. We must first see and accept the truth of that "excessive scepticism" in order fully to appreciate the real force of nature or the imagination over reason. And given our undeniable natural instincts, the process of following out the reasoning to that excessive scepticism can itself have good effects which cannot be achieved in any other way. It can lead to what Hume calls "a more *mitigated* scepticism or *academical* philosophy, which may be both durable and useful" when the excessive scepticism is "in some measure, corrected by common sense and reflection."[58] So the "excessive" position which Hume calls "Pyrrhonism" can have good and lasting effects even if it cannot be permanently believed or followed. To ask what those effects are, and why they are good, is to ask what Hume thinks *"mitigated* scepticism or *academical* philosophy" is, and why he recommends it.

First, it is important to see that "mitigated scepticism" as Hume understands it is not a set of doctrines or truths. It is something we can find ourselves with, or a state we can find ourselves in, when the reflections leading to excessive scepticism have been tempered or mitigated by our natural inclinations. So mitigated scepticism is not just a qualified or watered-down version of the complete or excessive scepticism which Hume arrives at in his uncompromising, negative philosophizing. In particular, it is not the thesis that we can never be absolutely certain of anything but can at most have beliefs which are only probable.[59]

Popkin calls Hume a Pyrrhonist, but Hume speaks of Pyrrhonism as an unacceptable "excessive" form of scepticism. When he is in his study and follows those "profound reasonings" that lead to it he finds himself fully convinced, so he does not regard Pyrrhonism as "excessive" in the sense of going beyond the truth in what it says. It is rather because it cannot be put into practice; the "doubts or scruples" it rightly arrives at cannot in fact have "any constant influence on the mind."[60] A Pyrrhonist "must acknowledge, if he will acknowledge anything, that all human life must perish, were his principles universally and steadily to prevail."[61] Of course, there is no danger of that. The inevitable force of nature is always too strong for the Pyrrhonian conclusions to be put into effect. So on Hume's view, no one could possibly be a Pyrrhonist. In particular, Hume himself could not. He too, like everyone else, must follow nature.

Popkin acknowledges that what he calls "epistemological Pyrrhonism" is the only possible outcome of philosophizing in Hume's way, and he agrees with Hume that it can never cause us to adopt what he calls "a practical Pyrrhoninian attitude."[62] But he nevertheless regards Hume as a Pyrrhonist, in fact as a "consistent Pyrrhonist," because he simply does what comes naturally and so follows the ancient sceptical or Pyrrhonian tradition of living under "the guidance of Nature" alone. For Popkin, "the true Pyrrhonist is both a dogmatist and a sceptic,"[63] but of course not at the same time. It is a matter of alternating "moods," even of "split personality."[64] Since he is led to believe things by the force of nature, the Pyrrhonist will be "as dogmatic and as opinionated as one is naturally inclined to be."[65] In one mood, the necessities of nature overcome him, and he is "dogmatic"; he asserts and believes things. In another mood, the obstacles to reliable knowledge impress him, and he is "sceptical"; he sees there is little or no reason to assert or believe anything. But both moods are produced by natural forces. "In being entirely the product of nature he welds his schizophrenic personality and philosophy together. He believes whatever nature leads him to believe, no more and no less."[66] This is said to yield a "quietude" or peace of mind that is not open to what Popkin calls the "orthodox Pyrrhonist." Such a person would want to be undogmatic and to suspend judgment about everything, but that would put him into continual conflict with nature, and he could not succeed. Nature would inevitably force on to him the very beliefs he officially doesn't want. And he would be unhappy at his failure. But the Humean Pyrrhonist as Popkin sees him will have a "peaceful attitude" towards any "dogmatic view" he adopts, "since how he feels about it will be natural, and there will be no attempt to combat his inclinations."[67]

I think this picture of an easy-going, peaceful way of life does not really capture everything that Hume is getting at in his recommendation of "the sceptical philosophy." Following nature is certainly involved in being a mitigated sceptic, but that is not all there is to it. Someone who was "sceptical" only some of the time, and "dogmatic" the rest of the time, would not really be following a sceptical way of life. He would simply be a creature of nature. And every creature is a creature of nature. But not everyone leads a sceptical way of life. What is required for the kind of scepticism Hume recommends is not just following nature, but following nature while at the same time acknowledging or realizing nature's inescapable force. We can achieve that realization only by first becoming convinced of the "profound reasonings" of the philosophers. We see that we can have no reason to believe any of the things we so naturally believe, and then we find, in our very thoughts and actions as we leave our studies, that those undeniable negative conclusions immediately give way in the face of the overwhelming power of nature. We cannot continue to endorse or express those conclusions in the ways we live our lives, but they nevertheless continue to have certain effects.

This living in the acknowledgement of, or acquiescing in, both the profound philosophical "doubts" and the natural "solution" of those doubts is what Hume calls "mitigated scepticism." It is something that is *"consequent* to science and enquiry."[68] It is a "natural result of the Pyrrhonian doubts and scruples,"[69] and it could not have been achieved without them. It is a state which arises when "excessive" Pyrrhonism is tempered or mitigated by our natural inclinations, as it inevitably will be. And it is therefore a state we can find ourselves to be in all the time. It is not just a passing mood; it can be a way of life. But it would not be possible without both of the ingredients Hume stresses. What he calls Pyrrhonism alone is impossible; it cannot be lived. But without the startling effects of that excessive Pyrrhonism our natural inclinations operating on their own would not lead to a truly sceptical way of life either. They would not give us anything like the tranquillity or quietude or peace of mind sought and perhaps even found by the sceptics of antiquity.

Hume in effect explains how his mitigated scepticism might lead to a kind of tranquillity. He distinguishes two different sorts of durable and useful effects which the pursuit of excessive scepticism and the inevitable force of our natural inclinations can combine to produce. The first is a greater "modesty and reserve" in all our thoughts and reasonings. Simply following the urges of nature is not best for "the greater part of mankind"; they "are naturally apt to be affirmative and dogmatical in their opinions."[70] They are uneasy and impatient with indecision, hesitation, or balance of opinions. They "throw themselves precipitately into the principles, to which they are inclined."[71] But Hume thinks that "a small tincture of Pyrrhonism might abate their pride" and help such people achieve or at least approach that "degree of doubt, and caution, and modesty, which, in all kinds of scrutiny and decision, ought for ever to accompany a just reasoner."[72] Following the "profound researches" of the Pyrrhonist can lead to greater easiness in

the face of ignorance and uncertainty, less precipitousness in adopting beliefs simply in order to free oneself from indecision, and less obstinacy in holding on to the beliefs one has.
That is only one kind of beneficial effect.

> Another species of *mitigated* scepticism which may be of advantage to mankind, and which may be the natural result of the Pyrrhonian doubts and scruples, is the limitation of our enquiries to such subjects as are best adapted to the narrow capacity of human understanding.[73]

The humbling experience of becoming convinced of the imperfections of our faculties brought out by the Pyrrhonian reasoning will tend to confine our reflections more modestly "to common life, and to such subjects as fall under daily practice and experience" and to lead us away from "all distant and high enquiries."[74]

> While we cannot give a satisfactory reason, why we believe, after a thousand experiments, that a stone will fall, or fire burn; can we ever satisfy ourselves concerning any determination, which we may form, with regard to the origin of worlds, and the situation of nature, from, and to eternity?[75]

In emphasizing the indispensability of philosophical reflection to the truly sceptical way of life Hume seems to me closer to the ancient sceptical conception of the quest for *ataraxia* or tranquillity than is Popkin's fully natural, but possibly unreflective, way of life. Pyrrhonism as Sextus Empiricus describes it is not just any natural way of life. It involves a certain mode of inquiry which, if successful, can lead to tranquillity. The beginnings of the sceptical way of life lie in the perplexity which inquiring minds naturally get into when they seek the truth. They begin with the idea that finding and grasping the truth will give them tranquillity, but they quickly find themselves torn between conflicting opinions and are unable to determine which of them are true. The sceptical strategy is to exploit those very contradictions or conflicts, to oppose every argument with an opposite one of equal weight. This "main basic principle of the Sceptic system" is what eventually leads inquirers to tranquillity by encouraging them to suspend judgement and to cease dogmatizing.[76]

It is true that the sceptic simply follows nature or goes along with appearances. But that natural form of life arises only for someone who has already followed the sceptical inquiry and has subjected himself to the sceptical tropes that are said to produce the required suspension, so it is available only to those who begin with reflection. A blissful peasant who never reflected or who never felt or was moved by anxiety about his lack of understanding of the way things are would not lead a sceptical life, however blindly and calmly he was carried along by his natural instincts.

It is the sceptical, and not simply the natural, way of life that Hume recommends. The life of a blissful peasant is not something most of us can even aspire to, let alone achieve. Most of us, like Hume himself, are "naturally *inclin'd* to carry [our] view into all those subjects, about which [we] have met with so many disputes in the course of [our] reading and conversation. [We] cannot forbear having a curiosity" about the sources of our beliefs and actions.[77] We are "uneasy" to think of what we do "without knowing upon what principles [we] proceed."[78] For almost all of us, then, Hume thinks that what he calls the sceptical or philosophical way of life would be best.[79]

Why would that way of life be best? Even if Hume is right that reflection on the "profound" Pyrrhonian reasoning would in fact result in what he calls mitigated scepticism, why is that a reason for us to engage in that kind of sceptical reasoning? And is it really true, as Hume says, that the doubt, caution, and modesty which he thinks we would achieve is something that *ought to* be found in every "just reasoner"? Why is that so? Is there any good reason for us to resist our natural temptation to go beyond common life and experience into "distant and high enquiries" about creation and eternity and fate? Why would that be the best way to live? And how can Hume, of all people, presume to tell us what is the best way of life for human beings?

Hume has answers to all these questions. I think they reveal even more clearly his affinity with the sceptics of antiquity. The answers all rest on human nature. He knows that " 'tis almost impossible for the mind of man to rest, like those of the beasts,[80] in that narrow circle of objects, which are the subject of daily conversation and action."[81] We will inevitably venture out beyond them into "distant and high enquiries" some of the time. Since we know that for most of us such journeys are inevitable:

> we ought only to deliberate concerning the choice of our guide, and ought to prefer that which is safest and most agreeable. And in this respect I make bold to recommend philosophy, and shall not scruple to give it the preference to superstition of every kind or denomination.

We know that "the *imagination* of man is naturally sublime, delighted with whatever is remote and extraordinary."[82] Given free rein, it creates a fertile field for the "embellishment of poets or orators" or "the arts of priests and politicians."[83] Such manipulators thrive on superstition, which exploits our fears and our ignorance, and pushes the mind farther in a direction in which its natural bias or propensity already leads it.[84] New worlds of undreamed-of and inaccessible beings are invented to answer our anxious questions and allay our fears. To follow the high-flying imagination in this way and to go along with superstition would be to yield to some of our natural inclinations, but Hume finds it the wrong thing to do simply because "superstition seizes more strongly on the mind, and is often able to disturb us in the conduct of our lives and actions."[85] Philosophy cannot do that. That is why he recommends philosophy over superstition.

There are admittedly certain kinds of philosophy which "may only serve, by imprudent management, to foster a predominant inclination, and push the mind, with more determined resolution, towards that side which already *draws* too much, by the bias and propensity of the natural temper."[86] So not just any kind of philosophy will be a sufficient antidote to superstition. Hume regards "the Academic or Sceptical philosophy" as most harmless and innocent in this respect.[87] It flatters no natural passion but the love of truth, and it encourages modesty, doubt, and suspense of judgement in matters too large for our easy comprehension.

> Nothing, therefore, can be more contrary than such a philosophy to the supine indolence of the mind, its rash arrogance, its lofty pretensions, and its superstitious credulity.[88]

Hume recommends, not philosophy in general, or any old philosophy, but non-pretentious, non-superstitious philosophy: "the Academic or Sceptical philosophy."

What is important in understanding Hume's defense of this form of scepticism is not just the recommendation he makes of a philosophy and a way of life, but also the basis on which the recommendation is made. He does not justify it on the grounds that by giving completely free rein to the imagination we would be led into beliefs that are false, to a tissue of errors and illusions. He is in no position to say that profound, careful philosophy is superior in that respect. Nor does he suggest that the conclusions of the sceptical philosophy are supported by good reasons while elaborate superstitious pictures of the world are not. He says simply that superstition "seizes more strongly on the mind, and is often able to disturb us in the conduct of our lives and actions."[89]

> Philosophy on the contrary, if just, can present us only with mild and moderate sentiments; and if false and extravagant, its opinions are merely the objects of a cold and general speculation, and seldom go so far as to interrupt the course of our natural propensities.[90]

That is why errors in philosophy are only ridiculous while those in religion are dangerous, and that is why philosophy is always to be preferred.[91] We will be better off with it: less disturbed, more content, and more balanced.

I suggest that much of *An Enquiry Concerning Human Understanding*, and certainly its opening and its closing sections, represents a defense of and a plea for the sceptical philosophy on just these grounds. Different species of philosophy are distinguished in Section I, and "many positive advantages" of "an accurate scrutiny into the powers and faculties of human nature" are listed.[92] And Section XII makes a case for the superiority of mitigated scepticism in securing those advantages. In defending the study of philosophy, the *Enquiry* can also be seen as a justification of Hume's more youthful *Treatise* which had fallen "*dead-born from the Press; without reaching such distinction as even to excite a Murmur among the Zealots.*"[93] "Profound and abstract philosophy" of the kind he pursued there, he admits, is "painful and fatiguing," and it is often obscure,[94] but it should not be rejected entirely on that account alone. There is indeed a plausible objection against a great portion of "profound reasonings, or what is commonly called *metaphysics*";[95]

> that they are not properly a science; but arise either from the fruitless efforts of human vanity, which would penetrate into subjects utterly inaccessible to the understanding, or from the craft of popular superstitions, which, being unable to defend themselves on fair ground, raise these intangling brambles to cover and protect their weakness.[96]

But even if that is true of most philosophy, especially of lofty, pretentious, system-building philosophy, it is no reason for philosophers to abandon the field and "leave superstition still in possession of her retreat,"[97] heaping "religious fears and prejudices"[98] on defenseless minds. It is all the more reason to enquire carefully into the nature and extent of the human understanding, to pursue as profound and abstract an investigation as is needed to "discover the proper province of human reason."[99]

> We must submit to this fatigue, in order to live at ease ever after: And must cultivate true metaphysics with some care, in order to destroy the false and adulterate.[100]

In saying what we must do Hume does not argue here that careful, profound reasonings are likely to lead to the truth, while superstition and prejudice are not. He says only that the proper study of the human faculties will enable us to live at ease in a way that superstition and prejudice will not. Sheer "indolence" or lack of interest might protect a few people from the effects of a "deceitful philosophy,"[101] but for most of the rest of us it will be "overbalanced by curiosity."[102] And although the philosophical reflection we cannot avoid might well lead at first to "despair," it "may give place afterwards to sanguine hopes and expectations."[103] The point is that we will sometimes raise our minds above the matters of common life and experience, and in doing so we need a guide.

> Accurate and just reasoning is the only catholic remedy, fitted for all persons and all dispositions; and is alone able to subvert that abstruse philosophy and metaphysical jargon, which, being mixed up with popular superstition, renders it in a manner impenetrable to careless reasoners, and gives it the air of science and wisdom.[104]

These are large claims to be made in the name of philosophy as Hume understands it. His support for them comes from his view of human nature and of what is necessary for a good human life. He knows that "the mere philosopher" is widely believed "to contribute nothing either to the advantage or pleasure of society."[105] But on the other hand "the mere ignorant is still more despised."[106] Each represents only one extreme of what is essential to a balanced human life. Human beings are reasonable, and so need science and learning as part of their "proper food and nourishment."[107] But they are also sociable beings, as well as active beings, and they need business and occupation. They need relaxation and enjoyment as well.

> It seems, then, that nature has pointed out a mixed kind of life as most suitable to the human race, and secretly admonished them to allow none

of these biases to *draw* too much, so as to incapacitate them for other occupations and entertainments. Indulge your passion for science, says she, but let your science be human and such as may have a direct reference to action and society. Abstruse thought and profound researches I prohibit, and will severely punish, by the pensive melancholy which they introduce, by the endless uncertainty in which they involve you, and by the cold reception which your pretended discoveries shall meet with, when communicated. Be a philosopher; but, amidst all your philosophy, be still a man.[108]

Hume recommends the pursuit of the sceptical or academical philosophy as the best or perhaps the only way to achieve this most natural and therefore most blissful human condition. It represents not only the best way to be a philosopher, given that one is human, but also the best way of being human, given that one will inevitably try to understand oneself and the world. The pursuit of the sceptical philosophy is the best way of giving adequate expression to all the tendencies or propensities which constitute human nature. It will lead temporarily to "Pyrrhonism, or *excessive* scepticism," but, given our natural instincts, there is no danger that that will paralyze us. And our recognition of the superior force of those natural instincts will provide a somewhat bemused detachment from the empty pretensions of reason alone. Unlike the beasts, we will raise our minds from time to time beyond "that narrow circle of objects, which are the subject of daily conversation and action," and so to some extent we will satisfy our curiosity about "high and distant" matters. But we will do so without giving the imagination alone completely free rein, or simply indulging a predominant bias or inclination in our natural temper. With philosophy as our guide, we will be immune to the disturbances of religion and other forms of superstition. We will have achieved a happy "determination" in which no side of our nature "*draws* too much."

What is behind Hume's defense of the sceptical philosophy is nothing more than his views about the nature of human beings. Doubt, caution, and modesty—the effects of the sceptical enquiry—*ought* to be found in every "just reasoner," not because that is our God-given duty, but because we will be better off that way. We will be less disturbed, more completely satisfied, more balanced. For the same reason we ought to restrain the inflamed imagination and overcome superstition. Not because there is some *a priori* imperative for us to do so, but because more potential sources of turmoil and distress in human life will be avoided that way. For Hume those are the only sorts of facts which could ever lie behind any just claim about how people ought to live. In that respect too he is fully in accord with the sceptics of antiquity.

Unlike those ancient sceptics who tried to avoid all convictions or beliefs, Hume is not reluctant to believe or even to state the facts of human nature on which his conception of the best kind of human life depends. His acceptance of those facts is not inconsistent with the kind of scepticism he advocates. In fact, he cannot help believing them. Or if he does occasionally feel a certain doubt or reluctance, it is only during the "momentary amazement and confusion" brought on by intense philosophical reflection. And for him, as for the rest of us, that "delirium" soon passes away.[109]

Notes

1. D. Hume, *A Treatise of Human Nature,* ed. L. A. Selby-Bigge (Oxford: Oxford UP, 1958), 263.
2. *Treatise,* 264.
3. Ibid.
4. *Treatise,* 265.
5. Ibid.
6. *Treatise,* 266.
7. *Treatise,* 273.
8. Ibid.
9. *Treatise,* 265.
10. *Treatise,* 225.
11. D. Hume, *Enquiries Concerning Human Understanding and Concerning the Principles of Morals,* ed. L. A. Selby-Bigge (Oxford: Oxford UP, 1966), 159 (my italics).
12. *Treatise,* 265–66.
13. *Treatise,* 266.
14. *Treatise,* 265.
15. *Treatise,* 266.
16. *Treatise,* 267.
17. *Treatise,* 266.
18. *Treatise,* 267.
19. Ibid.
20. Ibid.
21. *Treatise,* 268.
22. *Treatise,* 217.
23. Ibid.
24. *Treatise,* 165.

25. *Treatise*, 209, 217.
26. *Treatise*, 253.
27. *Enquiry*, 160.
28. *Treatise*, 268 (my italics).
29. Ibid.
30. *Treatise*, 272.
31. *Treatise*, 269.
32. Ibid.
33. D. Hume, *Dialogues Concerning Natural Religion*, ed. N. Kemp Smith (Indianapolis: Bobbs-Merril, 1947), 132.
34. Ibid.
35. *Dialogues*, 133.
36. *Enquiry*, 39.
37. *Enquiry*, 41–52.
38. *Enquiry*, 43.
39. *Enquiry*, 46.
40. *Enquiry*, 46–47.
41. *Enquiry*, 47.
42. *Treatise*, 187.
43. *Enquiry*, 160.
44. Ibid.
45. *Enquiry*, 162.
46. *Treatise*, 186.
47. *Treatise*, 187.
48. *Treatise*, 268.
49. *Treatise*, 218; *Enquiry*, Section IV.
50. *Enquiry*, 162.
51. *Treatise*, 269.
52. Richard E. Popkin, "David Hume: His Pyrrhonism and His Critique of Pyrrhonism," *The Philosophical Quarterly* 1 (1951). Reprinted in V. C. Chappell, ed., *Hume* (Garden City, NY: Doubleday, 1966). Page references here are to the Chappell volume.
53. Popkin, 89.
54. *Treatise*, 270–71.
55. *Treatise*, 271.
56. *Treatise*, 269.
57. *Enquiry*, 161. Whether Hume is historically correct in calling the view he has in mind "Pyrrhonism," and whether Pyrrho or any of his followers were in fact "excessive" sceptics in this sense, are questions I do not try to answer here.
58. *Enquiry*, 161.
59. Popkin describes Hume's mitigated scepticism this way in his entry "Scepticism" in *The Encyclopedia of Philosophy*, ed. P. Edwards (New York: Collier-Macmillan, 1967), vol. 7, 455.
60. *Enquiry*, 160.
61. Ibid.
62. Popkin, 94.

63. Popkin, 95.
64. Popkin, 98.
65. Popkin, 95.
66. Ibid.
67. Popkin, 94.
68. *Enquiry,* 150.
69. *Enquiry,* 162.
70. *Enquiry,* 161.
71. Ibid.
72. *Enquiry,* 161–62.
73. *Enquiry,* 162.
74. Ibid.
75. Ibid. Similar words are put into the mouth of Philo in *Dialogues Concerning Natural Religion,* 131–32: "Let us become thoroughly sensible of the weakness, blindness, and narrow limits of human reason: Let us duly consider its uncertainty and needless contrarieties, even in subjects of common life and practice: Let the errors and deceits of our very senses be set before us; the insuperable difficulties, which attend first principles in all systems; the contradictions, which adhere to the very ideas of matter, cause and effect, extension, space, time, motion; and in a word, quantity of all kinds, the object of the only science, that can fairly pretend to any certainty or evidence. When these topics are displayed in their full light, as they are by some philosophers and almost all divines; who can retain such confidence in this frail faculty of reason as to pay any regard to its determinations in points so sublime, so abstruse, so remote from common life and experience? When the coherence of the parts of a stone, or even that composition of parts, which renders it extended; when these familiar objects, I say, are so inexplicable, and contain circumstances so repugnant and contradictory; with what assurance can we decide concerning the origin of worlds, or trace their history from eternity to eternity"?
    76. Sextus Empiricus, *Outlines of Pyrrhonism,* trans. R. G. Bury (Cambridge, MA: Harvard UP, 1976) I, 6, 9.
    77. *Treatise,* 270.
    78. *Treatise,* 271.
    79. He mentions only one exception: "I am sensible . . . that there are in *England,* in particular, many honest gentlemen, who being always employ'd in their domestic affairs, or amusing themselves in common recreations, have carried their thoughts very little beyond those objects, which are every day expos'd to their senses. And indeed, of such as these I pretend not to make philosophers, nor do I expect them either to be associates in these researches or auditors of these discoveries. They do well to keep themselves in their present situation; and instead of refining them into philosophers, I wish we cou'd communicate to our founders of systems, a share of this gross earthly mixture, as an ingredient, which they commonly stand much in need of, and which cou'd serve to temper those fiery particles, of which they are compos'd." (*Treatise,* 272).
    80. And perhaps those gentlemen in England.
    81. *Treatise,* 271.

82. *Enquiry,* 162.

83. Ibid.

84. *Enquiry,* 40.

85. *Treatise,* 271–72.

86. *Enquiry,* 40.

87. *Enquiry,* 41.

88. Ibid.

89. *Treatise,* 271–72.

90. Ibid.

91. See Philo's question in Part XII of *Dialogues Concerning Natural Religion* (p. 220): "How happens it, then, . . . if vulgar superstition be so salutary to society, that all history abounds so much with accounts of its pernicious consequences on public affairs? Factions, civil wars, persecutions, subversions of government, oppression, slavery; these are the dismal consequences which always attend its prevalency over the minds of men. If the religious spirit be ever mentioned in any historical narration, we are sure to meet afterwards with a detail of the miseries which attend it. And no period of time can be happier or more prosperous, than those in which it is never regarded, or heard of.

92. *Enquiry,* 13.

93. "My Own Life," in *The Letters of David Hume,* ed. J. Y. T. Grieg, 2 vols. (Oxford: Oxford UP, 1932) vol. I, 2.

94. *Enquiry,* 11.

95. *Enquiry,* 9.

96. *Enquiry,* 11.

97. *Enquiry,* 12.

98. *Enquiry,* 11.

99. *Enquiry,* 12.

100. Ibid.

101. Perhaps those gentlemen in England are safe.

102. *Enquiry,* 12.

103. Ibid. This is precisely the course of Hume's own sentiments as reported so dramatically in the first person in the "Conclusion" of Book One of the *Treatise.*

104. *Enquiry,* 12–13.

105. *Enquiry,* 8.

106. Ibid.

107. Ibid.

108. *Enquiry,* 9. Nature here appears to be speaking directly to the youthful author of *A Treatise of Human Nature.*

109. In the end perhaps the best recommendation of scepticism or of any other way of life is to be found not in confirmation of the general facts of human nature on which it is thought to be based, but on the actual lives of its practitioners. If we take Hume's own life as an expression of his scepticism, Adam Smith's description of that life is a strong recommendation indeed: "His temper, indeed, seemed to be more happily balanced, if I may be allowed such an expression, than that perhaps of any other man I have ever known. Even in the lowest state of his fortune, his great and necessary frugality never hindered

him from exercising . . . acts both of charity and generosity. . . . The extreme gentleness of his nature never weakened either the firmness of his mind, or the steadiness of his resolutions. His constant pleasantry was the genuine effusion of good-nature and good-humor, tempered with delicacy and modesty, and without even the slightest tincture of malignity . . . And the gaiety of temper, so agreeable in society, . . . was in him certainly attended with the most severe application, the most extensive learning, the greatest depth of thought, and a capacity in every respect the most comprehensive. Upon the whole, I have always considered him, both in his lifetime and since his death, as approaching as nearly to the idea of a perfectly wise and virtuous man, as perhaps the nature of human frailty will permit." (*Dialogues*, 247–48)

Selected Bibliography

The following are monographs or anthologies covering Locke, Berkeley, and Hume:

Bennett, J. *Locke, Berkeley and Hume. Central Themes*. Oxford: Clarendon Press, 1971.
Woolhouse, Roger. *The Empiricists*. Oxford: Oxford University Press, 1988.
Martin, C. B., and D. M. Armstrong. *Locke and Berkeley*. Garden City: Doubleday Anchor, 1967 (repr. Garland, 1988).

Locke

The standard edition of John Locke's *An Essay Concerning Human Understanding* is edited by Peter H. Nidditch (Oxford: Clarendon Press, 1975).

The following are selected books written about Locke's *Essay*:

Alexander, Peter. *Ideas, Qualities and Corpuscles: Locke and Boyle on the External World*. Cambridge: Cambridge University Press, 1985.
Ayers, M. R. *Locke*. 2 vols. London: Routledge, 1991.
Colman, John. *John Locke's Moral Philosophy*. Edinburgh: Edinburgh University Press, 1983.
Jenkins, John. *Understanding Locke: An Introduction*. Edinburgh: Edinburgh University Press, 1983.
Mabbott, J. D. *John Locke*. London: Macmillan, 1973.
Mackie, J. L. *Problems from Locke*. Oxford: Clarendon Press, 1976.
Wolterstorff, Nicholas. *John Locke and the Ethics of Belief*. Cambridge: Cambridge University Press, 1996.
Woolhouse, R. S. *Locke* Brighton, Sussex: Harvester, 1983.

254 Suggested Bibliography

Yolton, John. *Locke on the Compass of Human Understanding*. Cambridge: Cambridge University Press, 1970.
Yolton, John. *Locke: An Introduction*. Oxford: Blackwell, 1985.

The following are multi-author anthologies about Locke:

Chappell, Vere, ed. *The Cambridge Companion to Locke*. Cambridge: Cambridge University Press, 1994.
Tipton, I. C., ed. *Locke on Human Understanding*. Oxford: Oxford University Press, 1977.

Berkeley

The standard edition of Berkeley's works is A. A. Luce and T. E. Jessop, eds., *The Works of George Berkeley, Bishop of Cloyne*, 9 vols. London: Thomas Nelson and Sons Ltd., 1948–1957. A readily accessible collection of Berkeley's works is M. R. Ayers, ed. *George Berkeley, Philosophical Works, Including the Works on Vision*. London: Everyman, JM Dent, 1975.

The following are selected books written about Berkeley's *Principles of Human Knowledge* and *Three Dialogues between Hylas and Philonous*:

Berman, David. *George Berkeley: Idealism and the Man*. Oxford: Clarendon Press, 1994.
Bracken, H. M. *Berkeley*. London: Macmillan, 1974.
Dancy, J. *Berkeley: An Introduction*. Oxford, Blackwell, 1987.
Grayling, A. C. *Berkeley: The Central Arguments*. London: Duckworth, 1986.
Muehlmann, R. G. *Berkeley's Ontology*. Indianapolis: Hackett Publishing Co., 1992.
Pitcher, G. *Berkeley*. London: Routledge and Kegan Paul, 1977.
Tipton, I. C. *The Philosophy of Immaterialism*. London: Methuen, 1974 (repr. New York: Garland, 1988).
Warnock, G. J. *Berkeley*. Harmondworth: Pelican, 1953 (repr. 1969).
Winkler, K. P. *Berkeley: An Interpretation*. Oxford: Clarendon Press, 1989.

The following are multi-author anthologies about Berkeley:

Muehlmann, Robert G., ed. *Berkeley's Metaphysics: Structural, Interpretive and Critical Essays*. University Park: Pennsylvania State University Press, 1995.

Sosa, Ernest, ed. *Essays on the Philosophy of George Berkeley*. Dordrecht: D. Reidel Publishing Co., 1987.

Turbayne, C. M., ed. *Berkeley: Critical and Interpretive Essays*. Minneapolis: University of Minnesota Press, 1982.

Hume

The best edition of Hume's *Treatise of Human Nature* is edited by L. A. Selby-Bigge with revisions by P. H. Nidditch, Oxford, Clarendon Press, 1978. The best edition of the *Enquiry Concerning Human Understanding* is also edited by L. A. Selby-Bigge with revisions by P. H. Nidditch, Oxford, Clarendon Press, 1975.

The following are selected books written about central issues in Hume's *Treatise* and *Enquiry*:

Baier, Annette. *A Progress of Sentiments: Reflections of Hume's Treatise*. Cambridge, Mass.: Harvard University Press, 1981.

Beauchamp, Tom L., and Alexander Rosenberg. *Hume and the Problem of Causation*. Oxford: Oxford University Press, 1981.

Flew, A. *David Hume: Philosopher of Moral Science*. Oxford: Blackwell, 1986.

Fogelin, R. J. *Hume's Skepticism in the Treatise of Human Nature*. London: Routledge and Kegan Paul, 1985.

Garrett, Don. *Cognition and Commitment in Hume's Philosophy*. New York: Oxford University Press, 1997.

Livingston, Donald. *Hume's Philosophy of Common Life*. Chicago: University of Chicago Press, 1984.

Norton, D. F. *David Hume: Common Sense Moralist Skeptical Metaphysician*. Princeton. Princeton University Press, 1982.

Pears, David. *Hume's System: An Examination of the First Book of His Treatise*. Oxford: Oxford University Press, 1990.

Penelhum, Terence. *David Hume: An Introduction of His Philosophical System*. West Lafayette, Ind.: Purdue University Press, 1992.

Stroud, Barry. *Hume*. London: Routledge and Kegan Paul, 1977.

Wright, J. P. *The Skeptical Realism of David Hume*. Minneapolis: University of Minnesota Press, 1983.

The following are selected multi-author anthologies about Hume:

Chappell, V. C., ed. *Hume: A Collection of Critical Essays*. New York: Doubleday, 1966.

Norton, David Fate, ed. *The Cambridge Companion to Hume*. Cambridge: Cambridge University Press, 1993.

Norton, David Fate, Nicholas Capaldi, and Wade L. Robison, eds. *McGill Hume Studies*. San Diego: Austin Hill Press, 1976.

Authors

Michael R. Ayers is Professor and Fellow in Philosophy at Wadham College, Oxford. He is the author of *Locke* (Routledge, 1991), the co-editor of *The Cambridge History of Seventeenth Century Philosophy* (Cambridge, 1997), and the editor of *George Berkeley: Philosophical Works* (Everyman, 1975). He is also the author of numerous articles.

Phillip D. Cummins is Professor of Philosophy at the University of Iowa. He is the coeditor of *Minds, Ideas and Objects: Essays on the Theory of Representation* (Ridgeview, 1993), and the author of many articles in the history of philosophy.

Robert Fogelin is Professor of Philosophy at Dartmouth College. He is the author of *Hume's Scepticism in the Treatise of Human Nature* (Routledge, 1985) and of numerous articles.

Don Garrett is Professor of Philosophy at the University of Utah. He is the author of *Cognition and Commitment in Hume's Philosophy* (Oxford University Press, 1997), the editor of *The Cambridge Companion to Spinoza* (Cambridge University Press, 1995), and the author of numerous articles on Hume and Spinoza.

Charles McCracken is Professor of Philosophy at Michigan State University. He is the author of *Malebranche and British Philosophy* (Oxford University Press, 1983) as well as numerous articles on Berkeley and Descartes.

Edwin McCann is Associate Professor and Director of the School of Philosophy at the University of Southern California. He is the author of many articles on Locke and Kant.

George Pappas is Professor of Philosophy at the Ohio State University. He is the coauthor of *Philosophical Problems and Arguments* (Hackett, 1992), the coeditor of *Essays on Knowledge and Justification* (Cornell University Press, 1978), and the editor of *Justification and Knowledge: New Studies in Epistemology* (Reidel, 1979) as well as the author of numerous articles.

G. A. J. Rogers is Professor of Philosophy at the University of Keele. He is the founding editor of the *British Journal for the History of Philosophy* and is the author of many articles on the history of philosophy and the editor of many volumes. He is currently editing three volumes of the Clarendon edition of Locke.

Barry Stroud is the Mills Professor of Philosophy at the University of California at Berkeley. He is the author of *Hume* (Routledge, 1977), *The Significance of Philosophical Scepticism* (Routledge, 1984), and of many articles.

Ian Tipton is Reader in the Department of Philosophy at the University of Wales, Swansea. He is the author of *Berkeley: The Philosophy of Immaterialism* (Methuen, 1974), the editor of *Locke on Human Understanding* (Oxford University Press, 1977), and the author of many articles.

Margaret D. Wilson is Professor of Philosophy at Princeton University. She is the author of *Descartes* (Routledge, 1978) and the editor of *The Essential Descartes* (New American Library, 1969). She is also the author of many articles on philosophers of the early modern period, including Spinoza, Leibniz, Berkeley, Kant, and Descartes.

Kenneth Winkler is Professor of Philosophy at Wellesley College. He is the author of *Berkeley: An Introduction* (Oxford University Press, 1989), the editor of *The Cambridge Companion to Berkeley* (Cambridge University Press, forthcoming), and the author of many articles on the history of modern philosophy.